ANDRÉ MALRAUX
Metamorphosis and Imagination

ANDRÉ MALRAUX
Metamorphosis and Imagination

GUEST EDITORS
FRANÇOISE DORENLOT   MICHELINE TISON-BRAUN

NEW YORK LITERARY FORUM

NEW YORK • 1979

General Editor JEANINE PARISIER PLOTTEL
Hunter College, C.U.N.Y.

Managing Editor JANE ROGERS TONERO

Copy Editor CECIL GOLANN

Associate Editor ADELE GREEN

Special Editor MARGOT VISCUSI

EDITORIAL ADVISORY BOARD

MICHELINE TISON-BRAUN
Hunter College and the Graduate
Center, C.U.N.Y.

LeROY C. BREUNIG
Barnard College

MARY ANN CAWS
Hunter College and the Graduate
Center, C.U.N.Y.

HANNA CHARNEY
Hunter College and the Graduate
Center, C.U.N.Y.

MAURICE CHARNEY
Rutgers University

TOM CONLEY
University of Minnesota

SERGE GAVRONSKY
Barnard College

JEAN HYTIER
Columbia University

HARRY LEVIN
Harvard University

HENRI PEYRE
The Graduate Center, C.U.N.Y.

MICHAEL RIFFATERRE
Columbia University

ALBERT SONNENFELD
Princeton University

Copyright © New York Literary Forum 1979
All rights reserved

Library of Congress Cataloging in Publication Data
Main entry under title:

André Malraux, metamorphosis and imagination.

    (New York literary forum; v. 3 ISSN 0149-1040)
    Bibliography: p.
    Includes index.
    1. Malraux, André, 1901-1976—Criticism and interpretation—Addresses, essays, lectures. I. Dorenlot, F.E., 1934–   II. Tison-Braun, Micheline. III. Series.
PQ2625.A716Z565   843'.9'12   77-18629
ISBN 0-931196-02-7

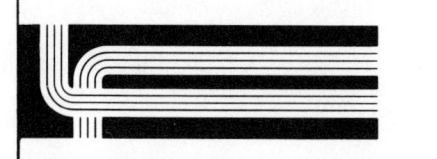

CONTENTS

List of Illustrations vii

Preface ix

PART 1. THE RHETORIC OF METAMORPHOSIS

1. The Voice of the Poet 3
   W.M. Frohock

2. Dialectics of Character in Malraux 15
   Hanna Charney

3. The Haunted Model 21
   Françoise Dorenlot

4. André Malraux and the Metamorphosis of Literature 27
   Henri Peyre

PART 2. CONSCIOUSNESS AND EXPERIENCE

5. Metamorphosis and Biography 37
   Jean Carduner

6. "Figures in the Carpet" of Malraux's *Le Miroir des Limbes* 55
   James Robert Hewitt

7. Timesless Geography 67
   Martine de Courcel

8. Malraux and Death 75
   Pierre Bockel

PART 3. PHILOSOPHICAL GLEANINGS

9. Agnosticism and the Gnosis of the Imaginary 85
   Edouard Morot-Sir

10. Framing Malraux 125
    Tom Conley

PART 4. FANTASY AND IMAGINATION

   11. Poetics and Passion **143**
       Mary Ann Caws

   12. Archetypes: Dissolution as Creation **149**
       Bettina Knapp

   13. The Artist as Exemplar of Humanity **155**
       Micheline Tison-Braun

PART 5. THE SEMIOSIS OF HISTORY

   14. Malraux and Medellin **167**
       Walter Langlois

   15. Life Made into Fiction **189**
       Philippe Carrard

   16. Visual Imagination in *L'Espoir* **201**
       Brian Thompson

   17. Malraux's *Storm in Shanghai* **209**
       LeRoy C. Breunig

   18. Malraux's *El Nacional* Interview **215**
       Robert S. Thornberry

PART 6. TEXTS AND DOCUMENTS

   19. "Professions délirantes" from André Malraux's *L'Homme précaire et la littérature*, translated by Jeanine P. Plottel as "Flaubert: The Writer's Library" **229**
       Jean Hytier

   Chronology **241**

   Bibliography **245**

   About the Authors **253**

   Index **257**

LIST OF ILLUSTRATIONS

"I am in art as one is in religion" Frontispiece
Photo by Roger Parry. Gallimard

A note by Malraux, with a sketch of a cat—typical of the way he signed his letters to close friends 13
Walter Langlois

... the secret of identity and of life/Malraux at Verrières 19
Photo by Jacques Robert. Gallimard

Malraux (standing at far right) in a class at Bondy, where he prepared for entrance to Lycée Condorcet 19
Walter Langlois

As a child, about 1905 51
Florence Resnais

"Le fond de tout, c'est qu'il n'y a pas de grandes personnes ..." 51
Florence Resnais

"Art feeds on what it brings and not on what it abandons" 63
Florence Resnais

The public servant, 1945 71
Florence Resnais

The private citizen, about 1962 71
Photo by Michel Roy. Gallimard

The "Démon des prix littéraires"—a signed ink sketch by Malraux 74
Walter Langlois

Colonel Berger at the end of World War II 79
Photo by Jack Le Cuziat. Florence Resnais

Colonel Berger, 1944 79
Florence Resnais

Colonel Berger, 1944 81
Florence Resnais

General De Lattre de Tassigny confers Legion of Honor on Colonel Berger, 1945 81
Gallimard

"Human reality belongs to the imaginary"—Five faces of Malraux 100-101
Photo by Jacques Robert. Gallimard

Manuscript page of *Les Conquérants* 116-117
Françoise Dorenlot

Malraux at the Ministry of Cultural Affairs, about 1961 121
Gallimard

Malraux at home in Boulogne, 1948 133
Photo by Yale Joel. Florence Resnais

Malraux with some statues he brought back from Afghanistan, about 1933   137
Walter Langlois

One of Malraux's sketches decorating "Chapter Four" of a book   148
Walter Langlois

The sculpture Malraux "acquired" in Indochina and which figures in *La Voie royale*   153
Florence Resnais

One of Malraux's sketches on a title page   154
Walter Langlois

Malraux with Albert Beuret and Jacques Vandier, curator of Egyptian antiquities at the Louvre, 1947   161
Florence Resnais

Malraux at the time of *L'Espoir*, 1937   177
Florence Resnais

The reporter and/or writer   181
Florence Resnais

Malraux at the time of *La Condition humaine*, 1933   183
Florence Resnais

One of Malraux's ink sketches done on the "Author's Preface" of a book   188
Walter Langlois

Malraux in 1944.   193
Florence Resnais

Malraux at Verrières, 1971   197
Photo by Jacques Robert. Gallimard

Malraux at the shooting of *Sierra de Teruel (L'Espoir)*, 1939   205
Gallimard

André Malraux and Jean Grosjean at Verrières, 1971   211
Photo by Jacques Robert. Gallimard

"Essuie-Plume"—an ink sketch by Malraux   214
Walter Langlois

Malraux at Verrières   233
Gallimard

Malraux with Hemingway (at left) and Robert Haas of Random House, 1934   233
Walter Langlois

Malraux and Gide, 1934   237
Gallimard

Malraux, Gorki, and Koltzov in the USSR, 1934   237
Florence Resnais

Preface

For a number of years Malraux had been ranked as one of the foremost French writers of this century. Then as Malraux the controversial public figure began to dominate the French cultural and social scene, the literary reputation of Malraux the artist seemed to degenerate. In this volume of *New York Literary Forum*, some of the greatest contemporary critics of Malraux and modern French literature hope to convince you that Malraux is a misunderstood and undervalued *writer* deserving serious reconsideration. Whereas many books and articles about him either praise or stigmatize, our authors have avoided evaluations linked solely to political factions and fashionable trends. Their emphasis is on understanding how a writer converted the events of his life, his obsessions, and his fantasies into literature.

Metamorphosis may be understood on the aesthetic plane as the transformation of life into art. Metamorphosis may also refer to the dialectics of change and identity within a single text or in a succession of works. But, above all, metamorphosis includes imagination, the effect of fantasy in the creative endeavor. In Malraux's words: "Metamorphosis is not an accident, it is the law of the life of the work of art itself." ("La métamorphose n'est pas un accident, c'est la loi même de la vie de l'oeuvre d'art.")

An outstanding intertextual prelude to our Malraux study has already appeared in *New York Literary Forum*, volume 2, with Germaine Brée's structural study: "The Archaeology of Discourse in Malraux's *Anti-memoirs*."

Part 1 of this volume about Malraux, "The Rhetoric of Metamorphosis," explores some imaginary modes at play in Malraux's writings. From a subtle analysis of several figures of speech, W. M. Frohock infers the poeticity of Malraux's essays on art. Henri Peyre's reading and interpretation of Malraux's posthumous (and difficult) book *L'Homme précaire et la littérature* actually heightens our understanding of Malraux's general attitude toward literature. Struck by the ambiguity inherent in psychological approaches, Hanna Charney finds in language itself the key to Malraux's description of characters. Françoise Dorenlot's essay shows the structure underlying Malraux's fascination with models.

In Part 2, "Consciousness and Expression," the stress is on the autobiographical, and interrelations between life and work are brought to the foreground. Both Jean Carduner and James Hewitt insist on the consubstantiality of life and writing: Jean Carduner presents a wide-ranging discussion that, to a certain extent, prolongs W. M. Frohock's analysis of metamorphosis; James Hewitt enters into an examination of some stylistic cues (metaphors and structures) found in *Le Miroir des limbes.* Martine de Courcel demonstrates that Malraux's fascination with the arts and cultures of all epochs takes root in his metaphysical quest. Reverend Father Pierre Bockel, a very close friend of Malraux, delicately portrays a little known secret aspect of Malraux when confronted with death and the question of God.

Part 3, "Philosophical Gleanings," examines the theme of metamorphosis from several perspectives. Edouard Morot-Sir decodes the significance and function of the lexemes *metamorphosis* and *imaginary* in a far-reaching linguistic analysis. To better define "The Gnosis of the Imaginary," he sets his observations against a background of texts by Ribot, Sartre, Bachelard, and Lacan, all focusing on the imaginary. Tom Conley's psychoanalytical scrutiny of how the *Mona Lisa* and the *Wicker-Screen Madonna* are used in *L'Irréel* and *L'Intemporel* to illustrate the text leads yet to another interpretation of the concept of "irréel," the imaginary.

Part 4, "Fantasy and Imagination," specifically turns to Malraux's view of art styles. Mary Ann Caws develops the fundamental issue posed in *Les Voix du silence*: "What is art?" ("Ce par quoi les formes deviennent style.") Bettina Knapp plunges into the unconscious, collective or individual, of the artist and comes to grips with a Jungian concept of metamorphosis. Micheline Tison-Braun examines the Socratic function of art and shows that Malraux's artist embodies mankind's highest ideals.

Part 5, "The Semiosis of History," features historical criticism in which the historical facts themselves are contrasted and compared with their representation in Malraux's fiction. Malraux's narration of the battle of Medellin is analyzed by both Walter Langlois and Philippe Carrard. A thorough investigation of the actual events enables Walter Langlois to ascertain some historical points and to draw a clear line between the actual events and their artistic expression in *Man's Hope*. Philippe Carrard's textual analysis of the same episodes revolves around the formal distinctions between journalistic reportage and a work of fiction. Also dealing with *Man's Hope*, Brian Thompson dwells on the light/darkness opposition and suggests how Malraux's power of transfiguration manifests itself by such antithesis. LeRoy C. Breunig's essay on *Storm in Shanghai* traces the American critics' opinion of *Man's Fate* from the 1930s to the 1950s and shows how politics interweaves with art. "The Semiosis of History" closes with a historical document, the text of a previously untranslated and unavailable interview given by Malraux to the Mexican newspaper *El Nacional* on March 1, 1937. Statements on Spain, the revolution, Trotsky, the Soviet Union, and Malraux's own involvement in the war, together with the extensive analytical annotations and comments of the translator, Robert Thornberry, cast a vivid light on the little known aspects of Malraux's personality.

In Part 6, "Texts and Documents," *New York Literary Forum* is honored to present another heretofore unpublished translation by Jeanine P. Plottel of Malraux's posthumous book *L'Homme précaire et la littérature*, preceded by a brilliant commentary by Jean Hytier. In chapter 9, the key chapter of the book, Malraux explains, using Flaubert and Dostoyevsky as examples, that just as paintings are created from museums without walls, so masterpieces of literature are born from the writer's inner library.

ACKNOWLEDGMENTS

We wish to thank Florence Resnais, Walter Langlois, and Gallimard for letting us reproduce photographs from their private collections. We also wish to thank Gallimard for granting permission to translate "Professions délirantes" and especially Albert Beuret for his interest and support.

PART 1

THE RHETORIC OF METAMORPHOSIS

PART 1

STOIC

METAMORPHOSIS

The Voice of the Poet

W. M. FROHOCK

> *How, marry? Tropically.*
> Hamlet

At the heart of the argument about the nature of art and the function of the artist that Malraux adumbrated in an article[1] in 1934, developed in detail in *La Psychologie de l'art*, revised in *Les Voix du silence*, and amplified and refined in the two versions of *La Métamorphose des dieux*, is a sheaf of tropes that cluster around the master-metaphor, metamorphosis. They recur over and over, and the mention of one seems always to evoke several others: rarely does one appear alone on a page, and it is far from unusual to find three or even more figuring in the same sentence.

Metamorphosis itself—in nominal or verbal form—turns up twenty-five times in *Le Surnaturel*, twenty in *L'Irréel*, and fifty-one times in *L'Intemporel*, which makes a total of ninety-six in the 1,080 pages of *La Métamorphose des dieux II* to be added to sixty-six occurrences in the 640 pages of *Les Voix du silence*.[2] However fallible the count (or the counter), the magnitude of the total suggests that it would be a miracle if the meaning Malraux attached to the word remained constant, and even a cursory examination of the contexts confirm that the nuances are almost infinitely varied. Subject to metamorphosis are not only the characteristic art styles of various cultures but also the cultures themselves, individual works of art, artists, the idea of art we entertain, Malraux's own "Imaginary Museum," and so on down a long list that at times seems to include everything not absolutely immune to change. The process can be active, as when an artist like Picasso seizes upon another artist's work and transforms it into something of his own, or passive at least in the sense that a change takes place without perceptible agency or cause. Often it appears that the antithesis of metamorphosis—and the only possible alternative to it—is death: the art that doesn't metamorphose simply perishes. Yet at the same time that metamorphosis rescues and resuscitates, it also destroys, because the older work of art the artist subjects to metamorphosis dies in the process. Rarely does Malraux show an awareness of the multiplicity of meanings he gives the word.

This multiplicity is, of course, the subject to which my colleagues address themselves in the present publication. It would be arrogant of me to believe that I could add anything significant to their exegeses. I would like, quite simply, to insist that the multiplicity is itself multiplied by Malraux's persistent use of figure.

On rare occasions Malraux himself seems to want to avoid the figurative, as, for example, when he remarks in *Les Voix du silence* that there is a "continuity" from the Kore of Euthydikos to the art of Lung-Men but that the continuity is less a matter of influence than one of metamorphosis *"in the precise meaning of the word."*[3] (The emphasis here is mine but the words are Malraux's.) He continues: "The life of Hellenistic art in Asia is not that of a model but that of a chrysalis." Whatever he may mean by "precise" in this sentence, it is hard to believe that he intends a synonym for "literal." But what else can one conclude?

A crawling insect spins itself into a cocoon and after a period of dormancy emerges as a winged one. This is the precise *and* literal meaning of the word. (He is not concerned, nor shall we be, with the kind of extended meaning, familiar since Apuleius and Ovid, in which, for example, Philomela, so rudely forced by the barbarous king, becomes a nightingale.) And as no style in art is capable of growing wings or spinning a cocoon, he is really saying that this is the instance in which the change effected by a succession of artists is most closely comparable to the change effected by nature. In brief, he serves up as a statement of identity what is, in fact, an analogy, and what he calls "the precise sense" of the word turns out to be an entomological metaphor.

Meanwhile, before this passage occurs in *Les Voix du silence*, the word *metamorphosis* has already occurred some twenty times; and a reader who is at all disposed to hold Malraux to the logical implications of what he says has some excuse for suspecting that on these other occasions he has been as deeply involved in the figurative as he has in this one. Such a reader will be right.

As the purpose of this essay is to identify the element of poetry in Malraux, it is in order here to risk seeming at least vaguely Empsonian—and thus somewhat out-of-date—by suggesting that *metamorphosis* is peculiarly freighted with ambiguity and multiple meanings when applied to art. Perhaps strangely, it is much less so when applied to poetry—to the point that one hesitates to apply it at all. Take, for example, what happens in "Ash Wednesday."

Eliot opens his poem with the heavily allusive, Dantesque (actually from Guido Cavalcanti's familiar *ballata* [ballad]) variations on "Because I do not hope to turn again," with their insistence that the speaker can neither turn aside from the path he is on or go back along the way he has come. The tone is one of a man weighed down by what Malraux himself calls the sense of the "irremediable"—whoever enters here abandons hope. And now Eliot inserts the familiar "Desiring this man's gift and that man's scope"; Shakespeare juxtaposed with Dante!

But the line from Sonnet XXIX undergoes a radical change of meaning. Shakespeare's speaker, the "I," who beweeps his outcast state, is saying that no matter how depressing life may become and how black the prospect, he has only to think of one beloved person to dissipate his depression—all becomes right with the world and with his adjustment to it. Eliot's speaker enjoys no such advantage: he is so deep in the Slough of Despond that only divine help can get him out of it. In short, by inserting Shakespeare's verse in the new context, Eliot is making it "say" what Shakespeare doesn't.

At this point an advantage of working with verbal art, as contrasted with the visual, becomes manifest. We know enough about contexts, "magnetic fields," the effect on one word of the proximity of another, and what the young have taken to calling "intertextuality" for us to be able to specify the change of meaning and how it was obtained.

Now this is metamorphosis in one of the senses Malraux frequently assigns to this word. As he insists so often, the art of one culture can absorb something from a predecessor only if it perceives something in the earlier one that contemporaries were unaware of. (For example, our time didn't resurrect Romanesque architecture because of the faith it expressed for the men it was created for, but because it expresses a value that Romanesque man didn't feel, the value of Art itself.)

Of course, a paradox lurks in this particular notion of metamorphosis, at least if we persist in taking Malraux literally. He maintains that a radical change has taken place, and indeed we know what he means. But at the same time we look back over our shoulders and see that, in spite of what we have been told about how metamorphosis destroys what it appropriates, the Romanesque is still there. The paradox disappears only if we understand Malraux to be saying not that Romanesque has changed but that *our idea of art* has gone through some sort of transformation.

In other words, a piece of art changes its "meaning" when inserted in a new context, just as Shakespeare's verse does when Eliot appropriates it.

If we feel no temptation of talk of metamorphosis in the instance of "Ash Wednesday," the reason is probably that we can see so well what has taken place. As a term, *metamorphosis* might seem too pretentious; the metaphor, too palpable and at the same time high-flown. It would lack the element of mystery that surrounds it in Malraux's treatment of art.

Such an element of mystery remains even in so clear a case as Georges de La Tour's appropriating so much of Caravaggio and making it so thoroughly characteristic of himself by—as Malraux explains—his handling of light. In fact, a good case could be made for holding that something mysterious in the survival of art from one culture to another accounts for his preference for *metamorphosis* over the available synonyms Malraux used from time to time. *Mutation, transformation,* and so on down to *change* don't imply mystery in the same degree.

What goes on within the darkness of the cocoon is the workings of a god. Nature and the gods are secretive by definition, and the instinctive wisdom of the race cautions against prying into the secrets.

And it is also true that the word seems to offer more poetic flexibility than do its synonyms. It can be more easily personified. On occasion it can be enabled to exert force, endowed with unfettered determination (*acharnement*), and can even commit rape. It can be "corrosive" and "bite." It can "obsess" an artist and fill him with "rage." It also "speaks" with a voice of its own. And it loans itself to envisioning a world from which violence is never long absent.

The same flexibility is associated with the metaphors that cluster around *metamorphosis* and doubtless explains Malraux's preference for them as against the possible synonyms, for example, *annex* and *annexation.*

The words are almost as indispensable to Malraux's central argument as is *metamorphosis.* "The creative act, in civilizations that have a history, consists of wresting what it represents from the world of appearance, death, fate, in order to annex it to a world that our civilization is the first to know in its totality, the one we call the world of art."[4] This peremptory declaration wouldn't be out of place anywhere in the essays on art, but there may be an added significance in the fact that it appears so late in the development of Malraux's work, when he returns in *L'Intemporel* to his eternal burden, the way one culture "speaks" across the gulfs of time to another, or, in the case of an individual artist, what the latter takes from a predecessor and transmutes into his own originality.

Politically, annexation is most often *Anschluss:* the army of one country marches into another with the result that the second country or some part of it loses its separate identity and merges with the first. In some contexts, of course, the term doesn't connote quite such aggressive national behavior: countries have been known to purchase land to add to their own territory. But history records relatively few instances when the transaction was entirely voluntary on the part of the seller. And in such cases we tend not to speak of annexation but to save it for those cases that have an aura of imperialism about them and at least a hint of force and duress.

Because artists aren't armies on the march or land-hungry nations, *annex* has to be a metaphor; but the metaphor makes the artist an imperialist nonetheless. He simply takes what he wants without asking—and, in Malraux's lexicon, without amenity. As has very frequently been remarked, the metaphor appears constantly in context with another that means grab, snatch, or wrest away.

There is no way to make *arracher* (to tear up, wrest) a gentle—not to say gentlemanly—word. We tear up an offending weed, pull a tooth, snatch a handful of hair from the head of an adversary, or wrench something from his grasp, because we want it and are stronger than he. This verb is the characteristic first step toward the metamorphosis that must in turn precede annexation. There are times, however, when he prefers the less graphic term *conquest.*

Conquest has the special interest of having emerged very early in his discussions of art. "Art is Conquest," the essay already referred to, dates from 1934, when it revealed to many of his readers what would continue to be the dominant tendency of his ideas on art throughout the rest of his life. Like the other metaphors we have been contemplating, *conquest* suggests an imagination dominated by images of struggle—as is surely not inappropriate to a writer of tragedies, for the center of any tragedy is the *agon* or struggle. One likes to believe that Sir Ernst Gombrich wasn't being merely facetious when he thanked Malraux, in print, for revealing that his experience of art has been a "traumatic" one.[5] (It may also not be irrelevant to this discussion that some very interesting pages of *La Corde et les souris* ("The Rope and the Mice") are devoted to the career of Alexander of Macedon.)

This ennumeration of Malraux's metaphors could be extended. Veteran readers of the essays on art will doubtlessly miss several of their favorites from the list cited here. Where for example is *rupture,* important because his artists never merely leave their masters and go off on their

The Voice of the Poet

own, but always break away; the relation of one artist to his predecessors or those between an earlier and a later art are usually an adversary one or, at very least, a rivalry. And why omit *The Voices of Silence* from the list? How do they sound across the milennia? Why, in the more recent essays, do they not *speak* but *sing*? And why are they most audible in the dusk, when the harsher light of day turns crepuscular?

But once the prevalence of metaphor has been established, there is less need to extend the list than to insist that the use he makes of an individual metaphor keeps it alive. It could be argued, for instance, that *conquest* is no longer figurative in any important way: most of us feel that we can "master" a skill without doing it violence or a bad habit without holding a knife to its throat. We know that what were once vivid metaphors lose their metaphorical potential with passing time and fall back into useful but unspectacular literalness: my watch "runs" on my wrist and the hot water runs in the kitchen. This is part of the whole process of cognition.

The really remarkable thing about Jakobson and Harris's famous study of aphasia and its revelation that metaphor and metonymy are fundamental in the cognitive process is that we had to have the fact pointed out to us. But it is no less true, for all that, that in literary language a so-called dead figure can be restored to life and that one way of doing so is to associate it with a group of other words of which the metaphorical nature is more immediately perceptible. Let *conquest* lead to *metamorphosis*, and *metamorphosis*, in turn, to *annexation*, and we are surely in the realm of living metaphor.

Much of the resistance to Malraux's view of art has been inspired no less by his use of various metaphors than by his dependence on metonymy, especially as one of these reveals itself at the very core of his argument: *expression, to express*. Nothing has caused him more trouble with the useful but generally sober people to whom he refers regularly as "the specialists." As a race they are averse to broad generalization and to sentences that begin, "no art ever . . ." or "all art must . . ." And it happens that Malraux's theory that art is, above all, expressive, is just such a generalization. If my impression is right, the art books have drawn far more approval and much less adverse criticism from professional writers and the general run of informed critics than from the professional and highly respected academics, many of whom want no part of his expressionism.

For Malraux the importance of expressiveness in art is, of course, capital. The cardinal value that a given civilization "expresses" is, according to him, what undergoes metamorphosis. Without this metamorphosis of a value there can be no communication between one civilization and another. The value is expressed by the civilization's art.

But how can we be sure what a given art expresses? How do I know that the intuition of the sacred I feel when I look at a Romanesque sculpture emanates from the sculpture and is anything different from my personal response to it? And why do I feel nothing at all when I view the heads of the Kings of Judah in the Musée de Cluny, although I would probably respond to them if I saw them back in their place on the facade of Notre Dame? And what would I feel if I hadn't learned from people like Malraux himself? He provides little help when he attempts to answer such questions in *Le Surnaturel* and comes up with what turns out to be only another figure of speech. We all have dreams, he explains, in which a snatch of song we have heard during the day or a postal card we have seen becomes a magnificent passage of music or a sublime picture. The postal card doesn't become more beautiful and doesn't "cause" the feeling of sublimity. Instead it releases it, serving as a *déclenchement* (release). In this way, one gathers, a work of art "releases" the feeling of the sacred or manifests the otherwise inexpressible in the same way that the postal card manifests the sublime. We are left in our quandary: is what is "released" in us anything that wasn't there already?

For us the problem may be complicated by an inherent difference between the French and English languages. In normal English, expression is the exteriorization of an idea or an emotion by means of word or gesture or the exercise of any of the several arts; something inside us comes out. Current French allows a much greater latitude in that the object of the verb need not be so relentlessly specific. Whereas we would rarely write that a novelist or poet "expresses man"—we would write that he expresses man's hopes or aspirations or something of the sort—Charles de Gaulle writes exactly this in his *Mémoires de guerre*. In the instance we know perfectly well what he means: he has only used the kind of metonymy the ancients called synecdoche, the container for what it contains. But when Malraux, exercising the same license, writes that Cézanne expresses the light, we are by no means sure of his meaning. For what has Malraux substituted the word *light*? One suspects that he means Cézanne's impression of a light-effect, something like what Emily Dickinson called "a certain slant of light." But one is not sure.

The difficulty shouldn't, of course, be exaggerated. In numerous instances, whether one agrees with him or not, one knows well enough what Malraux means by *express*. The man who chisels the stone for a *tympan* may not know that he is an artist, but he knows that his subject is the Truth. The Truth happens to be hidden behind the world of appearance, but it is no less real; in fact, it is all that is real. And what the sculptor asks of his skill is to give visible form to what he feels the invisible Truth must be. This is surely what Malraux means by expressing the sacred. The notion has been implicit in his work since the beginning.

But in numerous instances his meaning is much less clear, because his reader isn't exactly sure of the object of the verb *express*, and when at long last, in *L'Intemporel* (pp. 351-353), he pauses to consider the ambiguities that inhere in the word, he does so for all the world as if he hadn't been contributing to their number himself for more than three decades. The fundamental difficulty, he alleges, arises from the current belief in a "Will to express" on the part of the artist. This belief has replaced the older ones that share the need to realize a universal ideal of beauty. Like so many capital notions (such as God, death, love), the "Will to express" is founded on a word of so many meanings that, according to Malraux, it may be taken to mean that the artist is trying to express the forms in his work or the feelings of his model or his own feelings or his personality. "Does a painting of Van Gogh express a twilight, the twisting of a branch, the suffering of Van Gogh, or the personality of Vincent?" It was high time to raise the question.

And perhaps to answer it. One can see how a painting can express a twilight, but only in the sense that a poet expresses one by writing that over all the mountaintops is peace and thus transfers his inner serenity to the world outside. It is no easier to see how a painting of a gnarled and twisted piece of still growing wood expresses the wood, although in the role of something like Eliot's "objective correlative" it may assume a meaning for an observer who wants, like the old man in Bernanos's *Monsieur Ouine*, "to grow old like a tree." This seems quite different from the meaning of *express* when what is expressed is Van Gogh's suffering—which is just as possible as that one inchoate animal cry should express the pain and horror of Oedipus—or from expressing the aggregate of the urges, needs, repulsions and such that make up a personality. The first two examples, twilight and branch, entail metonymy, whether the two others do or not. One can conclude that, a good part of the time at least, Malraux uses *express* as a trope. To the extent that he does so, this key-verb joins his metaphors in a structure built largely of figures.

But aside from the undeniable fact that a structure of tropes confuses the resolutely literal-minded reader, why use so much time and paper establishing the point? I suggest that Malraux's literary behavior in this respect should determine the general approach any of us should adopt to all his writing on art. In other words, these books should not be read as if they were ordinary prose discourse.

Many years ago I wrote that Malraux's art was "an art of ellipsis." *Les Voix du silence* was very new, and the remark was prompted by a first reading of it, followed by an obsessed rereading of the novels; I had been left with the impression of a mind that leaped from idea to idea so abruptly that his reader inherited the task of supplying the transitions, in particular the causal ones. And this, in turn, seemed related to the way his novels so often seem to exist for the sake of scenes imbued with inspired intuition, like Katow's final exit, Kassner's return to Prague, the Descent from the Mountain, the perspective of the walnut trees at Altenburg. Now that we have the complete *Métamorphose des dieux*, *Le Miroir des limbes*, and *L'Homme précaire* the impression is all the stronger.

In a passage near the end of the "Lazare" section of *Le Miroir des limbes* (pp. 621-622), Malraux himself notes that someone has pointed to the way his memory seems to linger over moments that play the role of epiphanies. Far from taking exception, he lists a number, including several of these mentioned just above. The fact of his having revived a number of these "moments" by reprinting them, after revision, in one volume or the other of *Le Miroir des limbes* suggests that he has accepted, although perhaps belatedly, a view of a special gift that has been on the market for twenty-five years.

One doesn't generally look to a writer who is especially attuned to epiphanies for a patiently expository discussion of any subject such as, say, art. Epiphanies are, after all, instances of intense intuition and insight. And the possessor of such an intuition is likely to feel it to be self-evident or, at least, not nearly so in need of demonstration as it seems to us. For him, figurative language will be adequate, and he will frequently surprise and delight his reader with sentences like: "L'adolescence éternelle des matins de l'Ile de France, le bruissement d'Odyssée de l'air frémissant de Provence ne s'imitent pas, ils se 'conquièrent' " (The eternal adolescence of the mornings of the Ile de France, the Odyssean rustling of the shimmering light of Provence cannot be imitated, they have to be 'conquered.'). (*Les Voix du silence*, p. 351).

The sentence is, of course, only a reiteration of one of Malraux's central ideas: the painter doesn't copy external reality but somehow transforms it. And one of the verbs is the metaphor Malraux calls upon so often, to conquer. But although what he says can't be copied is actually light or two different qualities of light, the word itself is unmentioned. What we have instead reports the responses to the effect of light on a delicate and imaginative sensibility—the youth and freshness in one case, the Odyssean rustle of the shimmer in the other. It would be hard to say that these aren't minor epiphanies in themselves. At any rate, they aren't examples of direct, expository prose. In the process of saying that the light must cease to be light and become color, Malraux has succeeded, I would suggest, in a conquest of his own in another medium, winged words.

I happen to be writing this paragraph in Provence. The sun rose an hour ago over the Montagne Sainte-Victoire, although I didn't see it do so because lesser but nearer hills cut off the view. Even so, the light outside my window is that same light, and it does shimmer, although I am not sure that I would recognize an "Odyssean rustling." I find the sentence extremely moving and thus effective. But possibly this is because I am an amateur of poetry and not a specialist in the fine arts.

Nobody today will seriously dispute Jonathan Culler's contention that we approach poetry otherwise than we do prose. The poet disposes of a number of "signals" that precondition us. A special effect of typography, a way of grouping lines, a wantonly uneconomical use of white space, a "rough right," perhaps the size of the volume itself or even the title may inform the reader, before he has read a line, that a special set of expectations is appropriate. All but the most hardened survivors of (American) New Criticism would concede this now and indeed always would have done so. But what about the poets who don't put out many signals?

So far as I can discover, Malraux displays only one warning: his constant recourse to figurative language. There are cryptopoets as well as self-avowed poets, and to reveal the presence of a cryptopoet, one clear, insistent signal is probably enough. The proliferation of figurative language in the earlier sections of *Les Voix du silence* warns us that we are reading no ordinary prose; because of it we feel no radical break—no abrupt change in tone—when we pass from the primarily demonstrative prose of the early parts to the heightened discourse of the pages at the end in which Gaëtan Picon was the first to recognize the admirable "Hymn to Man." We have become so habituated to moments of recurrent heightening in the earlier pages that we are fully prepared for the elevation of the later ones.

The presence of the "Hymn to Man" at the end of *Les Voix du silence* left addicted readers of Malraux's writing on art in a state of uncertainty as to what to expect of the first *Métamorphose des dieux*. Read with due regard to its inherent poetry, *Les Voix* led to a sort of culmination in which art becomes the ultimate accomplishment in which man confirms his greatness and the artist emerges as the Representative Man, in Emerson's sense, who has liberated humanity from "the condition of being a man," which is the bondage of time, history, and death.[6] Like a successful tragedy, *Les Voix* becomes a poem in which death is swallowed up in victory. After this apotheosis, one wondered what Malraux could possibly say, in addition, on the subject.

Because it was incomplete, the first *Métamorphose des dieux* provided at most a partial and unsatisfactory answer. Indeed, some of us took it to be an amplification of ideas already proposed in *Les Voix*. And when, toward the end of his life, we learned that we would have a second and different *Métamorphose*, it was excusable for us to ask ourselves whether, nearly twenty years since the first version, this did not have to mean that Malraux's way of looking at art (*son regard*) had not changed.

My conviction is that it had not. The Malraux of the three-volume version is still guided by the familiar, fundamental concerns—the nature and function of styles in art, the idea of style itself, the mastery of originality, the varying relations of an art to the culture for which it "spoke."

What had changed was his perspective. In 1951 his capricious health may have given him reason to feel that *Les Voix* would perhaps be his last book. If he did suspect this, he was, happily, wrong. His life continued ... and, after the apotheosis, art continued to change. *Les Voix* had been based upon the study of masterpieces made available through necessarily expensive photographic reproduction, in other words upon that costly luxury product, the album. Now other, less expensive and more flexible means of reproduction, in particular the "audiovisual," were making accessible not only the masterpieces but also the secondary works of the individual styles—thus altering the nature of the "Imaginary Museum" itself. And at the same time the world had become aware of those other

A note by Malraux, with a sketch of a cat—typical of the way
he signed his letters to close friends

forms of art that do not result from conscious creative effort—the "aleatory," the "ready-made," the accidental, including even the flotsam we drag home to decorate our living rooms. Even our *idea* of art was subject to change: the "modern," from Manet through Picasso, had assumed that where other values failed, art itself was an absolute, the expression of a creator. As it turns out, the assumption characterizes a given culture—ours, transitory like the others.

There is still, in *La Métamorphose des dieux*, an abundance of figurative language. Even in Malraux's ultimate attempts to refine upon the notion of conscious human Will, so implicit in all his work, figure intrudes itself; see his distinction between *Volonté d'expression* (will to express) and *Volonté d'accession* (will to attain, rise to). And, not surprisingly, Malraux has not abandoned the role of poet. Let anyone who doesn't believe so try to reduce the final paragraphs on Rembrandt to a paraphrase. As the late John Crowe Ransom cautioned us years ago, paraphrase a poem and you get . . . only a paraphrase. The poem itself evaporates.

Poetry, yes, but no final peal of triumph. One does not write hymns in praise of metamorphosis.

I have no intention of subverting Malraux's reputation as a thinker. To do so would be a ludicrous critical error. But not to recognize the poetic dimension of his work is a critical error also and one that it would be good to avoid more frequently than we do.

Notes

1. "L'Art est une conquête," *Commune*, 13, 14 (September-October 1934). *Les Voix du silence* is dated 1935-1951.
2. I have chosen arbitrarily to refer to the titles of the French originals. With the exception of *Le Musée imaginaire*, which infelicitously becomes *Museum without Walls*, the titles of the English translations merely adopt the English cognates of the French. Where I have quoted Malraux in French, my context (I believe) reveals the content.
3. *Les Voix du silence*, p. 167: "la vie de l'art hellénistique en Asie n'est pas celle d'un modèle mais d'une chrysalide . . ." (the life of Hellenistic art in Asia is not that of a model but of a chrysalis . . .). References to *Les Voix* throughout are to the original edition.
4. *La Métamorphose des dieux III. L'Intemporel*, p. 75.
5. Sir Ernst Gombrich, "André Malraux and The Crisis of Expressionism," *The Burlington Magazine* (1954), pp. 374-378.
6. Here once again Malraux falls into a figure. Surely we are not "delivered" from our destiny: we continue to live in time and to die in time, and we do not escape history. But see Perken's often quoted "ce qui pèse sur moi c'est ma condition d'homme" in *La Voie royale*. We are relieved not of our human condition but of the burden of it—literally its weight that bears upon us. Metonymy thus appears at the center of Malraux's work.

Dialectics of Character in Malraux

HANNA CHARNEY

In the paradoxes of love and personal identity, Malraux repeatedly and poignantly rejected the kind of resolution that Pascal proposes in the following "Pensée" or "Thought":

> Un homme qui se met à la fenêtre pour voir les passants, si je passe, par là, puis-je dire qu'il s'est mis là pour me voir? Non, car il ne pense pas à moi en particulier. Mais celui qui aime une personne à cause de sa beauté, l'aime-t-il? Non; car la petite vérole, qui ôtera la beauté sans tuer la personne, fera qu'il ne l'aimera plus: et si on m'aime pour mon jugement, ou pour ma mémoire, m'aime-t-on, moi? Non; car je puis perdre ces qualités sans me perdre, moi. Où est donc ce *moi*, s'il n'est ni dans le corps ni dans l'âme? Et comment aimer le corps ou l'âme, sinon pour ces qualités, qui ne sont point ce qui fait le *moi*, puisqu'elles sont périssables? Car aimeroit-on la substance de l'âme d'une personne abstraitement, et quelques qualités qui y fussent? Cela ne se peut, et seroit injuste. On n'aime donc jamais la personne, mais seulement les qualités.[1]

(If a man goes to the window to see the passersby, and I pass by, can I say that he went there to see me? No, for he is not thinking of me in particular. But he who loves a person because of her beauty, does he love her? No; for smallpox, which will take away the beauty without killing the person, will make him no longer love her. And if one loves me for my judgment, or for my memory, does one love me, myself? No; for I can lose these qualities without losing myself. Where, then, is this *I*, if it is neither in the body nor in the soul? And how does one love the body or the soul, if not for these qualities, which are not what makes the *I*, since they are perishable? Would one love the substance of a person's soul abstractly, and whatever qualities were to be there? That cannot be, and would be unjust. Thus one never loves the person, but only the qualities.)

This "Pensée" leads most directly into the paradoxical presentation of character in the novels of Malraux, except that the facile conclusion, "Thus one never loves the person, but only the qualities," does not apply. One does love the person, in Malraux, but whom does Gisors love in the person of his son Kyo? Even if, as has been shown, paternal love in the works of Malraux is the most complete form of acceptance, what and who is Kyo for a father to whom he does not fully reveal his most important strategic plans? Whom and what do Kyo and May love in each other? "Une certaine complicité" (a certain complicity) or an inalienable self-hood? In *Les Noyers de l'Altenburg (The Walnut Trees of Altenburg)*, Walter says he loved his brother Dietrich, who has just committed suicide. What is the love of an enemy brother, separated by hostility and now by death? When Gisors, in *La Condition humaine (Man's Fate)*, is said to have loved a Japanese woman for her "tendresse" or tenderness, "tendresse" is a "quality," as Pascal puts it, a characteristic that must have been pleasing to him. His daughter-in-law, May, "à demi virile" (half-virile), was probably not his type of woman and ran counter to his taste. Yet he is drawn to her through the love she has for his son and the son's love for her.

The Role of Contradictions in Malraux

Character in the fiction of Malraux reproduces the same irreconcilable oppositions that permeate his concept of man, situated at the chance encounter of birth and individual consciousness, dying a death that is his own death although it wears the mask of the universal; communicating through word and action but never reaching the other. Individual freedom and the determinism of history follow and oppose each other in a dialectic without resolution (a non-Hegelian dialectic, as it were) and of which dialogue—as in Pascal's "Pensée"—is a characteristic expression. The much debated question of antinomies in Malraux can—and should—be debated further; it issues forth into the "mystère," the mystery of man's birth, the creation and history of a character or a painting. Blanchot, in *La Part du Feu* ("The Fire's Part"), shows how Tchen, from *La Condition humaine*, faces Berger from *Les Noyers de l'Altenburg:*

> Tchen et Berger sont ainsi l'un en face de l'autre, tous deux porteurs d'un secret, tous deux devant un univers qu'ils ne reconnaissent plus, et pour l'un, ce secret c'est la joie, pour l'autre c'est l'impossibilité de vivre.[2]

> (Tchen and Berger are thus facing each other, both bearers of a secret, both before a universe they no longer recognize; and for the one, this secret is joy, whereas for the other it is the impossibility of living.)

The secret that binds *and* opposes these two characters, the secret of their identity and their life in the world and in the novel springs from the same paradox as the resounding and reechoing question of suicide. Suicide, which Camus, in *Le Mythe de Sisyphe (The Myth of Sisyphus)*, will turn into "the only serious philosophical problem," sounds the first notes of *Les Noyers de l'Altenburg*, just as the act of killing starts *La Condition humaine.* At the beginning of Part II, the theme is resumed through its variations in the dialogue. Walter asks the narrator's father if he could enlighten him on the possible reasons for Dietrich's suicide. Further ambiguity results. Two days before his death, speaking of Napoleon, Dietrich had remarked that, whatever might happen, he would want no other life but his own. The choice of self seems to transcend all the reasons for despair and even death, in a contradictory but overwhelming feeling of identity.

Paradox and Irony in Malraux

This unique choice—paradoxically again—is often articulated in the encounter with another character, in dialogues where language alternates with the voices of silence. The "douleur du dialogue" (pain of dialogue), as Blanchot calls it, this often painful confrontation describes harmonics in which voices intersect and separate, rise and fall, punctuate each other in an abrupt, "nervous" rhythm constantly opening up onto the vast voice of silence behind it. Whatever the context—practical, philosophical, strategic, revolutionary—replies often fall like meteorites "chus d'un désastre obscur" (fall from an obscur disaster), in Mallarmé's words, unto the white page of the book.

As Merleau-Ponty said so well, in Malraux's language "le sens n'apparaît . . . qu'à l'intersection et comme dans l'intervalle des mots"[3] (meaning appears only at the intersection and as it were in the interval of words). Toward the beginning of *La Condition humaine*, it is in the interval between words that Tchen comes to discover his fate in his dialogue with Gisors. It is a masterfully orchestrated dialogue, prepared by the timing of this visit, which takes place after Tchen has committed his first murder. Other scenes, during which Tchen's planned visit to Gisors is repeatedly mentioned by several characters, intervene. At four o'clock in the morning, the insomniac Gisors, who was expecting Tchen, listens to him as Tchen starts: "C'est moi qui ai tué Tang-Yen-Ta"[4] (I am the one who killed Tang-Yen-Ta). The directness of their talk is real, but ironic. Gisors understands perhaps better than anyone else, but Tchen is alienated and separated forever by his murder. He does not understand himself better than Gisors does; it is to him, Gisors, that he went for an answer, which only the exploratory movement of the dialogue itself will give. But the answer only perpetuates the paradox:

—Je serai bientôt tué.
«N'est-ce pas cela surtout qu'il veut?» se demandait Gisors. «Il n'aspire à aucune gloire, à aucun bonheur» . . .
—Si tu veux vivre avec cette . . . fatalité, il n'y a qu'une ressource: c'est de la transmettre.
—Qui en serait digne? demanda Tchen, toujours entre ses dents.
[p. 55]

(I will soon be killed.
"Isn't that mainly what he wants?" wondered Gisors.
"He aspires to no glory, no happiness" . . .
—If you want to live with this . . . fatality, there is only one resource: to transmit it.
—Who would be worthy of it? asked Tchen, still between his teeth.)

It is no longer the return to the individual that is the problem of modern painting according to Merleau-Ponty in his commentary on Malraux; it is "le problème de savoir comment on peut communiquer sans le secours d'une Nature préétablie" (the problem of knowing how one can communicate without the help of a preestablished Nature). This seems eminently true in its application to Malraux. It is in this light that one can consider the question of "l'espoir"—of hope and despair—in his work. What does it mean that *La Condition humaine* ends on despair, whereas *Les Noyers de l'Altenburg* affirms life at the end? Is there a progression? In a sense, there undoubtedly is. But if we look at the way in which Kyo and May, in *La Condition humaine*, clash and battle in their dialogue about love and the paradox of individual freedom and see how they are for a time reunited by a common love through the thought of love-in-death, then separated again by events that lead to Kyo's death alone, we can pursue *this* paradox to the end of the novel, where Gisors, Kyo's father, and May, his widow, talk about Kyo.

...the secret of identity and of life...
Malraux at Verrières

Malraux (standing at far right) in a class at Bondy, where he prepared for entrance to Lycée Condorcet

[Gisors speaks:] —La seule chose que j'aimais m'a été arrachée, n'est-ce pas, et vous voulez que je reste le même. Croyez-vous que mon amour n'ait pas valu le vôtre, à vous dont le vie n'a même pas changé?

—Comme ne change pas le corps d'un vivant qui devient un mort...
[p. 283]

(—The only thing I loved has been torn away from me, hasn't it, and you want me to stay the same. Do you believe that my love was not worth yours, when your life has not even changed?

—As a living body that is turning into a dead one does not change.)

If Kyo's life and identity are the theme here, they are paradoxically affirmed and confirmed, in different and opposite ways, by Gisors and May. To come back to Pascal's "How does one love the body or the soul, if not for these qualities," *La Condition humaine* seems to answer: Gisor's Kyo and May's Kyo, diverse as they are, are mysteriously Kyo nevertheless. This seems to be, in Malraux, the irony of life as well as of death, closer to Pascal perhaps than Pascal himself. The final note of *Lazare*, "irony," echoes the irony of *Les Noyers de l'Altenburg*, where, at the end, the old peasant woman smiles a slow smile, when "elle semble regarder au loin la mort avec indulgence, et même ... avec ironie ..."[5] (she seems to look at death in the distance with indulgence, and even ... with irony).

The final irony is not, I think, a romantic resolution. It is rather an affirmation, similar to Nietzsche's desperate yea-saying, of the consciousness of the beholder. Thomas Mann showed, in his essay on "Freud and the Future" (1936) that "irony resides in the gazer and not that at which it gazes." In Malraux, too, irony affirms existence: of man, of art, of character.

Notes

1. Blaise Pascal, *Pensées* (Paris: Garnier, n.d.), p. 277.
2. Maurice Blanchot, "Note sur Malraux," *La Part du Feu* (Paris: Gallimard, 1949), p. 215.
3. Maurice Merleau-Ponty, "Le langage indirect et les voix du silence," *Signes* (Paris: Gallimard, 1960).
4. André Malraux, *La Condition humaine* (Paris: Gallimard, 1946), p. 51.
5. Idem, *Les Noyers de l'Altenburg* (Paris: Gallimard, 1948), p. 291.

3

The Haunted Model

FRANÇOISE DORENLOT

In a speech protesting the Italian conquest of Ethiopia, Malraux gave the following definition of civilization: "La civilisation, c'est de mettre le plus efficacement possible, la force des hommes au service de leurs rêves, ce n'est pas de mettre leurs rêves au service de leur force."[1] (Civilization means allowing man's strength to be the servant of his dreams in the most efficient possible way rather than allowing his dreams to be the servant of his strength.) Almost thirty years later, in 1963, in an utterly different context (inaugurating the French Book Fair in Montreal), he said: "Les hommes doivent unir leur force et leurs rêves, et faire ensemble que la force soit digne des rêves."[2] (Men should unite their strength and their dreams and work together so that strength be worthy of their dreams.) I should like to allude to a number of Malraux's observations whose striking convergence shows his fascination with "dreams," dreams that have been embodied in exemplary figures or ideas, models so to speak.

Had Malraux believed in God, his work would have followed a different path. Such was not the case. Hence, for him, the spiritual vacuum of our time and man's despair:

Pour avoir détruit Dieu, et après l'avoir détruit, l'esprit européen a anéanti tout ce qui pouvait s'opposer à l'homme: parvenu au terme de ses efforts, comme Rancé devant le corps de sa maîtresse, il ne trouve que la mort.[3]

(Because it destroyed God and after having destroyed Him, Western intellect has abolished all which might have stood in the path of man: having reached the limits of its efforts, it finds only death, like Rancé before the corpse of his mistress.)

That statement from *The Temptation of the West* is echoed in *Lazarus:*

Le chrétien, à travers Saint Paul, participe du Christ; l'homme quelconque, comme disaient les Italiens, ne participe pas de la relativité, ni du monde, à travers Einstein.... Le Christ, le Bouddha, Mahomet s'adressaient à lui. La science, non.... Ce qui rendait compte du monde avait formé les hommes ... La formation de l'homme passe par le type exemplaire: saint, chevalier, caballero, gentleman, bolchevik et autres. L'exemplarité appartient au rêve, à la fiction.[4]

(The Christian, through the medium of St. Paul, partakes of Christ; the average man doesn't partake of relativity or the universe through Einstein.... Christ, Buddha, Mohammed addressed themselves to him. Science doesn't.... What used to explain the world was what had molded men ... Modern man has been fashioned on the basis of exemplary stereotypes: saint, chevalier, caballero, gentleman, Bolshevik, and so on. The exemplariness belongs to the realm of fancy, of fiction.

In the span of forty years that separates both those works, Malraux ceaselessly and obstinately quested after possible models for man. So, for instance, was born *Man's Fate*: "J'ai cherché des images de la grandeur humaine—je les ai trouvées dans les camps des communistes chinois écrasés, assassinés, jetés vivants dans les chaudières..."[5] (I sought out images of human grandeur—I found them in camps where Chinese Communists were smothered, murdered, thrown alive into furnaces...) The writer's aim is made explicit in the preface to *Days of Wrath (Le Temps du mépris)*: "... on peut aimer que le sens du mot art soit tenter de donner conscience à des hommes de la grandeur qu'ils ignorent en eux."[6] (One may wish the word *art* to mean an attempt to give men a consciousness of their own hidden greatness.) As if the artist were to fill the spiritual void of today's society.... Quite paradoxically, the very artist who, for lack of a transcendental principle, finds himself unable to build either a temple or even one tomb,[7] does perceive some "greatness" in man. His own eventual fulfillment takes place through the formative function of the work of art. He uses whatever mold suits his purpose best—essay, novel, or play.

No wonder then that, as a novelist, Malraux portrays characters that other characters take as their models. Such is Gisors in *Man's Fate*. He is his son's pride: "This speech is *my father's* speech."[8] As a matter of fact, fathers are privileged figures in Malraux's world: Gisors, Alvear, Vincent Berger. Grandfathers, too: old Vannec, Dietrich Berger. And, to a lesser degree: Garine's and Kassner's fathers, Clappique's grandfather, Perken's uncle. Strangers may play just as important a role. Rebecci is "midwife" or rather midhusband to Hong's political birth; Grabot is emulated by Perken; Perken, by Vannec; Gisors, by Tchen; Peï, by Souen; Ximenes, by Manuel; Garcia, by almost every other character in *Man's Hope*. Also, Möllberg is emulated by his colleagues (although on a somewhat different plane). Actual admired historical figures may be at the root of this striving to imitate. Mayrena is pervasively present in *The Royal Way*, as Lenin, Napoleon, and Saint-Just are in *The Conquerors;* Bakhunin is in *Days of Wrath;* and Nietzsche is in *The Walnut Trees of Altenburg*.

Such overtowering figures, reappearing in both volumes of *Le Miroir des limbes* (*Antimémoires* and *La Corde et les souris*) include Mao, Nehru, Gandhi, Ho Chi Minh, victims of the concentration camps, the shadow of Jean Moulin, Senghor, Alexander the Great, De Gaulle, Picasso. Yet it should be noted that, however important these figures may have been, they were not without a precedent. For example, would Picasso's art be what it has developed into had there not been a "little Man from the Cyclades"?[9] In *Felled Oaks*, a book unquestionably devoted to De Gaulle, here and again Malraux conjures up the figure of Napoleon. Some allusions are made in passing; others are rather lengthy discussions. Let us take an example that illustrates the relations among politics, metaphysics, and the imaginary:

> Une de ses phrases [il s'agit de Napoléon] m'a toujours troublé, parce qu'elle est magnifique et incompréhensible: 'Je fais mes plans avec les rêves de mes soldats endormis'. Il a rétabli l'ordre—ou plutôt il l'a établi, car ce n'était pas le même. Il portait en lui le besoin de transformer la confusion en ordre, comme tous les hommes de l'Histoire qui ne sont pas des hommes de théâtre . . .[10]

> (One of his remarks [Napoleon's] has always troubled me because it is splendid and incomprehensible: "I make my plans out of the dreams of my sleeping soldiers." He reestablished order—or rather, he established it, for it was not the same order, like all men of history who are not theatrical figures . . .)

We previously alluded the presence of Napoleon in *The Conquerors*, published in 1928, that is, two years after *The Temptation of the West*. We should also note the publication two years later of an anonymous biography about the French emperor. Its editor was no other than the author of *Man's Fate*.[11] *The Temptation of the West*, for one, stresses the overwhelming force of the unconscious, therefore, the excessive vulnerability of western youth: "... nous sommes pour nous-mêmes des êtres en qui dort, mêlé, le cortège ingénu des possibilités de nos actions et de nos rêves."[12] (... we are, in our own eyes, creatures in whom is dormant an unsophisticated and jumbled procession of the possibilities of act and dream.) Of all the "dreams" that capture the imagination (according to this text), the Napoleonic one stands out: "Nous avons tous senti la fraîcheur et la brume du matin d'Austerlitz ... Le jeune français dont une heure de désoeuvrement a fait Napoléon accomplit les gestes de l'empereur qui l'ont ému, mais l'empereur, c'est lui."[13] (We have all felt the coolness and the mist of the morning of Austerlitz ... The young Frenchman whom one hour of boredom has transformed into Napoleon performs those deeds of the Emperor which have excited his imagination, but it is he who is the Emperor).

Such statements cannot be misleading. They do not express a nostalgia for the cult of the individual. Throughout his life, Malraux condemned individualism and was always careful to make a distinction between man and the individual. At no point did he admire Napoleon for his military career or his administrative organization. What he valued was his far-reaching concept of action, action akin to dream, very much like De Gaulle's. "Les personnages capitaux de notre histoire sont dans tous les esprits, parce qu'ils ont été au service d'autre chose que la réalité"[14] (The chief figures of our history remain in every mind because they served something beside reality) explains De Gaulle's historiographer in *Felled Oaks*. The influence of mythic figures was already underlined in *The Temptation of the West*: "L'esprit donne l'idée d'une nation, mais ce qui fait sa force sentimentale, c'est la communauté des rêves."[15] (Intellect molds the concept of a nation; what gives it emotional vitality is the community of its dreams.)

What might be interpreted as reminiscences of a bygone era should actually be understood as a fascination for transcending destinies, both historical or artistic. Strikingly, the Jean Moulin eulogy opens and closes on a direct appeal to French youth. The commemorative speech on the death of Joan of Arc, in a most lyrical and emblematic style, asserts: "... le tombeau des morts est le coeur des vivants."[16] (The tomb of the dead is the heart of the living.)

In a parallel manner the artist, too, transcends his condition. Art changes an artichoke into an acanthus, history into a chant. Malraux's recourse to images, here again, is "exemplary":

> L'humanité vivante transmet inexorablement ses monstres avec son sang, mais celle des artistes morts, lorsqu'elle nous transmet le fléau du monde: l'horreur assyrienne, malgré les rois tortionnaires de ses bas-reliefs, emplit notre mémoire de la majesté de *la Lionne blessée*. [And] ... s'il existait un art des fours crématoires tout

juste éteints ce jour-là, il n'exprimerait pas les bourreaux, il exprimerait les martyrs.[17]

(Thus, whereas living humanity transmits, from generation to generation, a legacy of "monsters" with its blood, the dead artists transmit another message, however cruel was the age they lived in. Despite these torturer-kings who figure in the bas-reliefs, it is by the majesty of its *Dying Lioness* that Assyrian art grips our imagination. [And] . . . had there been an art of the prison-camp incinerators, only that day extinguished, it would have shown us not the murderers but the martyrs.)

From the concept of social change as stated in *Man's Fate*

Une civilisation se transforme, lorsque son élément le plus douloureaux—l'humiliation chez l'esclave, le travail chez l'ouvrier moderne—devient tout à coup une *valeur* . . ."[18]

(A civilization becomes transformed, you see, when its most oppressed element—the humiliation of the slave, the work of the modern worker—suddenly becomes a *value* . . .)

to the very famous definition of humanism expressed in *The Voices of Silence:* ". . . nous voulons retrouver l'homme partout où nous avons trouvé ce qui l'écrase"[19] (. . . we wish to rediscover Man wherever we discover that which seeks to crush him to the dust) down to the last volume of *The Metamorphosis of the Gods* and *L'Homme précaire*, every single work, nearly every page vibrates with the same obsessive urge to change, transform, or transcend, that is, to negate one's condition and live in conformity with one's dreams. In that light, we understand Malraux's impassionate creation of Maisons de la Culture, meant to offset the materialistic environment of our daily lives, thus shaping and forming men's imaginary and intellectual universe: ". . . toute civilisation est menacée par la prolifération de son imaginaire, si cet imaginaire n'est pas orienté par des valeurs."[20] (Every civilization is threatened by the proliferation of its fantasies unless ideals orient these fantasies.) That sentence belongs not to *The Temptation of the West*, but to the speech of May 15, 1962, commemorating the fiftieth anniversary of the French Institute, in New York. Malraux never failed to seek substitutes to the absolute. With his tendency to think himself useful ("J'ai tendance à me croire utile . . ."),[21] he apparently considered himself bound to offer his contemporaries the "aftermath of the absolute."[22]

Notes

1. "Réponse aux 64," *Commune*, No. 28 (1935), p. 413.
2. Speech of October 11, 1963.
3. *La Tentation de l'Occident* (Paris: Grasset, 1951), pp. 215-216; *The Temptation of the West*, trans. Robert Hollander (New York: Vintage Books, 1961), p. 121.
4. *Lazare* (Gallimard, 1974) pp. 188, 189-190. *Lazarus*, trans., Terence Kilmartin. (New York: Holt, Rinehart and Winston, 1977), pp. 111-112, 113.
5. "Cinq minutes avec André Malraux" (an interview with Marius Richard), *Toute l'Édition* (9/12/1933), 1, 3.
6. *Le Temps du mépris* (Paris: Gallimard, 1935), p. 9; *Days of wrath*, trans. Haakon Chevalier (New York: Random House, 1936), pp. 4-5.
7. *Antimémoires* (Paris/ Gallimard, 1967), p. 11; *Anti-memoirs*, trans. Terence Kilmartin (New York: Holt, Rinehart and Winston, 1968), p. 2.
8. *La Condition humaine* (Paris: Gallimard, 1947). *Man's Fate*, translated by Haakon Chevalier (New York: Holt, Rinehart and Winston, 1976). Italics are Malraux's.
9. *La Tête d'obsidienne* (Paris: Gallimard, 1974); *Picasso's Mask*, trans. and annotated by June Guicharnaud with Jacques Guicharnaud (New York: Holt, Rinehart and Winston, 1976). The "little man from the Cyclades" is repeatedly used as a symbolic work of art. (Dated ca. 2000 B.C.) Its meaning is obviously lost. However, Picasso's admiration for that sculpture exemplifies the metamorphosis process constantly to be found in the development of art styles, according to Malraux. There definitely exists a stunning relation between the archaic idol and Picasso's style (as evidenced by the illustration on p. 134).
10. *Les Chênes qu'on abat* . . . (Paris: Gallimard, 1971), p. 110; *Felled Oaks*, trans. Irene Clephane (New York: Holt, Rinehart and Winston, 1972), p. 63.
11. This information was given to me by Robert Gallimard. The biography in question was published in 1930 for a collection called "Mémoires Révélateurs."
12. *La Tentation de l'Occident*, p. 101; *The Temptation of the West*, p. 52.
13. *Ibid.*, pp. 95-96, 98; *ibid.*, pp. 50, 51.
14. *Les Chênes qu'on abat* . . ., p. 224; *Felled Oaks*, p. 122.
15. *La Tentation de l'Occident*, p. 95; *The Temptation of the West*, p. 50.
16. *Oraisons funèbres* (Paris: Gallimard, 1971), p. 101.
17. *Les Voix du silence* (Paris: Gallimard, N.R.F., 1951), p. 623; *The Voices of Silence*, trans. Stuart Gilbert (New York: Doubleday, 1953), p. 625.
18. *La Condition humaine*, p. 426; *Man's Fate*, p. 352. Italics are Malraux's.
19. *Les Voix du silence*, p. 631; *The Voices of Silence*, p. 642.
20. In *Lectures choisies* of André Malraux, ed. Anne Prioleau-Jones (New York: Macmillan Modern French Literature Series, 1965), p. 191.
21. *Antimémoires*, p. 124; *Anti-memoirs*, p. 83.
22. Subtitle of one of the four parts of *The Voices of Silence*.

4

André Malraux and the Metamorphosis of Literature

HENRI PEYRE

From Plato to Heidegger—without making an exception for the allegedly logical French (Descartes, Pascal, or the Genevan Rousseau)—it ever was the privilege of influential thinkers to juxtapose contradictions and sedulously to refrain from defining their terms. Of that privilege, Malraux has superbly availed himself. *Absurdity*, *fate*, *transcendence*, and lately an even more elusive adjective taken as a noun, *l'aléatoire* for which it is hard to devise an adequate equivalent in English, are among his favorite terms. In his many writings on art and in his recent vaticinations on literature (Malraux would have felt flattered by the appellation of an inspired and inspiring *vates* [seer]), the word that recurred most obstinately was *metamorphosis*. Like the adjective *insolite* (unusual, strange, weird) which for a time was uttered ten times an hour by Frenchmen, like *le sacré* even dearer to that nation of alleged skeptics, *metamorphosis* is surrounded with an aura of mystery. Half a century ago, it had become a cliché to repeat that, in contrast with their German neighbors incessantly drawn to the *Werden* and delighting in their dynamic becoming, the French clung to the static, to stable and solid bourgeois values, and paid at least lip service to the Cartesian "clear and distinct ideas." If the present vogue of metamorphosis may serve as an index of their moods and if the awe-inspiring language of present-day thinkers such as Lacan, Derrida, and Deleuze is at all typical, a profound transformation has taken place in the country that boasted once that it had learned little and borrowed nothing from the Germans who occupied it for four years.

Malraux himself never claimed to be a philosopher and he seldom alluded to representatives of that revered species—Nietzsche being an exception. He was no expert in foreign languages. It is even doubtful if he pondered long on works dealing with art, ethnology, or aesthetics in which there appeared to be a premonition or an earlier version of views that he held and expounded with arrogant brilliance. Several Americans to whom he generously granted interviews, the present writer included, may testify to his patience, to his kindliness and, despite prejudices to the contrary, to his deep modesty. When, however, I courteously questioned him once or twice on the extent of Spengler's or Groethuysen's impact on his youth, he preferred to remain evasive. He was equally vague when I brought up the names of Worringer, whom he probably never read, and of two Frenchmen who might have fascinated him as having been long and deeply concerned with art as metamorphosis: the great essayist Elie Faure, whose high-flown speculations and lyrical prose frequently call Malraux's writings to mind, and a Sorbonne (subsequently Collège de France) professor, Henri Focillon, who was conspicuous for the rich and mellifluous language in which he clothed his ideas. *L'Esprit des formes* by Elie Faure, which constitutes the fifth volume of his widely read art history, came out in 1926, the very year when Malraux first won fame in Paris with his *Tentation de l'Occident*. It was republished, with additions, in 1933. The author, who was by profession a medical man, was, as Malraux was to be, obsessed by tragedy, by a Nietzschean will to triumph over the ubiquitous presence of death through a lyrical *amor fati* and through artistic creation. Focillon, probably the most oustanding of the historians and thinkers who studied Romanesque sculpture, dear to Malraux, had published in 1934 (one year after the Goncourt prize was given to *La Condition humaine*) *La Vie des formes*, a dense, often cryptic and highly suggestive volume on the fluid, ever-changing life of forms in art. Malraux did not deny having heard of those books, perhaps dipped into them. But he dismissed, and rightly so, the possibility of influences, just as he declared his utter lack of interest in the biographers who questioned him on "that paltry pile of secrets," which he wanted his adventures in China or over Arabia to remain. Unlike Gide, who misled critics and biographers through mentioning possible sources too generously and listing in his *Journals* too many books of which he had probably read but a few pages, Malraux, like Valéry, chose to hint that thinking and expressing views similar to those of one's contemporaries are the most normal of occurrences, in science as in art. Simultaneous polygenesis in the realm of ideas and of feelings would indeed prove a more rewarding field of studies for the historian of culture than the often sterile search for sources and borrowings.

Malraux's passionate interest in the arts did not precede his equally fervent concern with literature. He never completed his secondary education and, as the Belgian scholar Vandegans demonstrated, he never was a student at any of the "Grandes Ecoles." The freshness and the independence of his taste were perhaps preserved thereby. He did not have to be warned by lycée teachers and baccalaureate examiners against omitting transitions or making peremptory and unsupported assertions or blamed for not bothering to reconcile his contradictions. The most ungrateful service a sedate and prudent scholar could ever do Malraux (or Montaigne or Diderot) would be to argue that, despite appearances to the contrary, there were unity and consistency behind their variegated and at times desultory statements. The philosopher Alain, who, like most French moralists of the classical age (and like Suarès, Cioran, and René Char in our time), thought in, and through, unconnected aphorisms, was fond of saying that, when a system seems to stand in contradiction to the man who shaped it, it is the man who is right and the system that is at fault. Malraux's thought can easily be refuted: English and American art historians, far more attached to consistency than the illogical French, undertook such a refutation when *The Voices of Silence* first appeared. Some, like Ernst Gombrich, have not relented since in their strictures. But it is harder to refute or to confute the ardent and imperious personality throbbing behind Malraux's writings. He proceeds through avalanches of interrogations, and he throws fireworks of scintillating formulas. He lends his own elliptic language to the works of art and literature that face him with their own enigmatic questions.

The Attraction of Literature for Malraux

We may surmise, from his youthful editing and publishing ventures, what first attracted Malraux in literature; naturally enough, the works of his immediate predecessors: Max Jacob, Reverdy, the Cubist poets, and Baudelaire, who, from 1917 on, fifty years after his death, appeared in many cheap editions and was a revelation to the youth. The art of a remote past (the sculpture of the archaic Greek statues, that of Buddhist Asia, even the Romanesque porches of Moissac and Saint Gilles) may hold intense fascination for a young man of twenty. But he is seldom moved to his depths by the literary work of eight, or even six, centuries ago. Except for Pascal, with whom his affinities have always been marked, and for Laclos, Malraux never, until just before his death, had evinced much curiosity for the classical age of French literature, not even for Diderot and Rousseau. Yet he could have found in the last two the lineaments of the epoch-making concept of development, which Hegel and the German romantics were going to inherit and expand and which lies at the source of any study of metamorphoses.

Unlike several of his contemporaries, Malraux was too passionately eager to think forward as well as live forward, to busy himself with collecting every scrap of his past writings, or to prepare for the Pléiade series a full edition of his scattered works. He declined to encourage those of us who offered to him to collect and publish his reviews, done mostly between 1927 and 1936, and his subsequent addresses on political and cultural topics. Yet they would make up one of the most impressive volumes of minor pieces by any French writer of this century, at least equal to the best of Valéry's *Variétés* ("Varieties") or of Sartre's *Situations*. The maturity, the quiet and lucid wisdom of Malraux, then in his late twenties, reviewing for the *Nouvelle Revue Française* of June 1927 and June 1929 the books by Massis (*Defence of the West*) and by Keyserling (*Travel Diaries of a Philosopher*) are astonishing. They illuminate his early thinking on India and China. They also sketch, before any of Malraux's novels had received acclaim, the deepening that might accrue to fiction and the probable metamorphosis of that genre through "a dramatic conception of philosophy" such as Keyserling had propounded in his very original travel book.

The same obsession with the modern novelist's duty "to wrest from the tragic its unknown or alien elements" and to come to grips with fatality resounds in the pregnant reviews Malraux gave, in the same monthly magazine, in March 1928 and March 1934, of *L'Imposture* by Bernanos and *Les Traqués* ("The Hunted Down") by the Russian Michael Matveev. In the second of those articles, the recent Goncourt laureate spurned the temptation to bask in the security of his success and to turn into a candidate for academic honors: a metamorphosis that Mauriac, Cocteau himself, and Green would not reject and that was the pitfall open before Camus when death carried him away. Quietude is the enemy whose insidious lure is to be guarded against. "Man is an unknown animal who believed he could know himself in quietude. Let the drama be unleashed, and he discovers his power of dreaming, his specific madness." As early as 1928, before either Bernanos or Malraux himself had been imposed upon the reading public as the two French novelists who might be hailed as Dostoyevskyan, Malraux detected two features that have since become fundamental to his conception of modern fiction: "the intervention of Satan" suddenly transforming the character who has discovered "the Adversary" in himself and a technique through which it is not the characters who create the conflicts, but the conflicts that give birth to the characters. Much later, in the revealing marginal notes added to Gaëtan Picon's *Malraux par lui-même* (1953), Malraux was to assert forcefully:

> I do not believe it true that the novelist has to create characters; he must create a coherent and individual world, like any other artist . . .; not rival the Registry Office (Balzac's famous "Etat-Civil"), but transform reality.

In his posthumous volume on literature, Malraux boldly borrows, to apply it to authors, the formula that he had coined for the artists in his *Voices of Silence:* "Like the painter, the writer is not the transcriber of the world, he is its rival".

Between 1934 and 1975, while Malraux was living three or four lives in one, he had little leisure and probably little inclination to meditate or to write on literature. He inserted in his famous preface to *Days of Wrath* (*Le Temps du mépris*, 1935) a scathing condemnation of Flaubert, of his attitude toward his characters rather than of his art. Like Valéry and not a few others, he expressed a dislike of the novelist who was able to laugh, for years and years, at the puppet of *le Garçon* and to collect "received ideas" that he would use to ridicule the harmless pair of Bouvard and Pécuchet, "about whom he wrote all his life," we read in *L'Homme précaire* (p. 116). It really is too easy to select uncultured and unthinking fools of goodwill as one's target if the real aim is the vanity of all human knowledge! With the fairness that he brought to his judgments, Malraux reversed himself on Flaubert; he devoted penetrating pages to him in his posthumous volume on literature or on what may survive of it to bring comfort to that precarious creature, the man of the atomic age. Soon after World War II, in 1946, appeared the fragment of a work probably composed earlier: *Esquisse d'une psychologie du cinéma.* While the fighter of the Spanish civil war was working on his film on the battlefield and composing at the same time his novel *Man's Hope*, he was led to reflect on the differences between the two arts and their techniques. The remarks, concise, feverishly elliptic, formulated in that thin pamphlet, count among the most incisive penned by the author. They deepen our regret that Malraux never had occasion to return to the theme that he had broached there: the *mise en scène* of a great novelist. He defined that *mise en scène* as "the instinctive or premeditated choice of the moments to which the novelist gives his attention and of the means which he selects in order to bestow a special importance on them." Among those means, the passing from narrative to dialogue is the most significant. Another device is also at the novelist's disposal: "the linking of a crucial moment of his character with the atmosphere or the cosmos surrounding him. . . . Tolstoy drew from it one of the finest scenes of world fiction, the night when Prince André, wounded, contemplates the clouds, after Austerlitz."

Vast possibilities are left to the art of fiction, if only its practitioners would avail themselves of them. They can, better than the film directors, enter inside their characters, give expression to semiconfessions ("des demi-aveux") and to secrets suggested by the actions of the characters. Malraux, who had it in him to be a great movie producer and who was a strikingly effective wielder of the mass media, at the conclusion of his last volume, mourns the timidity of today's novelist. He has ceased to cherish and to nourish "l'imaginaire". He has failed to take advantage of his erstwhile privilege, that of probing into the inner man, and he has surrendered it to the psychoanalyst. He has not filled the gap left yawning by the disappearance of the sacred, which once inspired medieval sculpture. He seems resigned to the precariousness of man and almost ready to accept the disappearance of that creature, become "aleatory," abandoned to the chance of some random explosion. "In the presence of the aleatory, neither the world nor man has any meaning, since its very definition is the impossibility of a meaning, either through thought or through faith": thus concludes Malraux mournfully at the last but one page of *L'Homme précaire et la littérature*. Never had Malraux, the unbeliever who often wrote (and repeated to me firmly in April 1956) that he would never convert to any religion, sounded so nostalgic for some form of transcendence. Flaubert's worship of style and fanatic cult of the beautiful sentence would not satisfy him. Besides, Flaubert, who gave to the modern novel its letters of nobility and, in his own fashion, did for it what Racine had achieved for tragedy, was too lacking in any contact with the arts, too much of a bookish novelist, to win Malraux's unreserved admiration. The civilizations with which he felt most in sympathy were those that have left us no original images: Rome or Carthage.

The Meaning of Metamorphosis to Malraux

L'Homme précaire et la littérature, some sketches of which had appeared at the end of *Malraux, être et dire* by Mme. de Courcel and a score of contributors (Plon, 1976), was hastily and feverishly written by Malraux just as he was dying. Ever since the grave disease that had confined him to a hospital two years previously and from which he was astonished to arise like a Lazarus being granted a respite from the grave, the old fighter knew that his days were numbered. He could only jot down, with no concern for any consistently reasoned development, a few of his intuitive views on literature. The question that he implicitly asked himself and that others had probably asked him was why there should not exist an imaginary museum of literary works similar to the one of which he had dreamed for painting and sculpture. Could not a metamorphosis of the gods in the epic and in tragedy be conceivable, alongside the sumptuously illustrated one that Malraux had conjured up?

Malraux recalled how he had offered the lineaments of such a work when, in the 1930s, he had launched the project of a *Tableau de la littérature française (de Corneille á Chénier)*. In it, the authors were evaluated by the most prestigious men of letters in France. The basic principle was to renounce the chronological succession dear to professors and the concept of a progressive evolution of genres. The historical importance of a work of the past was taken to be secondary to the "presence" of that work or its impact upon us, today's readers. That very notion entails several metamorphoses.

Some genres disappear or cease to be relevant, and we cannot always explain why. Wear and tear? Lack of correspondence with a new taste?

Mere shift in fashion? Periphrases, which once were not devoid of complex charm and whose ambiguity lent some irony and wit to poetry, have given way to images. Imagination irrupted into our critical thinking with Diderot, Coleridge, and Schlegel. It has since been displaced by another term and a slightly different concept, *l'imaginaire*, itself in the process of serving as a facile and hardly meaningful catchword. The theater, once made exclusively or primarily in order to be seen, is now chiefly read. That is tantamount to depriving a religious ceremony of its liturgy. The dramatic genre, strewn with numberless failures in the nineteenth century and no longer to the forefront in our own, has been replaced by the novel. The Racinian triumph of order and of distanciation achieved through the stylizing skill of the dramatist came to be duplicated or paralleled by the Flaubertian novel. Unlike Balzac and even more Dostoyevsky, the author of *Madame Bovary* refuses any complicity with his readers. He keeps his characters at a remove and feels no admiration for any of them. Malraux in his older years did write more understandingly, even more reverently, on Flaubert than he had done in his impetuous years. But he could not commune with the cult of the artist of prose set so far above the hero and the saint. Flaubert may have at times called himself "an ascetic" and "a Catholic" of a sort. But he was not, like Malraux, haunted by a nostalgia for transcendence. The true religious spirit, Pascalian Malraux is fond of repeating, is "he who experiences in the very depths of his soul the anguish of being a man."

Other literary metamorphoses puzzle Malraux as they have puzzled others before him, not just the pettiness or the voluntary blindness of critics, such as Sainte-Beuve, whom Proust upbraided for it, but their honest inability to discern in the works of their contemporaries what posterity will one day read in them. Reviewers and critics often acknowledge and praise talent, but seldom the genius underlying the talent. Was that genius present there from the start? Or do we lend it to the work later, as that work takes on a changed personality? Racine was proud of the musicality of his lines, of the smooth succession of the scenes in his plays. His audiences may have relished "La fille de Minos et de Pasiphaé," but were they aware of the ferociousness of the passions depicted, of the monsters that the twentieth century likes to contemplate, unleashed and "seeking whom to devour" in *Bajazet* and *Phèdre*?

Between the author and his work, a metamorphosis—or several—takes place. Gide, in a subtle introduction to one of his early volumes, shrewdly refused to explain his baffling work. For, if an author may know what he intended to say, he never knows whether he said only that. And "one always says more than just that." Balzac thought he portrayed a society and wrote as a supporter of orderly monarchy. Dostoyevsky declared his love for Christ above truth, but he unleashed demons. One of the ablest critics of our age, Gaëtan Picon, who for several years stood close to Malraux (serving as "Director of Letters" under the Minister of Culture), has expanded those views in a suggestive volume of aesthetic speculation,

L'Écrivain et son ombre (Gallimard, 1953). A work inevitably undergoes metamorphoses as it passes from its creator to its public or rather to the multiple audiences that it encounters in diverse countries and through successive ages. It is also metamorphosed by what comes after it, at times having stemmed from it. It may become banalized, or, on the contrary, it stimulates other imaginations, fertilizes other intellects. Without probably having ever read it, Malraux here meets with a famous development of T. S. Eliot in "Tradition and the Individual Talent" (1917). A new work (a painting in a real or imaginary museum, a symphony, a striking novel such as Joyce's, Kafka's, or Proust's) transfigures and substantially alters all that is set next to it or what is read after it.

The literary work suffers from limitations that partly explain why Malraux's impatient and all-embracing genius always granted it less attention than he did to others arts (music excepted, to which he was much less sensitive). It is not a universal language, for it stands in need of translation, especially where poetry is concerned. It is dependent upon adaptations if it is a tragic or a comic play. It is more closely bound up with its time, its society, the mores observed around it than Leonardo, Rembrandt or Cézanne may have been. The literary author's presence is often more embarrassingly felt, perhaps more obstreperous (Montaigne, Corneille, Rousseau, Hugo) than that of Bosch, Vermeer, Chardin, or even Delacroix. And, for Malraux the agnostic, in search of "le sacré," that mysterious and revered element is more easily perceived in Sumerian and Egyptian, Romanesque and Gothic statues than in Dante (seldom mentioned by Malraux), in Shakespeare (who never seems to have been aware of Christ) or in Goethe. The last, however, was, after Ovid and Apuleius, the one among Malraux's predecessors who was most deeply concerned with metamorphosis: that of plants, on which he published a volume in 1790, and that of animals, to which he devoted another treatise in 1819.

"Stirb und werde!" Goethe used to say; "Die and become!" Malraux, who courted death so many times, has finally been claimed by it at the age of seventy-five. He had alternately seemed to be half in love with death, like Keats, and to be overawed by the definitive change it works in a mortal, "transforming life into destiny." To him, the creator was, not he who fixes and arrests change, but he who metamorphoses. In one of his very last pronouncements, on page 297 of *L'Homme précaire*, he declared: "It is one of the major characteristics of creation to dedicate a work to metamorphosis, hence to endow it with life." After the fascinating interpretations that he had proposed of Gothic sculpture, of Goya and Manet, he concluded his long career with a few pregnant pronouncements on Balzac, Flaubert, Zola. In an age in which literature has been vilified by its very practitioners more than once, Malraux had the courage to challenge such "miserabilism":

> The abjection of societies is saved only by their literature; for literary creation does not express men. It transcends then mysteriously, even when it rails at them.

PART 2

CONSCIOUSNESS AND EXPERIENCE

5

Metamorphosis and Biography

JEAN CARDUNER

The first pages of the *Antimémoires* are a vigorous indictment of autobiographical writing. This should not surprise any readers already familiar with Malraux's extreme reticence regarding any allusion to his private life. "Je ne m'intéresse guère" (I am not interested in myself). This is clear, and after the militant narcissism of so many contemporaries, such an attitude arouses sympathy and approval.

We know that Malraux began writing this book in the beginning of the summer of 1965 on the ship carrying him toward the Orient. A shock had been necessary to make him start writing again, a violent crisis that would pull him from the intellectual stagnation in which he had been caught since 1958, when he became cultural minister of General De Gaulle.[1] Moreover, it is this crisis that led his physicians to recommend this journey and pushed this man, who was not interested ("Je ne m'intéresse guère") in himself, to write some very violent letters to his wife, at the exact same time as he was writing the beginning of the *Antimémoires*:

De chaque escale, aux mots que lui fit parvenir ma mère, répondirent dans un crescendo impressionnant, des lettres débordantes d'accusations inimaginables dans leur disproportion. Quand il revint de son périple en Août, il intima à ma mère l'ordre de s'en aller.[2]

(At every port, he answered the notes my mother sent him with an impressive crescendo of accusations whose disproportion was unbelievable. In August, when he returned from his long tour, he gave my mother notice to leave.)

It seems that we are dealing with two distinct characters: the "JE" of the work, a lucid, well-constructed and coherent character—let us call him Malraux—and the "JE" of daily life—let us call him André— prey to the same difficulties as all of us, often incapable of rational and reasonable adult behavior.

This separation between André and Malraux, between the man and the legend is not new, and all readers of Malraux at one time or another have been fooled by it. Indeed Malraux created his own legend very carefully, and then upheld it, conforming to a well-established tradition in the literary world. It must be underlined that Malraux did not innovate in this domain (Gide was a good model), but he brought more talent and energy to this undertaking than the majority of his contemporaries. To state this does not at all help the critic if he or she settles for noting that one must not confuse the man and the author; however, a careful reading of the novels quickly reveals that André's own particular mythomania is very narrowly related to the creative genius of Malraux.

The publication of the *Antimémoires* (and a few years later of *Le Miroir des limbes*, of which they are the first part) allows one to state the problem in a new manner. Many of Malraux's fictional texts have often been perceived as autobiographical; but other texts, actually autobiographical, have been considered fictional. In *Le Miroir*, where he uses texts lifted from previous novels and combines them with his "mémoires," Malraux, for the first time, reveals his hand, and we may examine the complex relations between the imaginary, the experienced (*vécu*), and reality in his work.[3] All the more so because, for the first time, we are helped by the publication of written testimonies by Malraux's friends or relatives. That of his nephew, Alain Malraux,[4] offers us precious glimpses into Malraux's life after 1945, which, combined with *Le Miroir*, permits us to sketch the beginning of a true understanding of Malraux's creation. In particular, it permits the juxtaposition of an admirable prologue to the *Antimémoires* and raving accusations written at the same time by the same man. This can only prompt us to read again carefully this same prologue, which Philippe Lejeune has called the "dernier grand réquisitoire dressé contre l'autobiographie"[5] (the last great plea against autobiography).

André versus Malraux

Valéry, who, amongst those of his generation, is probably the fiercest enemy of the autobiographical genre, is the first author quoted in the text. Malraux's famous "que m'importe ce qui n'importe qu'à moi!" (of what importance is what is only important to me!) seems to echo Valéry at the beginning of *Propos me concernant*.[6] "Que me fait ma biographie? Et que me font mes jours écoulés? . . . Non, je n'aime pas les voies anciennes de ma vie." (What do I care about my biography? What do I care about days that have passed. No, I don't like bygone ways of my life.) Valéry and Malraux thus share a very firm critical attitude rooted in a clear concept of personality: we define ourselves only in so far as we project ourselves toward the outside, in the world and in action. This attitude is shared by Claudel, who stated it clearly at the time of his interviews with Jean Amrouche, published under the title of *Mémoires Improvisées*;[7] and we remember that Claudel is, among the authors of his generation, the one whom Malraux most admires (much more than Gide, who was one of his friends). One must accept the "je ne m'intéresse guère" of the beginning of the *Antimémoires* as the authentic expression of a personality theory that Malraux holds strongly, that he brings into play in each of his books, and shares with other important authors. This is a consequential choice since it defines its author in relation to a tradition and a literary practice. The references given in the text are revealing: Gide, Rousseau, Dostoyevsky, Saint Augustine, Saint-Simon, De Gaulle, T. E. Lawrence, Joyce, Proust, Freud. In explaining his choice, Malraux situates his work and himself amongst his peers.

The ever lucid Valéry, however, writes this paragraph in "Poésie et pensée abstraite," an article dedicated to poetic creation and appearing in *Variéte*:

> Je m'excuse de m'exposer ainsi devant vous; mais j'estime qu'il est plus utile de raconter ce que l'on a éprouvé, que de simuler une connaissance indépendante de toute personne et une observation sans observateur. En vérité, il n'est pas de théorie qui ne soit un fragment soigneusement préparé de quelque autobiographie.[8]

> (I apologize for exposing myself thus before you; but I think it more useful to tell about what has actually been experienced than to simulate a knowledge independent of any person and an observation without observer. To tell the truth, there is no theory that is not a carefully prepared fragment of some autobiography.)

Therefore, if Valéry is to be believed, (a reliable witness, since he is opposed a priori to any autobiography), any theoretical choice is also a sort of confession; as there can be no knowledge independent of the individual, neither is there any theory independent of its author. This is a trite statement; what makes it interesting is that it comes precisely from Valéry! Any violent rebuttal of the autobiographical genre is always suspect, in any case and, as Philippe Lejeune says, "beaucoup de ces réfutations sont à juger comme des conduites"[9] (many of these refutations should be judged as types of behavior).

It is, therefore, necessary to note every close relation between the personality theory and daily life, between memory and the text, between the inner "JE" (André) and the public "JE" (Malraux), between the individual and the character. In the prologue, Malraux approaches it straightforwardly, setting the problem of *être* and *faire*:

> Il est admis qu'un homme est d'abord ce qu'il cache. On m'a prêté la phrase d'un de mes personnages: "L'homme est ce qu'il fait." Certes, il n'est pas que cela; et le personnage répondait à un autre, qui venait de dire "Qu'est-ce qu'un homme? Un misérable petit tas de secrets...."[10]

> (It is assumed that, first of all, a man is what he hides. The sentence of one of my characters has been attributed to me: "Man is what he does." But he is not only that; the phrase was a reply to another character who had just said, "What is a man? A miserable small heap of secrets....")

As Malraux at this point quotes *Les Noyers de l'Altenburg (The Walnut Trees of Altenburg)*, a book that is partially integrated into *Le Miroir*, it is not without interest to quote the original text. It is situated at the beginning of the second part of *Les Noyers*, before the Colloquy. Walter Berger has come to greet his nephew Vincent, and he questions Vincent about his brother Dietrich Berger's suicide. After a reply in which Vincent explains that his father had written in his will, "Ma volonté formelle est d'être enterré religieusement" (It is my express wish to have a religious burial) but that erasures permitted the reading of the original phrase "ma volonté formelle est de n'être pas enterré religieusement" (it is my express wish not to have a religious burial) we read:

> —La crainte? ... suggéra Walter.
> —Ou la fin de la révolte: l'humilité.
> —Et d'ailleurs, que savoir jamais? Pour l'essentiel, l'homme est ce qu'il cache....
> Walter haussa les épaules et rapprocha ses vieilles mains, comme les enfants pour faire un paté de sable.
> —Un misérable petit tas de secrets.
> —L'homme est ce qu'il fait! répondit mon père, presqu'avec brutalité.[11]

> (—Fear? ... suggested Walter.

—Or the end of revolt: humility.
—Besides, what can ever be known? For what is essential, man is what he hides.
Walter shrugged his shoulders and brought his old hands close together, like children about to make a mudpie.
—A miserable small heap of secrets.
—Man is what he does! my father answered, almost with brutality.)

This scene is taken up once more in the first part of the *Antimémoires* (pp. 17-38), but Malraux suppresses the last words "presqu'avec brutalité" (almost with brutality) as if to attenuate the emotional reaction of Vincent Berger.

"On m'a prêté la phrase d'un mes personnages" (The sentence of one of my characters has been attributed to me), says Malraux. But this character is not just anyone. Vincent Berger is, in *Les Noyers*, a double of Malraux, who will choose to call himself Berger in the resistance in 1944 and who will christen his second son, born in 1943, Vincent. The suicide of Dietrich Berger, Vincent's father, is really the suicide of Fernand Malraux, which took place in 1931. Malraux says so further along, and Clara speaks of it in her own memoirs.[12] The opposition between *être* (being) and *faire* (doing) between *ce qu'il cache* (what he hides) and *ce qu'il fait* (what he does) is, therefore, not an abstract opposition, but rather a personal drama tragically lived by Malraux. Here the testimony of Alain Malraux must be cited. It is a bit long but revealing.

> André était de ces êtres qui, lorsqu'ils ne réagissent pas immédiatement à un choc important, enfouissent ce qu'ils ressentent au plus profond d'eux-mêmes et ne se permettent de la revive qu'à retardement, en général par transposition, réactions bien ultérieures mais alors redoutables, d'une violence inouïe, ravageant tout sur leur lancée, obscurcissant le jugement, et faisant parfois de celui qui en est l'auteur sa propre dupe. Ou encore, comme dans le cas de la relation avec De Gaulle, lui faisant adopter un tout autre registre, à la manière d'un peintre qui, réagissant à quelque chose d'imprévu, comme un brusque changement d'atmosphère, modifie abruptement le caractère de sa composition et supprime toute une perspective pour lui substituer un autre fond qui en fera une autre toile.
>
> La mort volontaire de mon grand-père, André l'avait, à son habitude, ensevelie, comme tout ce qui lui était essentiel. Il l'aimait en craignant, selon ses propres termes ce qu'il y avait d'imprévisible dans sa nature, sans se rendre compte que le phénomène se reformerait d'une manière identique entre ses enfants et lui. Ne m'a-t-il pas dit de son père, quatre ans après la mort de ses fils, ce que j'avais entendu presque mot pour mot à son propos de la bouche de Vincent: "Lorsqu'on lui disait au revoir, on n'était jamais tout à fait sûr qu'on le reverrait"?[13]

(André was one of those beings who, when they do not react immediately to an important blow, carry their feelings inside. They allow themselves only to relive such a blow much later, and generally by transposing it. Reactions come with hindsight, are all the more dangerous, incredibly violent, and destructive, clouding judgment: such people make fools of themselves. Or still, in the case of his relationship with De Gaulle, his tendencies made him use a completely different tone: he was like a painter reacting to something unexpected (for example, a sudden change of atmosphere) who quickly modifies the characteristics of his composition and omits a complete perspective and substitutes another background so as to fashion a different canvas.

André had willfully buried my grandfather's suicide the same way he did everything that was essential to him. He loved him, while, according to his own terms, being fearful of his own nature's unpredictability, unaware that the phenomenon would repeat itself in an identical way between his children and himself. Indeed, had he not told me something about his own father, four years after the death of his sons, something I had already heard about him, word for word from Vincent's mouth: "When saying goodbye to him, one was never completely certain ever to see him again."?)

We see, then, that at the very beginning of *Antimémoires*, there is a key episode of Malraux's deep, emotional life: the suicide of his father. Without trying for the moment to interpret the effects of this episode, let us remark that at the beginning of his last great book, Malraux presents with utter clarity the problematical relationship between his literary creation and his personal life. His theoretical hostility toward the autobiography can really be interpreted, as Valéry suggests, as a carefully concealed fragment of his biography, which the reader will have to decipher. It would require a book to attempt to unravel this hidden confession and to understand fully the global meaning of Malraux's creation. At this time I can only confine myself to the formulation of a few hypotheses, which I shall attempt to outline in this short article.

Metamorphosis and Malraux

In the prologue of the *Antimémoires*, Malraux recalls Dostoyevsky and writes:

> A supposer que *La confession de Stavroguine* fut réellement celle de Dostoievski, il aurait métamorphosé l'affreux événement en tragédie et Dostoievski en Stavroguine, en héros de fiction—métamorphose qu'exprime à merveille le mot héros. Il n'est pas nécessaire de modifier les faits: le coupable est sauvé, non parce qu'il impose

un mensonge, mais parce que le domaine de l'art n'est pas celui de la vie.... Cette métamorphose, l'une des plus profondes que puisse créer l'homme, est celle d'un destin subi en destin dominé.[14]

> (Supposing Stavrogin's confession—from *The Possessed*—was really Dostoyevsky's own, what he did was to transpose the appalling event into tragedy, and Dostoyevsky into Stavrogin, into a fictional hero—a transposition that is perfectly expressed by the word *hero*. No need to modify the facts: the guilty man is saved, not because he has imposed a lie, but because art and life are on different planes.... This metamorphosis of a fate undergone into a fate transcended is one of the most profound that man can create.)

We are here at the heart of the problem of artistic creation, according to Malraux. The word *metamorphosis* applied to the transformation of an actual event into fiction reappears three times in several lines and is linked to the creative power of the artist. It is, therefore, necessary to ask oneself about this word and to try to discern the meaning it might have for Malraux.

The word appears in French around 1530 as a common noun; from 1488 on, it was known as the title of the French translation of the poem of Ovid. Marot writes (quoted in Robert):[15]

> ... métamorphose est une diction grecque vulgairement signifiant transformation, et a voulu Ovide ainsi intituler son livre, parce qu'en celui-ci il transforme les uns en arbres, les autres en pierre, les autres en bêtes et les autres en autres formes.

> (... metamorphosis is a Greek word whose ordinary meaning is transformation. Ovid wanted this name for his book because in it he transforms some into trees, others into stones, others into beasts, and others in other shapes.)

The etymology is perfectly clear: the word indicates a "changement de forme" (change of form). The first definition from *Robert* specifies:

> Changement de forme, de nature ou de structure si considérable que l'être ou la chose qui en est l'objet n'est plus reconnaissable.

> (Change of form, of nature or of structure which is of such considerable magnitude that the being or the thing involved can no longer be recognized.)

However, this extremely general and complete definition is illustrated by examples that all come from mythology: Metamorphosis of gods from Graeco-Roman mythology. Successive metamorphoses of Vishnu. Metamorphosis of a man into an animal. In each case, changes in form are caused by a magical or divine power. Consulting *Littré*, one discovers that the first meaning given is the same: "changement de forme en une autre opéré suivant les païens, par les Dieux" (change from one form into another that pagans ascribe to the gods). The meaning of the word that comes first to the mind of any cultivated man, its original meaning, is therefore linked to the realm of *sacré* (the sacred). It is not at all surprising that Malraux entitles his last three volumes on art: *La Métamorphose des dieux*.

Littré and *Robert* list secondly the definition used by the natural sciences, and the most common examples concern the transformations of caterpillar into butterfly or of tadpole into frog.

These two definitions of the word belong to the most general meanings given to it, but there are nonetheless profound differences between a Greek god's change into a human being and a tadpole's change into a frog. A complete inventory of every occurrence of the word and an analysis of the contexts in which it appears would be required to understand completely Malraux's concept of metamorphosis. Since this research has not yet been done, one can only rapidly reflect on different synonyms of the word *métamorphose* and wonder why Malraux thrust them aside. Let us consider *transmutation, conversion, avatar, transformation*, and *évolution*. Without being exhaustive, this list is instructive. *Transmutation* is too closely related to the vocabulary of alchemy; *avatar* has either a religious meaning (first meaning: incarnation of Vishnu) or a pejorative one in common use; *transformation* is too trite and *évolution* too exclusively related to biology. Metamorphosis has the characteristic of suggesting both the world of the gods (*avatar*) and the natural evolution of living beings. It thus offers a possibility of superimposing these two meanings (and eventually confusing them), and it is infinitely richer in possibilities. It seems, therefore, possible to advance the hypothesis that Malraux uses the word *metamorphosis* in two different ways (mythologically and biologically) depending on whether he is talking about the physical universe or the relation between life and artistic creation.

For Malraux, a work of art (sculpture, painting, poem, novel) is not a "work-in-itself" endowed with an immutable or eternally valid meaning because it throws light on an aspect of an essence called human nature. A work of art, on the other hand, is an infinite series of potential metamorphosis, which modify and enrich it constantly. Of course, the work itself does not change. A Gothic sculpture that we admire today in a museum is in reality the same artifact that was in a thirteenth-century cathedral. What has changed is the relation of this work to a totality. To simplify, let us say that the imaginary museum is today the totality to which the statue refers, and it has replaced the cathedral. We do not and could not attribute the same meaning to the statue as did a Christian during the Middle Ages. When the word *metamorphosis* designates this change, it, therefore, implies a change in the nature and structure rather than a change in the form. A change in the nature because the passage from Malraux's *l'imaginaire de vérité* (world of imagination as truth) to *l'imaginaire de fiction* (world of imagination as fiction) implies that the religious object (*sacré*) has become an art object. A change in structure because Malraux sees the work of art as an element of an ensemble including the artist, the value system in which he creates, and his public. This structure possesses an invariant: the work; but the other elements are, by nature, condemned to change, being linked to History, and thus to Time. The meaning of the work will necessarily change when any of the variable elements of the structure is modified. This is the meaning of "la métamorphose des dieux"[16].

In the mythological sense of the word *metamorphosis*, the cause of the change is outside of man: it concerns the gods (or Destiny). This change is, therefore, reversible: Jupiter changes himself into a swan and becomes mortal, to seduce Leda; his feat accomplished, he becomes Jupiter once again. In *La Condition humaine*, Ferral asks Gisors: "À votre avis, pourquoi les Dieux ne possèdent-ils les mortelles que sous des formes humaines ou bestiales?" (Why then, in your opinion, do the gods take on human or animal shape in order to possess mortal women?) And Gisors responds: "Un Dieu peut posséder . . . Mais il ne peut pas conquérir. L'idéal d'un Dieu, n'est-ce pas, c'est de devenir homme en sachant qu'il retrouvera sa puissance; et le rêve de l'homme, de devenir Dieu sans perdre sa personalité."[17] (A god may possess . . . But he cannot conquer. The ideal of a god is to become a man while knowing he can keep his power; and the dream of man, to become a god without losing his personality.) In other words, every man dreams of a reversible metamorphosis, becoming a butterfly while retaining the possibility of returning to the caterpillar state. The human condition makes this dream forever impossible, since it is precisely the biological meaning of the term *metamorphosis* that implies an irreversible evolution: every organism that hatches in a different form from the adult must submit to radical transformations to achieve the evolution programmed in the genetic code (and let us not forget that the genetic code is transmitted by the sire). If Malraux speaks only rarely of evolution, but nearly always of metamorphosis, it is because evolution is a gradual and continual transformation that spreads over a long period and whose successive stages are not separately perceived, whereas metamorphosis indicates a radical, often unexpected and unforeseen change when it concerns a man instead of a representative of the animal or vegetable kingdom. That which exists before the metamorphosis is irretrievable and unrecognizable after the change. If continuity exists, it is neither visible nor perceptible, but hidden, and one must discover it. We find the *problématique* of *Les Noyers* again. According to Möllberg, discontinuity is the law of history: "L'homme est un hasard et pour l'essentiel, le monde est fait d'oubli."[18] (Man is an accident, and fundamentally the world is made from oblivion.) Vincent Berger does not know what to answer, but his meditation in front of *les noyers* (walnut trees) gives him the idea of a "métamorphose sans fin," an idea that comes from Möllberg himself when, prior to stating the phrase I have just quoted, he says: "Peut-être l'aventure humaine ne se maintient-elle qu'au prix d'une implacable métamorphose." (Perhaps human adventure only maintains itself at the price of a relentless metamorphosis.) Could not one maintain that the opposition between Möllberg and Berger is exemplified by their use of the word *metamorphosis*? Möllberg qualifies it as "implacable": it is therefore fatal, inevitable, and, he would add, impossible to recognize or understand. Whereas for Berger the metamorphosis is *sans fin*: it is thus actually linked to life and not to a whim of destiny or history; it should then be possible to decipher the meaning of it. According to Möllberg, metamorphosis would belong to a mythological order; according to Berger, it would belong to a biological order. How could one avoid thinking of the last years of Malraux's life when he followed with excited interest the spectacular progress of molecular biology? However, if this analysis is accurate, the difference between Berger and Möllberg is infinitely less radical than had been believed. All Malraux's works since *Les Noyers* have attempted to find arguments to justify Berger's intuition rationally, but reading *L'Homme précaire* leads one to wonder whether Malraux did not side with Möllberg's pessimism at the end of his life.

We are here in the domain of ideas. In his work, Malraux always sought to bring the ideological world closer to the world of everyday life. On the one hand, he always sought to bring his ideas to life by embodying them in characters and concrete situations; on the other hand, he always lived according to his ideas and conceived his ideas according to his life. It is precisely this very personal dosage between thought and action, living and writing, that is the most evident characteristic of Malraux's work and life. To understand better the notion of metamorphosis at the heart of Malraux's work, we must examine what the idea owes to his biography.

Basically, There Are No Adults

As we saw earlier when he spoke of Dostoyevsky's transposition of true fact in the novel, Malraux uses three times in ten lines the word *metamorphosis*. We have just explained that the notion of metamorphosis implies a natural change, irreversible and definitive. If then the true fact is transposed in the novel, it will be, by this very transposition, forever deleted: the butterfly cannot become a caterpillar again. It is clearly seen that this metamorphosis is one of *destin subi* (fate undergone) into *destin dominé* (fate transcended): the true fact is that it is either an act of another person, and it is of course imposed on me; or it is an act of the author of the metamorphosis. Now, Dostoyevsky's example is illuminating: the act he mentions is a crime that haunts the life of the subject; it is not a voluntary act. For example, in Malraux's case, a voluntary act like his involvement in the war in Spain, was already the sign of *un destin dominé*. The act that signifies *un destin subi* is the one that instinct and irrational feelings impose on the subject. The word *act* must here be understood in its broadest sense. This act may very well never be actualized; it may be either a phantasm or simply the absence of an act [not to have done what I ought to have done]).

It is perhaps useful to quote "D'une Jeunesse européenne,"[19] the fundamental essay in which Malraux reveals very clearly his conception of "MOI" (EGO):

> Le MOI, palais du silence où chacun pénètre seul, recèle toutes les pierreries de nos provisoires démences mêlées à celles de la lucidité; et la conscience que nous avons de nous-même est surtout tissée de vains désirs, d'espoirs et de rêves. Notre vie involontaire—presque toujours bien loin d'être inconsciente—dominerait l'autre sans un effort constant.
>
> (The EGO, a palace of silence that each one of us enters alone, hides all the gems of our provisional insanity mingled with those of lucidity; and the consciousness we have of ourselves is particularly woven with vain desires, hopes, and dreams. Our involuntary life— almost always conscious—would dominate the other life without constant effort.)

In every human being there is a continuous struggle between involuntary life and voluntary life, purposefully conscious, ordered by freely chosen values. It is another formulation of the dialectics of *être* and *faire*; but the two forces are not equal, and the supremacy of the *faire*, of the voluntary life, can be achieved only by a constant effort. This *schème* (a word that Malraux uses in *Les Voix du silence;* one could also use *structure*) is sufficiently evident in each of Malraux's books and does not require further explanation. It does account for the constant activism of characters who can do nothing but die once they have ceased to act or to struggle. There are numerous anecdotes concerning Malraux's superb intellectual machine always functioning, and he himself has often explained how he used to select a subject of precise reflection about which he exercised his mind while he seemed to dream. Alain Malraux quotes a revealing statement from a context that is no less revealing:

> Pour Noël (c'est en 1964) nous changeâmes encore de palace, nous égarant au "Dolder" près de Zurich, où, l'été 61, après l'accident de Gautier et Vincent, nous avions fait un premier séjour. C'était là, appuyé au balcon de sa chambre, qu'il m'avait dit un jour: "Tiens, pendant une ou deux minutes, je crois que je n'ai pensé à rien; ça ne m'était pas arrivé depuis vingt ans.[20]
>
> (For Christmas (the year was 1964) we changed hotels again and

went astray in the Dolder near Zurich, where we had already stayed in the summer of '61 after Gautier's and Vincent's accident. It was there that, leaning on the balcony of his room, he said to me one day: "Well, for a minute or two I think I thought about nothing at all; that hadn't happened to me for twenty years.)

It is significant that this statement was made shortly after the death of his sons, right at the beginning of the nervous breakdown that would lead him to consult Doctor Bertagna. (There are some similar traits in the portrait of Garine!) Malraux's "ne penser à rien" (to think about nothing) always means abandoning himself to day-dreaming and is always perceived as threatening. It is opening the door of this "palais du silence" in which the "provisoires démences" (provisional insanity), which it conceals, rapidly become permanent if the will does not restart very quickly the intellectual machine, fixing for the mind a very precise territory to explore and a goal to reach. Malraux's "ne penser à rien" *always* means "subir son destin" (to submit to one's fate).

Just at this moment in his life, after 1961, for Malraux, "subir son destin" evidently meant accepting the death of his sons. This drama did not reside in the political domain or in the world of individual adventures. It therefore could not be overcome by just another act. It had to be "metamorphosized." And Malraux would have to wait until 1965 to be able to write again.

Malraux had experienced many dramas in his life. Imaginary dramas—by this I mean intensely dramatical situations—as well as very real dramas. These dramas always resulted in radical breaks with the past, as if the victim of humiliation needed metamorphosis in order to become a different person, a hero, if possible, and forget his humiliation. The psychological motivation of the air expedition attempting to find the queen of Saba's capital (an episode in Malraux's life that is very difficult to understand in any other way) should certainly be explained along such lines. This is not the time to count Malraux's successive breaks with the past. Visualizing the film of his life in our mind is sufficient for us to see that it was a series of metamorphoses; changes of the public figure, from adventurer in Indochina to Minister of Culture of the Fifth Republic, being the best known. Those of Malraux himself (of André in the sense in which he says enviously of the general: "il n'y a pas de Charles") are more carefully concealed but, without doubt, more important since they determine the other metamorphoses.

If the fictional transposition of an act transforms it, then a careful reading of the author's work reveals a certain number of scenes or episodes that are the metamorphosis of true, authentic acts. And since metamorphosis is linked to the radical change in the nature of the act in question, above all, the work's passages that are least obviously autobiographical must be analyzed. The author revealed himself more authentically in fiction than in memoirs. Was it precisely to put us on the wrong track that

Malraux used fictional texts in the *Antimémoires*? And when, in the closing pages of *L'Espoir*, he wrote about Manuel (who is not an aviator and, therefore, is often neglected when considering the Malraux of this period):

> Un jour il y aurait la paix. Et Manuel deviendrait un autre homme inconnu de lui-même, comme le combattant de la Sierra avait été inconnu de celui qui avait acheté une petite bagnole pour aller faire du ski dans la Sierra.
> . . . .
> Manuel entendait pour la première fois la voix qui est plus grave que le sang des hommes, plus inquiétante que leur présence sur la terre—la possibilité infinie de leur destin.[21]

> (One day there would be peace. And Manuel would become another man unknown to himself, just like the Sierra's combatant had been unknown to the one who had bought a small car to go skiing in the Sierra.
> . . . .
> For the first time, Manuel heard the voice that is deeper than men's blood, more worrisome than their presence on earth—the infinite possibility of their destiny.)

Was not Malraux speaking about himself?
Alain Malraux writes:

> A l'exception du général De Gaulle, figure tutélaire qui venait confirmer la règle, il n'y avait pas d'exemple que l'auteur de *L'Espoir* n'eût pas rejeté ses proches—femmes et enfants—les uns après les autres; pour longtemps ou pour toujours; la mort en avait frappé quelques uns à temps, avant que son système d'évictions successives n'ait pu leur être appliqué.
> La rupture était inscrite en lui....[22]

> (With the exception of General De Gaulle, a tutelary figure that confirmed the rule, every example showed that the author of *L'Espoir* would reject those close to him, wives and children, one after the other; for a long time or forever, death had struck down some of them before he could apply to them his system of successive evictions.
> The rupture was inscribed in his life....)

The original rupture happens during childhood, and Malraux often said that he detested his own, although no one ever actually knew why. When he spoke of T. E. Lawrence, saying, "La plus mince humiliation de son enfance est toujours prête à surgir; les actes éclatants qu'il a accomplis, il ne les retrouve que par une véritable prospection" (the slightest humiliations of his childhood were always ready to show through; as for the astonishing deeds that were accomplished by him, he found them only by thorough digging), he was certainly thinking of himself as well, especially when he claims he was convinced that "le processus créateur du romancier est lié à la nature du passé qui l'habite ou qui le fuit"[23] (the creative process of the novelist is linked to the nature of the past that inhabits him or that flees from him). We can, therefore, suppose that the successive breaks in his life were reactions to deeply felt humiliations. The humiliation was passive (*subie*); the rupture was an act of will: would this then be the origin of the *schème* allowing transformation of *destin subi* into *destin dominé*?

The break with Madeleine Malraux, about which we know the basic facts thanks to the evidence of her son, permits us to see the complexity of Malraux's psychological reactions. This break was linked to the accidental death of his sons, probably experienced as suicide, therefore a voluntary break with him. Alain Malraux reports to us André's last words to his son Vincent when Vincent came to tell him of his departure for Port-Cros with Gautier (they were going to study together for their exams at the home of an old friend): "Mets-toi bien dans la tête que tu peux faire ce que tu veux, cela ne me concerne pas." (You can let this sink into your head: you can do what you want; it doesn't concern me.) What a rejection! Throughout their adolescence, the two boys always felt unaccepted by their father. But this "it doesn't concern me" has, after the death of the boys, a tragic ring. It must be remembered that Malraux had not at first wanted the birth of his first son and that he had convinced Josette Clotis to have an abortion. Josette was unable to bring herself to do it and Malraux had reconciled himself to the idea of having a second child.[24] The roots of his first feelings of guilt were undoubtedly there, perhaps repressed by the dedication of *Les Noyers* to Gautier, whom he always preferred to Vincent (to compensate?). Gautier was, moreover, the only son whose name was Malraux, this because his Uncle Roland had recognized him, something André could not legally do because he was still married to Clara. Roland was Madeleine's husband when he was arrested by the Gestapo on March 21, 1944 (he died later in a concentration camp). Malraux did not actively enter the resistance until then, and we must remember that shortly before Roland's capture, he learned that his youngest brother, Claude, who was later shot by the Germans, had also been captured. Malraux did not enter the active resistance sooner because he had valid and excellent reasons. But it is possible that reproaching himself, the prestigious eldest, for being the only brother still free (and several months later the only survivor), he transferred his guilt on his second son, Vincent, born in November 1943, attributing his "nonengagement" to Josette's pregnancy. One may even wonder if, after the death of his brothers, Malraux does not reproach himself for having lived calmly and happily with Josette from the end of 1940 until 1944, as if he himself had experienced, after his escape from prison camp, the reflex he attributes in 1941 to Vincent Berger (his double), who, while he is dying, at the end of *Les*

As a child, about 1905

"Le fond de tout, c'est qu'il n'y a pas de grandes personnes..."

Noyers de l'Altenburg thinks:

> Il était possédé d'une évidence fulgurante, aussi péremptoire que ce sifflement ténu dans sa gorge: le sens de la vie était le bonheur, et il s'était occupé, crétin, d'autre chose que d'être heureux![25]

> (He was possessed by a fulminating evidence as decisive as the whistling caught in his throat: the meaning of life was happiness, and jerk that he was he had busied himself with other things.)

If one adds that Josette died tragically in 1944 while Malraux fought on the Alsatian front, the details of the drama are complete. André will marry his sister-in-law, Madeleine, in 1948; the simplest solution since after Malraux's return to Paris, she raised Josette's sons, Gautier and Vincent, with Alain, born several months before the death of his father. Being the mother of Malraux's sons must not have been easy; to be their stepmother, even less so. In any case, the death of his sons would fatally bring about the end of a marriage made for their sake and maybe also out of a sense of duty toward Roland.

If one considers the suicide of Malraux's father, all elements of the crisis are present. The father's death had been sublimated after many years, which shows the depth of the shock, by the choice of a father figure, General De Gaulle, to whom Malraux was absolutely loyal (to the point of totally rejecting his daughter Florence when she showed her opposition to the general's Algerian stand, by signing the Manifest of 121). But the death of his sons (perceived as suicide) reopened badly healed wounds, heightened his pain, and set off a destructive psychic mechanism that would have certainly shattered Malraux, had he not met Doctor Bertagna, who cured him and to whom all Malraux's admirers owe eternal gratitude for having permitted the birth of the second part of *Miroir des limbes*, the conclusion of *La Métamorphose des dieux*, and *L'Homme précaire* in the peaceful retreat in Verrières, where "André menait enfin la vie qui lui convenait: sans famille"[26] (where André finally led the life that suited him: without any family).

At the very beginning of the *Antimémoires*, Malraux quotes the priest whom he asked what confession had taught him: "... le fond de tout, c'est qu'il n'y a pas de grandes personnes" (basically, there are no adults), and he adds at the end of the following paragraph, to be quite certain that we understood, "Je suis d'accord avec l'aumonier des Glières" (I agree with the Glières chaplain). I believe this sentence is the key to the works and to the personality of Malraux. All the ruptures, all the changes, in his life, result in the "découverte d'un secret simple et sacré" (the discovery of a simple and sacred secret). This was the second to last sentence in *Les Noyers*. Why did Malraux, when transcribing this phrase once again in *Le Miroir*, qualify this secret as "très simple" and "intransmissible"? It is because, if the best thing man can do with his life is "transformer en conscience une expérience aussi large que possible" (change into consciousness an experience as wide as possible), in this "expérience" are some elements that can reach the level of consciousness only at the end of life and are, therefore, intransmissible. Gisors said: "Il ne faut pas neuf mois, il faut soixante ans pour faire un homme . . . Et quand cet homme est fait, quand il n'y a plus rien en lui de l'enfance ni de l'adolescence, quand vraiment il est un homme, il n'est plus bon qu'à mourir."[27] (Sixty years, not nine months, are needed to make a man. And when the man is made, when nothing of childhood or adolescence remains, when he is really a man, he is good only for dying.) He was thinking of his son, Kyo, who was lucky enough to die young and heroically. If Kyo had survived the revolution, if he had been able to witness its defeat (in Spain and elsewhere), if he had seen his father, his brothers, his sons, and his wife die, he would have undoubtedly been able to say, he who knew it all along: "le fond de tout, c'est qu'il n'y a pas de grandes personnes."

Notes

1. There is a fascinating book to write about Malraux as Minister. Something in him was not indifferent to the prestige of "officialdom." But, if he attended the cabinet meetings at the right of De Gaulle, he had to be happy to exercise power vicariously: in his own ministry he had no real power. He paid a very high price for his total faithfulness to De Gaulle.
2. Alain Malraux, *Les Marronniers de Boulogne* ("The Chestnut Trees of Boulogne") (Paris: Plon, 1978), p. 191. This is a remarkable book, very well written, and giving priceless details about Malraux's private life, without ever being tasteless. It is by far the best and the most touching portrait we have of Malraux so far.
3. The sentence written about Clappique in *Man's Fate* is here appropriate: "Ce n'était ni vrai, ni faux, mais vécu" (It was neither true, nor false, but lived). (*Romans*, Pléiade, édition de 1976, p. 498).
4. Alain Malraux is the son of Roland Malraux and Madeleine Lioux. He was born a few months before the arrest of his father. He is at present the only survivor in the family perpetuating the name of Malraux.
5. Philippe Lejeune, *L'autobiographie en France.* Paris: A. Colin, 1971, p. 80.
6. This text was first published in the book by Berne-Joffroy: *Présence de Valéry.* (Paris: Plon, 1944). It is reproduced in volume II of the Pléiade edition of Valéry's work, pp. 1515-1538. This quotation comes from page 1506.
7. Paul Claudel, *Mémoires Improvisés.* (Gallimard, 1954). See especially p. 198: "Je ne me suis jamais trouvé moi-même spécialement intéressant". In her book *La Fin et le commencement* (Grasset, 1976), Clara Malraux remembers a scene in Madrid, at the beginning of the civil war, when, in a café, Malraux quotes from memory, with José Bergamin, long scenes from *Le Soulier de Satin* (*The Satin Slipper*).
8. Valéry, *Oeuvres Complètes* (Pléiade), Tome I, p. 1320.
9. Lejeune, op. cit., p. 90.
10. *Le Miroir des limbes* (Pléiade), p. 8. All references to *Antimémoires* refer to that edition.
11. *Les Noyers de l'Altenburg* (Gallimard, 1948), pp. 89-90.
12. Clara Malraux, *Voici que vient l'été* (Grasset, 1973), pp. 172-174. She quotes the sentence: "Si je devais renaître, j'aimerais encore une fois être Fernand Malraux" (If I had to be born again, I would like once more to be Fernand Malraux). Malraux transcribed it in *Les Noyers:* "Eh bien, ma foi, quoi qu'il arrive, si je devais revivre une autre vie, je n'en voudrais pas une autre que celle de Dietrich Berger" (Well, whatever

happens, if I had to live another life, I would not want any other than that of Dietrich Berger). Clara also mentions the religious funeral requested by her father-in-law, which took place twice, first in Paris, then in Dunkerque.

13. Alain Malraux, op. cit., p. 93-94.
14. *Le Miroir des limbes*, pp. 6-7; *Anti-Memoirs*, trans. by Terence Kilmartin (New York: Holt, Rinehart, and Winston, 1967).
15. Paul Robert, *Dictionnaire alphabétique et analogique de la langue française*, Tome IV (1966), p. 387.
16. "Le monde de l'art n'est pas celui de l'immortalité; c'est celui de la métamorphose. Aujourd'hui, la métamorphose est la vie même de l'oeuvre d'art" (The world of art is not the world of immortality; it is the world of metamorphosis. Today, metamorphosis is the very life of the work of art). (*Le miroir des limbes*, p. 53).
17. *Romans*, pp. 483-484.
18. *Le Miroir des limbes*, pp. 34-38.
19. In *Ecrits*, (Texts) collection "Cahiers verts" (Grasset, 1927), p. 142.
20. Alain Malraux, op. cit., p. 185.
21. *Romans*, p. 992.
22. Alain Malraux, op. cit., p. 218.
23. Gaétan Picon, *Malraux par lui-même* (Le Seuil, 1953), p. 60, note 20.
24. The book by Suzanne Chantal, *Le Coeur battant* (*Trembling Heart*) (Grasset, 1976), tells the story from the point of view of Josette Clotis. Suzanne Chantal wrote this book, using and quoting abundantly Josette's letters to her and her diary. See pp. 182-196.
25. *Les Noyers*, p. 245. This text becomes in *Le Miroir* (p. 867): "il est possédé d'une évidence péremptoire, comme ce sifflement ténu dans sa gorge: il s'est occupé, crétin, d'autre chose que d'être heureux" (he is seized by a realization as **peremptory** as the thin hissing taking place in his throat: he has wasted his time, fool that he is, on other things besides happiness). Malraux has learned that the "sens de la vie" is not "le bonheur" (the meaning of life is not happiness). He attributes to De Gaulle this sentence "les gens ne pensent qu'au bonheur—qui n'existe pas" (people think only about happiness, which does not exist). And he quotes what De Gaulle is supposed to have said to d'Astier: "L'illusion du bonheur, c'est fait pour les crétins!" (The illusion of happiness is made for idiots!). (*Miroir*, p. 659).
26. Alain Malraux, op. cit., p. 221.
27. *Romans*, p. 566.

6

"Figures in the Carpet" of Malraux's *Le Miroir des Limbes*

JAMES ROBERT HEWITT

> *Quelle relation y a-t-il entre l'homme et le mythe qu'il incarne?*
> *André Malraux*, Hôtes de Passage
>
> *(What then is the relationship between a man and the myth that he embodies?)*
>
> *By their metaphors shall you know them.*
> *James Olney*, Metaphors of Self

There is a familiar *Paris-Match* photograph of André Malraux standing in the midst of a sea of art photos. It purportedly shows him in the process of comparing, juxtaposing, and matching the picture reproductions that comprise *Les Voix du silence*, documenting his theories on the metamorphosis of art. When Malraux published his curiously titled *Antimémoires* some years later, he seemed to be indulging in a similar process of manipulation and organization: in this case, autometamorphosis, the conscious structuring of select recollections, some of which had already been transformed in his novels, into a kind of memorial volume that bore little resemblance to conventional autobiography or memoirs.

Sequels were promised, presumably to be posthumous, yet four such appeared, in fairly rapid succession, during Malraux's lifetime and were eventually incorporated into a single text designated as volume II of *Le Miroir des limbes*. It is pertinent to note that *miroir*, both as signifier and signified, playfully resembles *mémoire*—the basic phenomenon of memory (f.) but also the literary form of reminiscence (m.), which Malraux repudiates. One notes, too, that the "limbo" reflected by the mirror of his title is not only an intermediary state between life on earth and life everlasting but also in non-Christian parlance a state that is by definition vague and uncertain, hence subject to ambiguity. It is just that note of ambiguity between two possible "realities," the lived and the recorded, that Malraux wished to strike.

Only the naïve had expected that Malraux would "tell all," that his "anti-memoires" would somehow take us behind the scenes of the legend and reveal the confidential man. Michael Beaujour has pointed out that Malraux avoids all discussion of the R.P.F., for example.[1] Malraux himself, following Proust's *Contre Sainte-Beuve*, took pains to emphasize that Bonaparte is not Napoleon, Charles is not De Gaulle, nor Victor, Hugo—and, implicitly, that Georges-André is not necessarily the "A.M." of the *Antimémoires*. What we may call the ensemble of Malraux's explicitly "memorial" writing, *Le Miroir des limbes*, was not intended to demystify but to mystify and mythify, as poets and shamans do, using mystification as revelation, *mythos* as plot and structure.

Malraux's "Intentions"

Although much contemporary critical thinking rejects as futile or illusory the concept of authorial intention, it is irresistible in instances of highly conscious (and in Malraux's case, highly unorthodox) autoportraiture, to seek out the psychological prime mover that generates the text, dictating its patterns and design: what Henry James called "the figure in the carpet."

In interviews discussing this final phase of his work, Malraux took to asserting that he had wanted to write an "anti-Proust" just as he felt that Proust had written an "anti-Chateaubriand." Typically elliptical, this would appear to mean that whereas Chateaubriand had romanced biographical reality, Proust had gone the distance, making a novel of his life. But Malraux's preoccupation with memory and transcendence, as well as characteristic aspects of his narrative technique—the manipulation of temporal structure, the pattern of calculated digression and intratextuality, his reliance on generative imagery, and his transparent pursuit of the mythopoeic—suggest that Malraux's method, if not his stylistics, is more "Proustian" than he would have us believe. Writing of Dostoyevsky and

Rousseau, Malraux seems in spite of himself to be characterizing Proust:

> Cette métamorphose, l'une des plus profondes que puisse créer l'homme, c'est celle d'un destin subi en destin dominé [A., 13].[2]
>
> (One of the most far-reaching metamorphoses that man can create is the transformation of a destiny suffered into a destiny surmounted.)

Yet there is evidence that he may also have been seeking to compose an "anti-Lawrence," that it may be T. E. Lawrence who prompted Malraux's opposition to traditional *mémoires*.

According to Malraux, in the one article he devoted to Lawrence of Arabia, the latter was overcome with disappointment on reading the proofs of *The Seven Pillars of Wisdom*.[3] He had hoped to achieve a work of "titanic proportions" but on seeing his own words in print, they seemed rather the pale memoirs of a retired army officer. None of the grandeur, none of the "reality" had been recaptured. The title of Malraux's article, "N'était-ce donc que cela?" (roughly, "Is that all there was to it?"), provides a further revealing cross-reference, for it is a recurring theme in *La Vie de Henry Brulard*, that pseudoautobiography in which Stendhal (Henri Beyle) struggled with the very problem of reconciling imagination and reality, finding language inadequate for the transcription of experience.[4]

Malraux did not want *his* reader asking, "Is that all there was?" In response to Stendhal's putative "mirror" of reality and what he believed to be the diarylike realism of Lawrence, Malraux sought a verbal "third dimension" wherein the writer transcends the quotidian, extracts the essence of events and encounters, and transforms them into their mythic counterpart. A classic instance would be the "return to the earth" that he experienced flying over the desert, fictionalized in *Le Temps du mépris*, and subsequently relives/recreates in *Les Noyers de l'Altenburg* (*The Walnut Trees of Altenburg*) and again in *Lazare*. A perceptive reading of *Le Miroir des limbes* calls for the correlation of certain key, recurring figures—as divergent as caves, cats, gallows, and snow—figures that clearly haunted Malraux and that make of his *Le Miroir* neither memoirs nor chronicle but rather a poetic *rêverie* rooted in metamorphosis and thanatopsis.

Time, Death, and the "Tombeau" Figure

The *Antimémoires* calls attention to its structure in two conspicuous ways. Four of five section headings bear titles of earlier Malraux works, signaling that fiction is at least partially the framework for decoding this unorthodox set of recollections. Secondly, individual chapter units have date headings such as 1958/1965, 1934/1950/1965, recalling Malraux's use of journalistic "datelines" in *Les Conquérants* and *La Condition humaine*, a documentary device to suggest the dramatic progression of time. The effect here is just the opposite. Multiple temporality is employed to evoke simultaneity of experience. The "present" 1965 text, recording visits to Hong Kong, Cairo, Benares, and so on, is meant to conjure the totality of Malraux's "encounter" with each place at several different points in time. The door is open to shifts of memory, elusive and barely perceptible, past and present being *superimposed*.

Malraux's oft quoted explanation that his "*anti*-memoirs" answer a question that memoirs do not ask, seems unduly elliptical and unsatisfying. The key to the work seems rather:

... la mémoire ... ne ressuscite pas une vie dans son déroulement. [*A*., 17]

(... memory ... does not revive one's life in chronological order.)

He will later refer to the "merry-go-round" of his memory (*C.S.*, 555). The structure of the *Antimémoires* is thus consciously antichronological, designed to take the reader outside temporal sequence and involve him or her in the writer's extratemporal meditation on death. From the first page on, death is unambiguously the *topos*, as it will be throughout *Le Miroir des limbes:*

Réfléchir sur la vie—sur la vie en face de la mort ... [*A*., 10]

(To reflect upon life—life in relation to death ...)

L'homme que l'on retrouvera ici, c'est celui qui s'accorde aux questions que la mort pose à la signification du monde. [*A*., 17]

(The man you will find here is one attuned to the questions that death asks of the meaning of the world.)

Ici je n'attends de retrouver que l'art, et la mort. [*A*., 51]

(Art and death are all I hope to recapture here.)

Le mot mort me gène, avec son battement de gong. [*A*., 64]

(The word *death* irks me with its gonglike boom.)

... la plus profonde métamorphose, celle qui aura changé en musée l'empire de la mort. [*A*., 81-82]

(the most profound metamorphosis of all, that which will have transformed the empire of death into a museum.)

... l'ennui sans fin de la mort. [*A*., 104]

(... the endless boredom of death.)

It is thus altogether natural that the dominant symbolism of Malraux's text should be that of tombs, temples, caves, and museums—all figures of repository, figures of monument and memorial. Deriding modern civilization for its failure to "invent" tombs and temples, Malraux pursues that communal image throughout the text, the text becoming in effect his own verbal *tombeau*.

The first critic to penetrate the surface of the *Antimémoires* was Michael Riffaterre, who underscored juxtaposition, simultaneity, and superimposition as the basic elements of the structure; and analogy, metaphor, and metamorphosis as constituting its essentially *poetic* quality.[5] Following loosely Riffaterre's model, one readily traces the *tombeau* figure in its various manifestations, including the library in the Altenburg priory, a tomb/museum of books and sculpture, and the Lascaux caves, where the *Antimémoires* end—and man began.

As Malraux reflects on the panorama of civilizations, his extraordinarily associative mind leaps through time and space. The pyramids of Egypt become the pyramids of Mexico, and these, in turn, are metamorphosed into modern-day museums. Versailles is also such a museum, history transformed into a monument. The glory of Versailles suggests the ignominy of St. Helena, and Napoleon serves to evoke another conqueror in exile: Hitler in the underground cave at Nuremburg. Early in the *Antimémoires*, Napoleon's funeral carriage emerges theatrically from a dusty Versailles warehouse; in the concluding "Lazarus" section of *Le Miroir*, a ghostly death carriage appears bearing a coffin. He had seen it in a Lisbon museum. By way of contrast with the "monumental," Malraux visits the simpler graves of Nehru and Gandhi, as he will visit Picasso's—suggesting, in turn, the tomb of El Cid. Every tomb is a potential museum, including the verbal one Malraux is shaping for himself.

In the closing pages of the *Antimémoires*, we find a rapid succession of tomb figures. The barren North Pole of Malraux's return flight to Paris cinematically "dissolves" into the tip of the Ile de Saint-Louis, where Notre Dame, the aboveground temple, is juxtaposed with the Crypt of the Deportees—and consequently with the superimposed figure of tomblike concentration camps. That December night becomes another December night when the ashes of Resistance hero Jean Moulin are being transported to the Pantheon, itself a tomb/museum. Just as excerpts from Malraux's memorial address for Moulin are being incorporated into his own memorial volume, the Pantheon is metamorphosed into the prehistoric Lascaux caves, where the maquis "buried" themselves and where man first recorded on walls the commemorative images of himself and the world outside.

"Thou Art No God"

> ... peut-être n'ai-je retenu de ma vie que ses dialogues. [*A.*, 561]
>
> (... all that I've retained of my life perhaps are its dialogues.)

Riffaterre rightly defines Malraux's "dialogues" in broad terms as the juxtaposition (opposition or superimposition) of his encounters, whether with persons, places, or events.[6] A great portion of the *Antimémoires*, however, is devoted to literal dialogues, reminiscent of the many discussions in his novels where characters pause to question and to clarify their actions, to define the revolution they are in the process of creating. Malraux had been grappling with the notion of leadership—and at the same time with the idea of death—ever since *Les Conquérants* and *La Voie royale* where the "chiefs" Garine and Perken die alone and alien. In the later novels, Kyo and Katow find fraternity in death; Manuel and Magnin, fraternity in life.[7]

The historic leaders with whom he has dialogued, Nehru, Mao, and De Gaulle, have all been "formed in combat" and seem to exemplify Malraux's concept of the conqueror who embodies the collective will of a people. His soliloquy on tombs and monuments thus alternates with what superficially seems political dialectic but which actually feeds to the metaphysics of his *rêverie*, his basic dialogue with death: the role of the "hero" as incarnation of an antidestiny and the myth of conquest over death.

It is, therefore, significant that in *Miroir II, La Corde et les souris*, Malraux chooses to conjure up Alexander the Great, only to dramatize that he was repudiated for his pretensions to immortality. The opening pages first prolong Malraux's dialogue series, focusing on Senghors as the poetic incarnation of Senegal, but in the chapter following there abruptly emerges from the mythic past the disconcerting "conqueror," Alexander; for forty-five pages, he then becomes the center of a supernatural detective story that is also a moral and political fable.

The Director of Museums brings Malraux the photo of an unidentified antique "object" that may be worth purchasing. They take it to a medium (!) who identifies the object as the bloodstained fragment of a garment belonging to Alexander. Although the Board of the Louvre will not hear of buying it (500,000 francs for a fourth century blood stain), the cloth of a conqueror just misses finding its "tomb" in a Paris museum. Reflecting on Alexander, Malraux recalls that he sought not so much to *possess* as simply to *conquer*—like Perken, in *La Voie royale*, who relished not the kingdom but the creation of the kingdom. Malraux then reminds us ironically that Alexander's claims to deity ended in his rejection by Callisthenes and the people: "Tu n'es pas un dieu" ... "Thou art no god." (*C.S.*, 83)

The tale is intriguing and ironic in itself; it takes on almost allegorical pertinence by its position in the text, leading directly to a chapter dated May 1968 on the student revolution and De Gaulle's subsequent fall from power. Minister Malraux is in conference with an old Spanish war crony who is denouncing Marx and Freud, our modern gods. Their dialogue keeps being interrupted by official dispatches describing the progress of antigovernment riots. It is as though the young Latin Quarter "conquerors" are echoing that distant cry: "Tu n'es pas un dieu." The next section, still more ironically, comprises Malraux's dialogue at Colombey with the retired General, while a "Merovingian snow" blankets the whole countryside:

> La cellule de Saint Bernard, ouverte sur la neige des siècles et la solitude. [*C.S.*, 154]

> (Saint Bernard's cell, opening out onto the snows of time and solitude.)

Like Saint Bernard, De Gaulle, too, had preached a crusade, but ultimately no one listened any more.

The section first published as *Tête d'obsidienne* finds Malraux at one point, after discussing *Les Demoiselles d'Avignon* in the museum at Avignon, listening to blue-jeaned youngsters who reject Picasso, negating his once revolutionary innovations. But Malraux sees in Picasso's quest that relentless *anti-destin* that smacks of the superhuman, the closest man comes to being godlike. Among Malraux's "conquerors," it is perhaps Picasso, the artist as hero, who wrests more from death than the warrior-statesman.

Although much of *Le Miroir* is written in the actual or historical present tense, the first-person present of the "Lazare" section takes on an alarming urgency. The reader knows, as Malraux himself suspected, that he is writing his last book. It is like reading the diary of a dying man. De Gaulle and Picasso gone, he writes in the shadow of their tombs.

The *tombeau* figure appears here in duplicate: the hospital room in which he is confined and the ambulance that brought him there. The ambulance, in turn, recalls the tank in which he was trapped in 1940 and from which he escaped to discover the dawn. That scene, recorded in *Les Noyers de l'Altenburg* and reproduced in *Antimémoires*, is only suggested here. But Malraux does devote nearly one-third of his closing section to a reedited version of the poison gas scene from *Les Noyers*, where Berger, in one of the novel's three "epiphanies," loses consciousness in a state of revelation: notably, that of man's fundamental brotherhood. In like fashion, Malraux claims that his own dying does not interest him, but rather the communal phenomenon of man's death:

> La mort ne se confond pas avec mon trépas. [*C.S.*, 536]
>
> (Death is something other than my dying.)

We have come a great metaphysical distance, apparently, from Perken's death in the final pages of the 1930 novel, *La Voie royale:*

> Il n'y a pas de mort. Il y a seulement . . . moi . . . moi . . . qui vais mourir.
>
> (There's no death. There's just . . . me . . . me . . . about to die.)

Despite Malraux's disclaimer, however, it is at this juncture in the text, just three pages later, that he remembers Napoleon's funeral carriage and the Lisbon museum death carriage. In the first instance, he was ruminating death; in the latter, he contemplates his own death.

Cat and Mouse

Malraux's state while hospitalized, as he describes it, alternates between fever and lucidity, which we may take as code words indicating the hallucinatory rush of associative memories and the clarity of thought needed to analyze and order them. But is this not the stylistic technique he has used throughout *Le Miroir!* Recollections of wars alternate with fragments of fiction—with, as their common denominator, the basic "escape from death" figure—and Malraux is at times quite conscious of their juxtaposition, commenting upon it.[8] Recalling the cyanide scene from *La Condition humaine,* Malraux gravely reports that he himself ("hélas!") would not have given his own cyanide to save a friend from a more agonizing death. He is simultaneously reminded of the scene from *Le Temps du mépris* where an anonymous comrade offers his life so that Kassner may be freed. Oddly enough, not many pages earlier, Malraux has introduced an anonymous hospital "neighbor" who, during the very same night when Malraux miraculously "returns to earth," dies. This seems almost a comparable "surrogate" death.

His sole real companions there are his doctor and a stuffed toy cat. The unnamed doctor, with whom he discusses life and death, is called only "the professor"; he is clearly the polarization of the malevolent "professor" in the poison gas episode: one, a giver of death; the other, perhaps, a giver of life. How fascinating, too, that Malraux finds in this life-giving physician a figure reminiscent of De Gaulle in 1940—just when the General had escaped to London to save France!

The stuffed cat, Fourrure, plays an even more decisively symbolic role. It seems an incarnation of Malraux's own pet cat, who ran across the room from him when he suffered the attack that led to hospitalization, and

"Art feeds on what it brings and not on what it abandons"

also the cat who followed him when he escaped from prison camp. It is the familiar Malrucian cat who scurries around dark corners in the streets of Shanghai or Madrid, marking a chapter ending—a "fade-out." And it is also the original stuffed cat with red balloons in Malraux's 1921 *Lunes en papier* where the Deadly Sins march off to murder Death. One thinks, too, of Clappique's cat (in the "Voie royale" segment of *Antimémoires*) named Essuie-Plume. The idea of "pen wiper" (or pen *as* wiper!) links the cat figure representing "escape from death" to the notion of *écriture* as deliverance.

Now this final cat, Fourrure, in its final metamorphosis on the last pages of Malraux's last book, becomes disembodied . . . becomes the smile of the Cheshire Cat in *Alice in Wonderland*, just as Malraux outstares death and watches it fade. He has gazed into the mirror of limbo, returned through the looking glass.

The *Lazare* passage is thus an escape from the tomb, incorporating within its text inevitable references to earlier wartime escapes. Like Proust's novel, *Le Miroir des limbes* is incessantly self-referential; the last page sends us back to the first, which begins, "Je me suis évadé. . . ." (I escaped) and proceeds to chronicle a lifetime of escapes. In addition to the nine-lived cat who seems to hover over its pages, *Le Miroir* also stands under the aegis of the elephant and the mouse. The epigraph of volume I, *Antimémoires*, is an elephant meditating its former lives. The epigraph of volume II, *La Corde et les souris*, is a brief fable of escape: the Great Artist is condemned to the gallows, hanging with his toes touching the sand; with one of them, he sketches mice who miraculously come to life and gnaw away the hangman's noose.[9]

It is words—words nibbling at the noose of time—that provide salvation and resurrection. As in the prison camp at Chartes: ". . . écrire est le seul moyen de continuer à vivre" (writing is the only way to stay alive). The words that transform experience simultaneously serve to metamorphose the writer into the monument of his designing: his mythopoeic temple, his *tombeau*.

The Gallows in the Snow

As a companion to the tomb configuration—and in addition to the gallows from which the Great Artist hangs—references to gibbets recur periodically throughout *Le Miroir:* Dostoyevsky's, Piranesi's, and the haunting gallows of German concentration camps. Undesignated, yet implicitly present, is that prototype gallows: Villon's. So, too, the "snows of yesteryear." Snow falls with remarkable recurrence on the pages of *Le Miroir*. White stretches over the North Pole mark Malraux's return from the East in the last pages of the *Antimémoires*, and this scene, as noted, "dissolves" into an icy December night when Moulin's ashes are ceremoniously moved to the Pantheon.

It is snowing when Malraux visits the medium who reveals the mystery of Alexander; that medium, in turn, recalls the "Merovingian Queen of Casamance" and the "kapok snow" of her magic tree, an image that recurs in both *Antimémoires* and *La Corde*. And that Paris snow recalls the snow "throughout all France" when Malraux lost Josette Clotis in a wartime train accident. In a reversal of the image, Picasso's widow remembers an April snow as she returns to Vauvenargues with her husband's coffin. The most memorable of all snows perhaps is the "Merovingian snow" falling incessantly, as though burying France, while Malraux holds his last dialogue with De Gaulle. It is not surprising that Malraux told André Brincourt that snow is the significant image in *Les Chênes qu'on abat*.[10]

In contrast to the warm Alsatian sunset and the pristine dawn that mark two of the "epiphanies" in *Les Noyers de l'Altenburg*, we now encounter winter and death. In opposition to tombs that are transposed into monuments, there remains still the figure of a gaping gallows and the snow that buries all. Its mythopoeic organization and design reveal *Le Miroir des limbes* as Malraux's ultimate metamorphosis of self in the face of immanent death, his redistribution of "successive selves." But in structuring their unity, he has uncovered the most menacing of figures; behind those "escaping" selves, oblivious to their metamorphosis, stands the gallows in the snow. Despite Malraux's parable of the artist and the mice, it lurks there, a bleak Beckettlike décor.

Images of Images . . .

"We must try at the outset to deliver the writer from the myth," declares one earnest Malraux biographer.[11] Nothing perhaps could be more foolhardy or less desirable. If a body of writing since Montaigne can be considered "consubstantial" with its creator, it is that of André Malraux. This was already apparent in his works of fiction, where a legendary writer and a writer of legends seemed to share a common *écriture*. In *Le Miroir des limbes*, Malraux and his "double" find even greater textual homogeneity.

Writing several years before Malraux had adopted the "mirror" of his final title, James Olney had applied the figure to Montaigne, looking in a mirror and describing "images of himself within images of himself."[12] The very consubstantiality of *Le Miroir* lies precisely in Malraux's multiple perception of self-in-metamorphosis, discovering his ultimate constancy, and in finding those mimetic verbal figures that permit us best to identify him.

Read separately, each part of *Le Miroir* stands as a meditation on death in the guise of an autoportrait, or is it rather an autoportrait in the guise of a meditation on death? In either case, the basic structural figure of the two-volume *Le Miroir* is thus: a man looking at himself and seeing death and/or a man looking at death and seeing himself. But we have no need to "deliver" the writer—his function is his own "deliverance."

The fact that the man is also a novelist of stature, a notoriously elliptical thinker, and a remarkably cunning stylist, obstinately refusing to distinguish between traditional forms of fact and fiction, gives *Le Miroir* its particular metaphorical lucidity and sometimes maddening elusiveness. Just as we now read *L'Espoir* (*Man's Hope*) not as war propaganda but as a contemporary *Iliad*, *Les Voix du silence* not as art history but as a modern *De Rerum Natura*, *Le Miroir des limbes* emerges neither as autobiography nor antibiography, but a Villonesque *Grand Testament*, the final stanzas of a lifelong poem on death.

Notes

1. Michel Beaujour, "Autobiographie et autoportrait," in *Poétique* (No. 32, November 1977), pp. 442-458. Cf. p. 455. Beaujour also seems to favor the view that Malraux's *Miroir* may correspond to that difficult-to-define "genre," the autoportrait (p. 443).
2. References in this article are to *Antimémoires* (Paris: Gallimard, 1967) and to *La Corde et les souris* (Paris: Gallimard, Folio editions, 1976). Quotations and page numbers will be identified in parenthesis as *A*. or *C.S.*
3. "N'était-ce donc que cela?" in *Liberté de l'Esprit*, Nos. 3, 4, 5 (April, May, June, 1949). I have been able to consult only the English translation: "Lawrence and the Demon of the Absolute," *Hudson Review*, VIII, No. 4 (Winter, 1956), pp. 519-532.
4. *La Vie de Henry Brulard*. Stendhal, *Oeuvres Intimes* (Paris: Gallimard Pléiade edition, 1955), p. 379: "Paris, n'est-ce que ça?" (Is that all there is to Paris?), p. 383: "Le Saint-Bernard, n'est-ce que ça?". The same verbal formula is also attributed to Lamiel after her initial sexual encounter. Stendhal is manifestly on Malraux's mind, for the key phrase "N'était-ce donc que cela?" is immediately preceded in Malraux's article by a reference to the scene in *La Chartreuse de Parme* where Fabrice betrays his wonderment that the Battle of Waterloo fails to live up to his expectations of grandeur.
5. Michael Riffaterre, "Les *Antimémoires* d'André Malraux," in *Essais de Stylistique Structurale* (Paris: Flammarion, 1971), pp. 286-306. Cf. p. 296 *et passim*. This study first appeared in English in *Columbia Forum*, XI, No. 4, 1968.
6. *Ibid.*, pp. 292-293.
7. In Malraux's last novel, *Les Noyers de l'Altenburg*, this opposition is preserved: Vincent Berger finds fraternity in death; his son, the narrator, finds fraternity in life.
8. At the very start of *Lazare*, Malraux claims not to understand why the poison gas scene has been reintroduced here. It is an obvious perpetuation of the "death revelation" motif.
9. The "fable" appears to have twofold origins. In *Antimémoires* (p. 573), Malraux describes the Nazis hanging deportees in just such a manner. In *La Corde et les souris* (p. 49), he refers to an apocryphal legend of the child Jesus who "molds" a dove, which comes to life and flies off.
10. "On Greatness and the Crisis of Our Time: An Interview with André Malraux," *Salmagundi*, No. 18 (Winter, 1972), pp. 7-8.
11. Cecil Jenkins, *André Malraux* (New York: Twayne Publishing, 1972), p. 13.
12. James Olney, *Metaphors of Self: The Meaning of Autobiography* (Princeton: Princeton University Press, 1972), p. 81.

7

Timeless Geography

MARTINE DE COURCEL

At a time when academic research is split into many specializations, Malraux challenges us to reflect on the whole of human artistic endeavors and to integrate art with our image of man engaged in a constant struggle with his destiny. It is difficult to explain Malraux's faculty for assimilating and integrating other cultures with his own, yet it is one of the most remarkable facets of his genius. Perhaps this tragic humanism can be deciphered by paraphrasing Pascal: he had already found what he sought in other cultures.

Malraux's entire work is a meditation about time and space, virtual or real, and therefore about the limits of man and about death. His dislike for the conception of death held by certain Christians played a large role in his alienation from the Christian religion. In his youth he was led to seek another vision of death in the Oriental philosophies.

His relationship with time was strange; through what might at first appear to be mechanisms of defense or denials he rejected traditional concepts of time. An unconscious rejection of death? Indeed, it was not

EDITOR'S NOTE: A similar version of this chapter was published in *Espoir*, June 1977.

particularly significant for him apart from the notion of "time-in-art," which he discovered early in his career. *La Voie royale* states that "in art it is as though time does not exist. What interests me, . . . is the decomposition, the transformation of these works of art, their innermost life, which is made from the death of men. All works of art tend to become myth."[1]

He returns to this idea in his last book, *L'Homme précaire*: "A statue of the Royal Portal at Chartres belongs simultaneously to the twelfth century, which conceived it, to eternity for the Christian who prays to it, to the present for the artist who admires it. The river of chronological time loses itself in the time of art, without upstream or downstream as in a lake with unknown shores."[2]

In the same sense that there is an Imaginary Museum, there is also an Imaginary Chronology and an Imaginary Anthology. Discontinuity of duration corresponds to Malraux's denial of time and allows him to exist in the company of thinkers, of great men, and of the artists of all centuries. So, too, his denial of spatial limitation allows him to live in the company of thinkers and creators from all countries.

There has been much debate about Malraux's distaste for introspection. That he was indifferent to "what was of interest only to himself" is masterfully illustrated by his allusiveness in dealing with his own life in the *Antimémoires*, much as a painter depicts a theme. Was this manner characteristic before his first contacts with China and India, or was it a question of a meeting, an anticipation fulfilled? Is it precisely this denial of the self, this indifference toward what is individual—an affinity with Taoism—that explains the astonishing availability of Malraux, the interior mobility that allowed him to identify not only with cultures but with individuals as well?

History as such fails to interest him; it is the significance of historic events and not the events themselves that are important to him. Again he seeks meaning. Why then should we be surprised that the same is true for his private life? There is always that distance, that self-detachment, however un-French we may find it.

He seems to have had the ability to create a vacuum within himself. It is tempting to relate this to certain Buddhist disciplines. Actually, the faculty seems to be innate in Malraux and allows him to let himself by inhabited as readily by Alexander the Great, by Rembrandt, or Picasso as by the most humble of his interlocutors. At times we get the feeling that in those moments Malraux was harking to another self, listening to the one whom he had welcomed and who inhabited him in the state that Hinduism calls depossession.

In India, Malraux found what is called there "a culture of the spirit," which was in some way natural to him in the sense that he was conscious of "the spiritual void of the West."[3] Indian philosophies led him to determine, if not actually discover, the notion of eternal change. He went beyond the idea of eternal return, which had so captivated him in Nietzsche, and directly apprehended the Hindu perception that intuits being as the eternal becoming of man. (Much later, in the same way, he was strongly interested in the idea of transmigration as it appeared in the novels of Mishima.)

A sentence in *Les Conquérants*—premonitory because written in 1928, two years before the well-known Salt March—endeared him to a whole generation of Indian revolutionaries: "If Gandhi had not intervened, India, which gives the world its loftiest lesson, would be no more than a country in revolt." It is to Nehru, moreover, that he confided, as he reports in his *Antimémoires*:[4]

> ... the resuscitated works of art, those that once would have been called immortal, alone seem strong enough to withstand the powers of sex and death. If nations did not appeal to those works, what would happen? In fifty years our civilization, which deems itself a civilization of science and is, would cease to be so and would become the civilization most subject to instinct and to elementary dreams that the world has known. It is there, I believe, that the problem of culture faces us.

If Malraux's conception of liberty and of culture may have affected the political Indians, his knowledge of the different forms of Indian art, which led him to comparisons like that of the bodhisattvas and certain Gothic statues, opened new perspectives to Indian art historians. And if Malraux was capable of writing that he felt perfectly at home in "the nocturnal garden of the great Indian dreams,"[5] reciprocally India, with the awarding of the Nehru Peace Prize in 1947, recognized him as one of its own.

Japan—another country that continued to fascinate him, where he chose to make one of his first trips as Minister of Cultural Affairs in 1958, and where he returned as a convalescent in 1974—was also very much taken with Malraux. The Japanese intelligentsia considered each of his trips an important event.

As early as 1930 he provoked a lively curiosity among his hosts when, on landing for the first time in Japan, he declared without preamble, "what interests me is *hara-kiri*, the intentional death." And the echo of that interest reappears in a phrase of *La Condition humaine*, published three years later: "to die is passivity, but to kill oneself is action."[6]

It is quite natural that a man for whom "the metaphysical character of death"[7] assumed a grave importance was fascinated by that voluntary and ritual death. Besides, let us not forget that the cult of the hero, for which—like Nietzsche, though to a lesser degree—Malraux felt a certain attraction, derives its code from the "Way of the Samurai," which also considers the problem of the purity of action, a frequent theme in his novels. He is finally more interested in revolt than in revolution and particularly in characters who knew how to say no, from Antigone to the unknown resistance fighter.

André Malraux's first journeys to Asia between 1925 and 1930 coincided with travels to the Middle East, to Persia and Afghanistan. The famous expedition to Yemen was in 1934. He used the knowledge about the art of the different civilizations acquired during those journeys for the Greco-Buddhist exhibition organized in 1931 at the Galerie de la N.R.F. and for the Gothic-Buddhist exhibition that he mounted as art director of Gallimard.

During the same period he also frequently went to Italy, to Central Europe, and most particularly to Germany, where he not only visited museums but also familiarized himself with German Expressionism, philosophy, and the psychoanalysis of Freud. In 1928 his wife, Clara, translated *The Psychoanalytic Journal of a Little Girl.*

Nor must we overlook his Russian journeys of the thirties and particularly his participation in the First Congress of Soviet Writers, which took place in Moscow in 1934. It was an opportunity for him to meet many intellectuals of the revolutionary and postrevolutionary periods, who were mesmerized by his knowledge of Russian literature.

In 1937 he went to the United States and Canada to raise funds for the Spanish Republicans. That propaganda tour, in the course of which he met Hemingway and other writers involved in the anti-Fascist struggle, was obviously not his first contact with American literature; his long interest is shown in, among others, the preface to Faulkner's *Sanctuary*, which he wrote in 1933.

Malraux was familiar with classic and contemporary English literature, but England itself did not particularly attract him. Perhaps this was because he first knew it through its Empire in the Far East, in India, or in Egypt and because the radical anticolonialist in him did not like that image. This reservation, however, did not prevent him from holding Shakespeare as one of the greats of all humanity or from speaking with enthusiasm of the English Romantics or from prefacing in 1932 *Lady Chatterley's Lover.*

After the war and his first ministerial mission under General De Gaulle, he began to travel again and never stopped, either in an official capacity or as a private citizen. In the fifties he went to Egypt and Iran several times and spoke in New York at ceremonies commemorating the anniversary of the French Institute. As Minister of Cultural Affairs he took many trips and made many speeches: Athens and Brasilia in 1959, Dakar in 1966, and Oxford in 1967.

In 1972, President Nixon, wishing to prepare for his first meeting with Mao Tse-tung, invited Malraux, who was now a private citizen, to Washington. In 1973 he returned once more to India, Bangladesh, and Nepal; and in 1974, to Japan. In 1975 he took his last trip, to Haiti.

It is clear that these trips were never touristic in the strict sense, any more than his participation in action had been simple adventure. This experience of the ubiquity of culture allowed Malraux to relate to the ac-

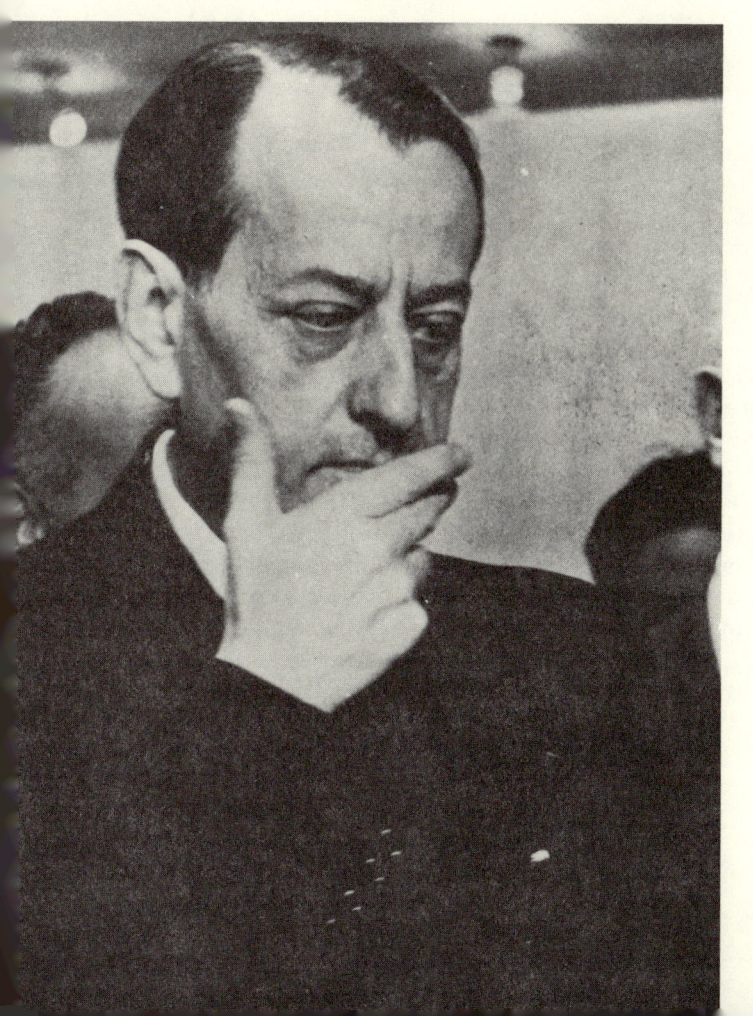

The public servant, 1945 (above)

The private citizen, 1962

quisitions of all humanity in a time and a space that he felt as immediate, in the intemporal, and it lends to his work a cosmic dimension that dismays some of his readers who reject the sublime by taking refuge in irony.

With Malraux's advance from the notion of eternal return to that of eternal beginning again, we find ourselves far from the Spenglerian pessimism that fleetingly tainted his first works. For he does not perceive this incessant change as a fatality of decline, but rather as the infinite possibility of new creations; he perceives it as antidestiny.

This explains his fascination with Dostoyevsky and even more with Picasso. What Malraux writes in *La Tête d'obsidienne* (*Picasso's Mask*) of the one he calls "the inventor of forms without peer" could as well be said of him: ". . . even the whole of his works, through the nature and sequence of the periods, is haunted by metamorphosis unlike the work of any other artist before him."[8] And further on, ". . . whereas all his great rivals were obsessed with the elaboration of their art, he alone is possessed by the passion to metamorphose his own."[9]

To carry this analogy a step further, we can ask ourselves whether the discovery that art was antidestiny was not important for his own development, for his own renascence. The death of God was certainly for him the tragedy of the modern era, but, unlike Nietzsche, he never rejoiced in the fact. "The dead gods came alive again in the statues . . ." There we cannot fail to perceive the Hindu influence, of which he wrote in *La Tête d'obsidienne* that "though indifferent to knowledge in the Occidental sense, this (Hindu) art is a means of revelation. It discovers and expresses the experience that chosen objects harbor; each of these essences reflects the supreme Essence . . . Asia considered art as a power for the penetration of the world, before it knew the sermon of Benares."[10] And the statements that he made to a French television reporter in July of 1975 can be seen in that context: "Indian thought interests me," he said. "I do not take it for my own: to assimilate the Vedanta to a Western philosophy is absolutely useless. The Vedanta is characterized by a communion with the cosmos. For the West there are ideas and concepts; for India there are states of being."

This revelation of art as antidestiny laid out in *La Métamorphose des dieux* was in itself a progression, an elaboration of the thought that came from *Le Musée imaginaire*, which is in turn extended through *L'Irréel* and *L'Intemporel* in which Malraux keeps listening to "the immemorial dialogue of creation."[11]

The renascence amounts to a new metamorphosis brought about not through the discovery of a concept, but through the audiovisual technology that, for Malraux, disrupts once again all of our acquired knowledge and casts doubt on not only the real museum but also the imaginary museum through its specific power, "that of restoring the lost unity."[12]

We can see that Malraux, who was often accused of fixating on the past, was actually involved in the most contemporary pursuits and inclined toward the latest research in the arts. He was a man who expected much from recent discoveries of cellular biology, as witness his speech addressed to Professor Hamburger on the occasion of his election to the Académie des Sciences. He was a man who took an active interest in movies—he made the film of *L'Espoir*, adapted from an episode of his novel and was twice forced to abandon the project of filming *La Condition humaine* with Eisenstein in 1934 and Zimmermann in 1970. He was a man who taped numerous programs for television—the reception accorded to "La Légende du Siècle" comes to mind as do two television films in the series made by Jean-Marie Drot, inspired by *L'Irréel* and *L'Intemporel* and commentated by André Malraux. This man, then, the multiple Malraux, believes that such techniques will revolutionize our conception of the world. Once they cease to be considered merely a means of information (message) and are seen as a means of expression (medium), the change brought about will be of the same order as the havoc caused by the alphabet.

What fascinates him is the power of these techniques to restore *simultaneously* the *entirety* of art for an enormous audience and to abolish the contingencies of space and time: "the past and the distant lands that brush against us lightly, the shattered chronology of the little screen—this is the epiphany of intemporality."[13]

Malraux's last books do not appear to close off his work, but rather to open it totally to the adventure of humanity in its becoming: "the vast resurrection of our time in which so many forms become united because they were the successive forms of the struggle of art against destiny . . ."[14] that "shows us what creative power is carried within the metaphysical interrogation posed by the means of Art alone."[15]

If Spengler deconstructed the mechanism of *The Decline of the West*, if Valéry demonstrated that civilizations, too, are mortal, then Malraux in his last pages leaves us a message that without contradicting the tragic humanism of his whole work entreats us not to despair of humanity. For if our civilization has lost the illusory certainties brought to it by the scientism of the nineteenth century and no longer knows the values on which it is based, this is less because it is passing through an unprecedented crisis than because it is at the very heart of the most fabulous metamorphosis and because "the major spiritual events have belied all predictions."[16] Perhaps only Malraux has given an answer to the question: what good is a soul if God does not exist?

Translated by Lee Leggett

Notes

1. *La Voie royale* (Paris: Grasset, 1930), p. 42.
2. *L'Homme précaire* (Paris: Gallimard, 1976), p. 280.
3. Review of *La Défense de l'Occident*, by Henri Massis in *La Nouvelle revue française* (June 1927).

4. *Antimémoires* (1967; rpt. Paris: Gallimard, Folio, 1969), p. 355.
5. *Ibid.*, p. 287.
6. *La Condition humaine* (1933, rev. 1946; rpt. Paris: Gallimard, Folio), p. 255.
7. *Lazare* (Paris: Gallimard, 1974), p. 102.
8. *La Tête d'obsidienne* (Paris: Gallimard, 1974), p. 120.
9. *Ibid.*, p. 131.
10. *Ibid.*, p. 201.
11. *Ibid.*, p. 223.
12. *Ibid.*, p. 361.
13. *Ibid.*, p. 391.
14. *L'Irréel* (Paris: Gallimard, 1974), Preface, p. vii.
15. *Ibid.*, p. 286.
16. *L'Homme précaire*, p. 330.

The "Démon des prix littéraires"—
a signed ink sketch by Malraux

8

Malraux and Death

PIERRE BOCKEL

Death, a source of fascination and ceaseless questions, has irrevocably clasped Malraux in its emaciated and fraternal arms. Death was his life's companion and also his work's central character, in turn, assuming fatality's impassive traits and heroic exaltation's mobile face. It took on the countenance of torture, but also the serenity of the life it consummated. Whatever death's semblance, Malraux's chant was one of incredible beauty.

How did death approach him? In his childhood, as the term of a path that had hardly been used? As a fundamental contradiction to the noblest desires of life? Did his father's suicide accentuate the dreaded presence? Malraux's extreme discretion about his past does not allow an answer.

Death's presence as André Malraux's familiar companion appears first in his novels through features of a hero who breaks down. Inscribed in the revolutionary scheme and suffered in terror, death is always fraternal: one dies so that others may live. And dying thus, the partisan fulfills the plenitude of his destiny and accedes to supreme liberty. "What would a life

EDITOR'S NOTE: This chapter originally appeared in French in *La Revue des Deux Mondes*, May 1978.

have been worth for which he had not been willing to die?" thought Kyo before his death. Dying always presents itself in a context of "desperate heroism" as the only escape from destiny. Death, be it self-destruction or a state sustained, is a gesture that curiously combines nobility and bitterness, fraternity and solitude, eternity and nothingness. From the depth of his prison, Kassner dreams about his death: "Beyond his cell, beyond time, existed a world victorious against pain, a twilight swept by primitive emotions where all that had been his life glided by with the invincible motion of worlds in a communion of eternity."

I only met Malraux in 1944, at the onset of adventures that were to lead us to Strasbourg, arms in hand. This first "complicity," as he liked to call it, was also the prelude of what later became a close friendship. The Vosges' combats were particularly murderous. And the coffins that lined up in the small Froideconche church in the Haute-Saône led to our most solemn exchanges.

Following the author of *La Condition humaine*, did Colonel Berger still gaze the same way upon death? Surely. Except that now a hero's death meant that such and such a comrade had fallen by our side. In the face of metaphysical questioning, the lyrical accent snapped. The mystery of death came forth spontaneously from the bloody fall. Perhaps my church affiliation encouraged him to engage me in a dialogue that soon became endless.

Death Struck Him with Blow upon Blow

And at the heart of this funereal hammering that inscribed itself in the logic of war, death approached Malraux in a most tragically unwonted way. He exposed himself to death daily and seemed not to fear it. To revenge itself for such contempt, death struck him with blow upon blow through his most cherished beings. Death aimed at his heart but never disturbed his stature. On November 11, 1944, the news came that a train had crushed his wife, Josette. It was "lightning," he said. A little later, he learned that the Germans had executed his brother Claude, that his brother Roland had disappeared in the Neuengamme concentration camp, and that Raymond Maréchal, his old companion of the Spanish civil war, had fallen in a commando attack. We then stopped talking about death. Silence united us more strongly than words, all the more so that a few days before Josette's death, I had witnessed their last kiss.

The war was ending. But death continued to strike the man it had fascinated so. In 1961, his two sons, Gautier and Vincent, were killed in an automobile accident. "Almost all those I loved were killed in accidents," he wrote. Then came the turn of Louise de Vilmorin, the friend he had found again; she was carried off by a heart attack in a few moments. And on November 9, 1970, De Gaulle, the great Oak of Colombey, collapsed. Each time Malraux returned to solitude.

An Offering to Death

In 1971, at the outbreak of the Bangladesh war, André Malraux decided to volunteer. He was stopped from joining the revolutionary army in time only by the rapid succession of events. I wondered what such a determination meant in depth. A priori there was nothing surprising for the officer of the *Frente Popular* or for Colonel Berger from the Alsace-Lorraine Brigade to find himself on the Bengal front. Our society's lethargic indifference towards humiliated nations certainly called for a spectacular witness. Malraux was ready to testify. But at his age and in his poor health? It seemed to me that a secret scheme was hidden behind this decision. Now that death had deprived him of so many affective attachments, he was weary of life. Strange misgivings came to me. Perhaps the hour had come for him to act out his old taste for suicide and for the fascinating death of the hero in an exemplary gesture. An opportunity to leave with nobleness? To make death an offering by exchanging his life for the liberty of a nation? I had written to him in this sense. His answer was immediate. In a letter of October 4, 1971, he wrote me: "Your point of view is more profound and more tragic than mine. But you should know that in everything that I do in the realm of what may be called the world's destiny, I believe myself more legitimate when I feel I am with you. For obscure reasons, if you are in the Sahara and I am in Bengal, we will die together—and you should know that you will help me die with nobleness."

A year later he was being urgently taken to the Saltpêtrière medical center.

After having reflected his own seductive face under traits of fallen heroes, after having cruelly conjoined with him through those closest to him, in 1972 death again came near, and its hallucinating stare gazed at him. "And now, it's between the two of us," had said Bernanos at the onset of his death-agony. Did he address himself to God or to Death? Bernanos thought about God, assumed Malraux. And himself? . . . "I hasten patiently toward death," he would write.

From this proximity of a death that only grazed him, André Malraux left us an important eyewitness account in which hope answers anguish: a glimmer in the night. Like Saint John's Lazarus, Malraux died a second time. Of his second death, the true death, we know and will know nothing besides the lights of faith for him who has faith. But *Lazarus* remains.

Man Face-to-Face with Judgment

"What is *Lazarus*?" I asked him the day before the book came out. "Lazarus," he said, "is man face-to-face with the mystery of Judgment." "Why this astonishing title?" André Dumas asked himself. He tried to explain this in an excellent article that appeared in *Réforme*. I hope I may be forgiven for quoting several passages that seem to shed light about this. In Chapter 11 of the Gospel according to John, writes André Dumas, Lazarus does not speak. Jesus speaks and, while on the subject, suddenly affirms his bond with the distress of Martha and of Mary. Without ceasing to be of this time and place—about which no one, including Lazarus, ever has anything to say—death then becomes the moment of life when brotherhood rises stronger than the end of such life. The meaning is probably that contrary to the immortality of the soul or to the person who would deny death, through resurrection comes about insurrection of brotherhood affirmed by God, between himself and his Son Jesus, in agony and in death. It is the brotherhood that Jesus promises for all men to live with him, the brotherhood that precedes us in Galilee, in Jerusalem and unto the extremities of earth and history. But speaking about resurrection is as difficult as speaking about death. No one has remembrance of death; only invisible God fulfills, sees, and announces resurrection. But about what men do with death and with resurrection, there is much to say. We are the only living species to know our mortality. Such knowledge is at the beginning of all human culture. Christians exist because they believe that their existence as human beings is identified with passage of Jesus Christ. Everything is born from such a mystery: culture and faith.

From the threshold of *Lazarus'* (in André Dumas's words) "door that skepticism doesn't close but that agnosticism doesn't enter either," Malraux, always in search of transcendence and the absolute, asks himself a series of questions about the day after death. Actually, because of the modesty that was a dominant trait of his character, he has persons with whom he pretends to be talking or other acquaintances from his past ask these questions.

First, before committing suicide, his father had left out for all to see an opened book with this sentence underlined: "And who knows what we will find after death?" Did Malraux, face-to-face with death, escape from the feeling that is everyone's lot? As one of his priest-friends confided, "At the end, believers or unbelievers, men always die in a tangle of fear and hope." From his Hindu friend Raja Rao, he learns that "death is a road toward light." And from his conversation with his doctor, we glean many statements that leave us perplexed about his lack of belief, statements that I myself could confirm by many astonishing utterances noted in the course of our conversations. We dealt with the death of skeptics who "almost never get away with it," with the meaning of life, the connection between explanation and meaning, the ability of science to fashion or change our planet but not man, of the absurdity of scientific truth conceived as supreme value. About science he declares: "The new god can do more than all the others because it can destroy earth. But he is a silent god," and he adds that if it were possible to "live according to Christ or Buddha, it would not occur to anyone to live according to Darwin or Newton or Einstein." Does he apply to himself this sentence of one of Dostoyevsky's character, a sentence he believes has been taken too lightly:

Colonel Berger at the end of World War II

Colonel Berger, 1944 (right)

"If I had to choose between Christ and truth, I would stay with Christ against truth"? An agnostic, Malraux recognizes that "all dialogue with death begins with the irrational," but that at the bottom, the irrational is not what is not real; and he adds that "a plausible explanation is well worth an absence of explanation."

Anguish and Hope

Such discussions constitute the revised version of the Salpêtrière experience. But the underlying feeling close to the nearness of death in which anguish and hope answer each other remains. We hear again Bernanos's words that had so struck him: "And now, it's between the two of us." At the end, who is the Other for Malraux? "You know better than I do that no one escapes God," he had admitted to me one day. But who is God? An unnamed transcendence at the heart of man? "This eternal part of man that within him goes beyond himself?" This transcendence Malraux called "brotherhood," the brotherhood that draws to its close in death and makes men free. "There is no greater love (or no greater liberty) than the offering of one's life," says Saint John. When Malraux talks about brotherhood in rigorous communion, is it in an oblique way to suggest the Source? Saint John says "Love"—"God is Love." After the day following Salpêtrière, Malraux also will translate brotherhood by love. And when he speaks about the "brotherhood that destiny does not erase," we think of Saint Paul affirming that though everything passes, only love remains. I now hear a clamor of hope in the words that he threw with his muted voice, a few weeks before living "Lazarus" in the woods of the former "maquis de Durestal," as he addressed former comrades of the Resistance: "You who are my companions of yesterday will perhaps be my eternal companions!"

"And now, it's between the two of us." I remember this harrowing cry from the death of anguish: "Ah, if later through radio and television, in front of men finally ready to hear, the last prophet screamed unto death: there is no nothingness!" Once calmness returns, he applies Victor Hugo's confidence to himself: "Je sens mon profond soir vaguement s'étoiler" (I feel my profound night become vaguely filled with stars).

"Meeting of doctors. Danger for the cerebellum: cure, paralysis or death." The outcome was cure; and more than cure, because the man who came back to us from his encounter with death was profoundly soothed. Meditation and combat seemed to have liberated him from a kind of febrile tension that was characteristic of his being. His reluctance toward emotions had considerably given way. His face seemed rested, no longer plagued by tics, and reflected kindness beyond its countenance. But nothing modified at all the flashing power of his thinking.

Malraux has now died for good. His brutal dive into a coma leaves us forever ignorant of his last glance toward death and its aftermath. One

Colonel Berger, 1944

General De Lattre de Tassigny confers the Legion of Honor on Colonel Berger, 1945

day, when I suggested to him that we might travel to Jerusalem together, his answer was: "To Benares or to Mecca, whenever you wish. But going to Jerusalem means going to Gethsemane, and there I will have to utter Christ's words." Was the Créteil hospital Gethsemane? No one will ever know.

The only word that we heard him mumble during the night of his death agony was an answer to someone close to him, who asked him if he were suffering. "It is an endless bore," he whispered. He was probably referring to the circumstances of his departure from life; while he was haunted by the mystery of death, he apparently did not fear it.

He dropped off to sleep forever with the sleep of Lazarus, "staring as he went by at the worn-out face of death," according to the last word of the book.

Translated by Jeanine P. Plottel

PART 3

PHILOSOPHICAL GLEANINGS

9

Agnosticism and the Gnosis of the Imaginary

EDOUARD MOROT-SIR

I propose calling "The Problematic of Universals"[1] the system that serves as a dynamic pattern throughout Malraux's published works and that gives them a steadily enveloping unity. That unity is achieved, despite the diversity of Malraux's texts, through a stylistic device: grouping words, phrases, and sentences around a single word—*imaginaire* (imaginary), which is both the most important signifier and its own domain of reference.[2]

The Malraucian problematic is based on an intuition of "concrete universals" that encompass the unique forms and lives of human civilizations; these are expressed by proper nouns. We discover and identify these universals through an awareness of *différence*. Our language is no longer the monologue of creative genius or even the desperate dialogue an individual uses in trying to establish contact and communication with others; our time and civilization have converted the ancient model of the symposium into the colloquium in which texts, with their infinite possibilities, have their differences transformed into harmonious coexistence and constructive confrontation. I believe Malraux develops this aesthetics of difference into a grammar of adjectival supremacy and a rhetoric of interrogation. Recognizing the stylistic coherence[3] of Malraux's works from *Lunes en papier* (1921) to *L'Homme précaire et la littérature* (1977) allows us to progress toward a deeper understanding of this author's linguistic originality.

Adoption of any set of aesthetic rules implies the progressive formation of a semantic consciousness tending to a more or less organized series of philosophical statements and leads to what was once called a *Weltanschauung*. The epistemological status of a world view has never been clear, and I do not intend to reconstitute that of Malraux. We do know that Malraux maintained an unfalteringly positivistic attitude, though he expressed it in negative terms: he never believed in the promise of metaphysics, and he frequently insisted on his agnosticism. In our times positivism has been closely related to agnosticism, thus implying a confidence in scientific knowledge. Were this true in Malraux's case, his works could be seen as contributing directly or indirectly to the human sciences, to history, psychology, sociology, anthropology. In fact, though, Malraux was never tempted by the scientific challenge. He emphasized more than once that he did not claim to be a historian of art or of culture. Consequently, his agnosticism hides an intent deeper than the usual one of denying the possibilities of metaphysics and glorifying science.

I would like to explore this very curious situation in which agnosticism promotes a knowledge neither metaphysical nor scientific. To suggest the peculiarity of this epistemological state of affairs, I use the word *gnosis* (without meaning to connect Malraux in any way with Christian or Manichean Gnosis). I propose to give the problem a linguistic formulation and to discuss it strictly at the level of the paradigmatic and syntagmatic relations between signifiers. This does not mean that I discard all references to the signified, but rather that I test the significance of each text through the actual use of signifiers in it.

With this perspective, I have limited my research to studying the following: the literary organization of the text around two words, *métamorphose* and *imaginaire*, and around two propositions, one cosmological, the other anthropological. These propositions are: "Any reality (human reality included) is subject to the universal law of metamorphosis," and "All human reality belongs to the Imaginary." It is my hypothesis that Malraux started with a cosmology of universal metamorphosis and little by little transmuted it into a poetic of the Imaginary.

The word *imaginaire* appears in semantic-stylistic constellations. Its presence can be qualified by its connections with other words. It gives rise to synonyms and antonyms. Even when absent, it continues to exercise its semantic power—an imaginary object or situation may be described without using the word *imaginaire*. *Imaginaire* belongs to what I propose calling the "imag-paradigm." As any French dictionary shows, this includes nouns, verbs, adjectives, and, more rarely, adverbs: *image* (image), *imagerie* (image making), *imagination* (imagination), *imagier* (image-maker), *imagiste* (painter), *imago* (*imago*), *imaginer* (to imagine), *imager* (to adorn with images), *imaginaire, imaginatif* (imaginative), *imaginable* (imaginable), with frequent nominal uses of the three adjectives and adjectival uses of the past participle *imagé* (full of imagery).

The normal system consists of the triangle: *imagination imaginer image.* The adjective *imaginaire* qualifies the value granted to the products of the triangle, which themselves belong to the real world. Neither our imagination nor our images are imaginary; to imagine is not an imaginary operation. The *Robert* dictionary recognizes three meanings for *imaginaire*: 1) existing only in the imagination, without reality (in this sense the word has several synonyms); 2) true only in a person's imagination (as in the French *malade imaginaire* [imaginary invalid]; 3) as substantive, the domain of the imagination. As the French language is commonly used, each element of the triangle implies the others; *imaginaire*, instead, is relatively independent. Finally, in the way in which, in our time, psychological vocabulary serves to designate and signify man's mental operations and states, the imag-paradigm participates in a very complex semantic pattern containing the words *sensation, perception, judgment, reason, sensibility, passion,* and so forth.

Here, then, is the definitive formulation of our problem: *What is the lexical situation of the imag-paradigm throughout the works of André Malraux?* I base my answer not on precise data about vocabulary concordances but on my own sampling and analysis. I do not suggest that my results are rigorous and definitive. Nonetheless, though details may be subject to revision, I believe that my general observations about lexical frequencies, relationships, and organizations are valid.

The Early Novels

Lunes en papier, that exercise in imagination, presenting a purely imaginary world, makes little use of the imag-paradigm. *Imaginaire* is absent. *Imagination* and *imaginer* appear with a meaning to be maintained in all other works: they designate the operation by which the human mind can create unreal worlds or represent to itself external aspects of the world. In each case, the words are related to the central word *conscience* (consciousness/awareness) and, more specifically, to the very frequent expression *prise de conscience*, in which *prise* has its original, literal meaning: to seize, to take possession of, as if the act of becoming conscious were like the acts of abduction, capture, and transport to another world.

Here are two examples from *Lunes en papier*:[4] "... tel que *l'imagination*[5] ne peut se le représenter sans émoi" (such as *imagination* cannot portray it to itself without emotion) (34; "it" stands for "a number of ridiculous couplets and stupid songs"), and "Et la Mort s'applique à *imaginer* un grand nombre de figures obscènes ..." (And Death works hard to imagine a large number of obscene forms) (45).

In *La Tentation de l'Occident* (1926), sampling reveals a more complex use of the *imag-paradigm*. *Imaginaire* appears twice—probably the first uses in Malraux's texts. In both cases it is an adjective subordinated to the word *rêve*, which will have an important function in the works to come: "La lecture, les spectacles, chez les gens sans culture, sont des sources de *vie imaginaire* (For people without culture, reading, plays are sources of imaginary life) (74), and "le général *imaginaire* prépare des plans logiques . . ." (the imaginary general prepares logical plans . . .) (75). Let us note in passing this first mention of a question that will become central later when Malraux meditates on the relationship between the Imaginary and popular culture.

In this work I have found many appearances of the word *image.* Among the most significant are: "nos *images* de la vie" (our images of life) (57); "devant sa plus belle *image*" (in front of its most beautiful image/reflection) (63; ambiguous reference: "its" refers to *marque* [imprint]); "Que d'*images* il faut à des hommes blancs pour leur donner une *image* nationale" (How many images white men need to give them one national image) (74); "Nous ne dessinons pas une *image illusoire* de nous-mêmes, mais d'innombrables *images*" (We don't sketch one illusory image/picture of ourselves, but countless images/pictures) (75); "la beauté des *images*" (the beauty of the images) (85; refers to Buddhist sculptures); "les *images* qui s'étaient attachées à la contemplation" (images that were attached to contemplation) (94; Taoist contemplation); ". . . le contraste entre les *images occidentales* de ses phrases de visionnaire et le calme de ses paroles . . ." (. . . the contrast between the western images of his visionary's sentences and the calm of his words . . .) (99).

The verb appears less frequently, with the meaning already found in *Lunes en papier:* "Tout le jeu érotique est là: être soi-même et *l'autre;* éprouver ses sensations et imaginer celles du partenaire" (The whole erotic game lies in this: to be oneself and *the other;* to experience one's own sensations and imagine those of the partner) (76; Malraux italicizes *l'autre;* this remark presages similar ones in *La Voie royale* and *La Condition humaine*); ". . . le Chinois *imagine*, si je puis dire, sans *images*" (. . . the Chinese imagines, if I can put it that way, without images) (77); ". . . l'idée du monde, du monde qu'il ne saurait *imaginer*, correspond pour lui à une réalité" (. . . the idea of the world, of the world that he wouldn't be able to imagine, for him corresponds to a reality) (78); "Mais je ne saurais *imaginer* sans trouble des méditations . . ." (But I wouldn't know how to imagine meditations without uneasiness . . .) (56; the expression *savoir imaginer* is typical—as we shall see, to imagine is the heart of knowledge.

The textual situation of the noun *imagination* in *La Tentation de l'Occident* is analogous to that of the verb, with a parallel meaning: "Des schèmes de vies célebres le dirigent, et courbent un instant *son imagination* docile qui tout à coup les domine à son tour" (Patterns of famous lives direct him and for a moment control his docile imagination which suddenly in turn dominates them) (75; "him" and "his" refer to the

Frenchman); "Car la rêverie, qui est encore action, est soutenue par une *imagination passive*, qui consiste en substitutions involontaires" (For dreaming, which is still action, is upheld by a passive imagination, which consists of involuntary substitutions) (76; the expression *imagination passive* probably comes from the *Essai sur l'imagination créatrice* by Th. Ribot); "Avec quelque force que je veuille *prendre conscience* de moi-même, je me sens soumis à une série désordonnée de *sensations* sur lesquelles je n'ai point prise, et qui ne dépendent que de mon *imagination* et des réactions qu'elle appelle" (No matter with how much force I want to become aware of myself, I feel I am bound by a confused series of sensations over which I have no hold and which are subject only to my imagination and the reactions it invites) (76). This last sentence is a very interesting example clearly showing the relationship between awareness of oneself, sensation, and imagination. Also, it establishes a close connection between *prendre conscience* (to become aware of) and *avoir prise* (to have hold): imagination is conquest and possession. Finally, in this work Malraux makes imagination subordinate to sensibility, a relationship he will maintain to the end, even when the human world is assimilated by the Imaginary: "Combien de siècles de sagesse nous ont conseillé de faire de notre *imagination* la servante toujours nouvelle de notre *sensibilité*" (How many centuries of wisdom have counseled us to make our imagination a constantly new servant of our feeling) (83).

Thus, in *La Tentation de l'Occident*, the imag-paradigm plays a secondary but significant role. The semantic center of the vocabulary is the word *conscience*, which denotes the act of apprehending. Around *conscience* the dominant lexemes are *culture, forme(s), rêverie(s), rêve(s)*, within the universal duality of knowledge and sensibility. This duality will never disappear. In fact, it will lead to discovery of the psychological and cosmic functions of the Imaginary.

Les Conquérants (1928) follows the same pattern. Here are a few examples: "L'*image* ridicule de l'animal ramassé, prêt à bondir, l'obsédait" (The ridiculous image of the rolled-up animal, ready to leap, obsessed him) (154); "il y a une *image*, un souvenir qui revient toujours" (there is an image, a memory that always returns) (270); "L'idée était alors dans l'air, et elle se reliait au jeu de son *imagination*, tout occupée de Saint-Just" (The idea was then in the air, and it was bound to the play of his imagination, completely occupied with Saint-Just) (153); "Je l'*imagine* tel que je l'ai vu" (I imagine him just as I saw him) (152). Malraux does not refer to the Imaginary, but to the world of the mind, of cultures, values, forms, dreams, and metamorphosis; he speaks of the succession of cultures, the differences and conflicts between them. Again there is a lexical grouping around *conscience;* occurring often are *connaître* (to know), *comprendre* (to understand), and a vocabulary related to perception, memory, and knowledge. Also centered around *conscience* is a vocabulary concerned with morality, which includes words to be found regularly in later texts: *liberté* (liberty), *destinée* (destiny), *action, passion*. The lexeme *culture* envelops historical and geographical words, with a constant passage from proper nouns to nouns used in the singular that signify unique incarnations of essences or differences. For the same signifier—for example, words like *destin, mort*—Malraux's text commutes between the two poles of the general and the unique; capitalization often indicates a singular having no plural form.

In *Royaume-Farfelu* (1928) the imag-paradigm is almost absent. Here are two rare appearances: "de pâles *images* se forment sur la mer de silence" (pale images take form on the sea of silence) (317), and "des éventaires chargés . . . d'écailles oblongues, de petits chevaux de papier, d'*images*, de sucreries . . ." (stalls full . . . of oblong shells, of little paper horses, of pictures, of sweets) (318). The two lexical groups, moral and psychological, dominate and organize the vocabulary used in descriptions and in narrative. In this exercise in pure imagination, the epistemological lexical system underlies all other vocabulary. The importance it receives implies that to write, even when one describes imaginary situations or narrates imaginary adventures, is to search for knowledge, a search ultimately leading to a *prise de conscience* or conquest.

In *La Voie royale* as well the imag-paradigm is almost absent, but it does make a few extraordinary appearances: "Arracher ses propres *images* au monde stagnant qui les possède" (Snatch his own images from the stagnant world that possesses them) (38; "his" is ambiguous—it designates Claude, or any human being, or the world itself); "*L'imagination*, quelle chose extraordinaire! En soi-même, étrangère à soi-même . . . *L'Imagination* . . . elle compense toujours . . ." (The imagination, what an extraordinary thing! By itself, a stranger to itself . . . the imagination . . . it always compensates . . .) (12; it would be interesting to study further this faculty for compensation and its links to the ambiguous status of the imagination, which is both out of the natural order of things and estranged from reality); "Il n'y a qu'une seule 'perversion sexuelle' comme disent les imbéciles: C'est le développement de *l'imagination*, l'inaptitude à l'assouvissement" (There is only one sexual perversion, as imbeciles say: development of the imagination, an inaptitude for satiety) (14); "Rêver ou lire? Feuilleter pour la centième fois l'*Inventaire*, jeter encore *son imagination*, comme la tête contre un mur, contre ces capitales de poussière, de lianes et de tours à visages, écrasées sous les taches bleues des villes mortes" (Dream or read? To leaf through the *Inventory* for the hundredth time, once again to fling one's imagination, like one's head against a wall, at those capitals of dust, lianas, and staring towers, crushed under the blue stains of dead cities) (17; Malraux italicizes "*Inventaire*"); "Soudain, son *imagination* le jeta à la place de Perken" (Suddenly his imagination threw him into Perken's place) (166). In this text Malraux seems to prefer the rêv-paradigm, and he frequently writes *rêves, rêveries, rêver*. The lexical situation has not changed: epistemological and moral patterns are combined with a vocabulary of obsession and dream.

The Later Novels

In dealing with these early works, I risk the following hypothesis: Before 1930 André Malraux is still attached to Spengler's vision of cultural metamorphosis. Later, thanks to his own epistemological intuition (that is, that to write is to become aware and, as a result, to know and to understand), Malraux will free himself from the spell of Spengler; he will master the antihistorical outlook that inspires the narrative techniques of the novels from *La Condition humaine* onward; becoming the dominant theme in *Les Noyers de l'Altenburg*, cultures will be more than the products of a universal metamorphosis—in their becoming, cultures challenge, each in its unique way, the absurdity and fatality of history.

In *La Condition humaine* (1933) I find no apparent change in the use of the imag-paradigm. Here are a few examples: "Malgré lui, il avait laissé là *l'image éclatante* de sa colère." (Despite himself, he left there the dazzling image of his anger) (362; "himself" refers to Ferral); "Cette force, *cette furieuse imagination* souterraine qui était en lui-même . . . était prête à prendre toutes les formes, ainsi que la lumière" (This force, this furious underground imagination that was in him . . . was ready to take every form, just like light) (227-228; Gisors meditating); "ce n'était pas une *imagination*, une loterie fantastique aux gagnants inconnus" (It wasn't an imagination, a fantastic lottery with unknown winners) (380; Clappique at the gambling house is winning). One finds rather frequent uses of *imaginer* meaning "to become aware of a person, a situation," and so on: "Il s'imagina elle, habitant son corps" (He imagined he was she, inhabiting her body) (274; "he" is Ferral, "she" Valérie); ". . . vous n'imaginez pas à quel point les magasins sont mal gardés . . ." (. . . you can't imagine how badly guarded the stores are . . .) (311); "*Toi, qui t'imagines si bien tant de choses, qu'attends-tu pour t'imaginer que tu es heureux?*" (You, who imagine so many things so well, what are you waiting for to imagine yourself happy?) (397; Clappique is writing to himself and is interrupted by Gisors's arrival; Malraux's italics); "Il *s'imagine* . . ." (He imagines himself . . .) (435; Kyo, in jail, is trying to picture himself dead). There is also a revealing use of *imaginaire:* "Roulant toujours sa cigarette *imaginaire* . . ." (Always rolling his imaginary cigarette . . .) (221; Gisors speaking with Tchen).

Epistemological and moral vocabulary again dominate the narration; awareness of life can cause only anguish, but the human mind, through knowledge, accedes directly to eternity: "l'esprit ne pense l'homme que dans l'éternel" (the mind imagines man only in the eternal) (464). This frequently expressed conviction in the power of the intellect could explain Malraux's reluctance to use the imag-paradigm as long as he has not mastered the full meaning of the Imaginary. Until then, he prefers the rêv-paradigm, which here designates an inferior form of consciousness and knowledge; later, he will contrast the world of dreams and reveries with the Imaginary.

In *Le Temps du mépris* (1935) the same situation obtains. Although a few texts on human creativity indicate that Malraux is meditating more and more on the function and nature of the artist, the uses of the imag-paradigm do not go beyond ordinary meanings. The combination *to see/to think* predominates. So does the duality *communion/différence*, seen as basic emotional experience; the latter forms a "monde de l'angoisse" (world of anguish)[6] (556). Malraux builds a synonymic chain typical of him with the verbs *créer* (to create), *inventer* (to invent), *se dépasser* (to transcend oneself), *se concevoir* (to conceive of oneself). Compared to these linguistic formations, the imag-paradigm is not very significant. *Imaginaire* is absent; *image* has no unusual meanings; *imagination* refers to the creation of an imaginary world, for example, "en imagination" (in imagination) (558), "dans l'imagination des hommes" (in the imagination of men) (560).

L'Espoir (1938) deepens the duality *being/acting* in the use of the verbs *être* (to be) and *faire* (to do). A look at the last section of the text shows semantic and stylistic play among the following: *sensation* (feeling), *réflexion* (reflection), *volonté* (will), *conscience de* (awareness of), *passé* (past), *projection* (projection), *homme* (man), *mort* (death), *vie* (life), *destin* (destiny), *présence* (presence), *parler* (to speak), *entendre* (to hear), *sentir* (to feel). Here are uses of *imaginer*: "*imaginer* le coup de grâce" (to imagine the finishing stroke) (775), "*imaginer* l'arrivée de 10,000 hommes démoralisés" (to imagine the arrival of 10,000 demoralized men) (779), "celui-ci ne pouvait *imaginer* sans peine que leur dernière conversation fût une discussion" (the latter could not imagine without sorrow that their last conversation was an argument) (810). Behind the ordinary meaning, one becomes aware of the obsessive effort human consciousness makes to escape the historical and sensorial given, the will it exerts to conquer another world, to control fatalistic time so that art and style can transmute a vision of the future into a passage to eternity. Through this effort, absence is converted into presence; it becomes the true presence. Malraux lived this drama intensely; it is at the heart of human creation. However, in his novels he seems to have been unable to give the imag-paradigm the full power it would have in his later writings. Or, rather, in these works he could not yet make the signifier *imaginaire* the point at which his linguistic projections converge and from which they disperse. It may seem paradoxical that this new use of *imaginaire* coincides with Malraux's abandonment of the language of pure fiction or of fiction combined with history. But is it not normal that an awareness of the Imaginary cuts short one's spontaneous use of a language of the Imaginary and invites one to use other languages in exploring it?

Malraux draws closer to an awareness of the Imaginary in *Les Noyers de l'Altenburg* (written in 1940),[7] although in this book the imag-paradigm is still less important than the rêv-paradigm. Here Malraux connects man's dreams and reveries with the concepts of culture and with man's artistic representations (*les représentations des hommes*). He emphasizes the pluralism of cultures, which he contrasts with the "*implacable métamorphose*" (142), and substitutes this pluralism for a linear philosophy of history.

First we note two uses of *imaginaire* as adjective. One is rather atypical: "C'étaient des animaux *imaginaires*" (It was some imaginary animals) (104; this is part of the description of Herman's room). The other deserves special emphasis: "C'est la table d'un *livre imaginaire* qu'il n'écrit pas, qu'il n'écrira jamais." (It is the table of an imaginary book that he is not writing, that he will never write.) (105; "he" designates Walter preparing the contents of the *Colloque*); Malraux concludes through the voice of Herman: "Il contraint les autres à le parler" (He compels others to speak it) (105; "it" refers to the imaginary book. Note the passage from writing to speaking). Here Malraux is close to his great philosophy of the Imaginary. Observe that he uses *livre imaginaire* before *musée imaginaire.* He never uses *livre imaginaire* again, although he retains the idea of the colloquium as the ultimate form of human language, which gathers together the disseminated monologues and dialogues of past cultures.

In connection with the imag-paradigm, he names Pascal twice (97 and 289); he quotes the famous fragment: "*Qu'on s'imagine . . . c'est l'image de la condition humaine*" (Let us imagine . . . it is the image of the human condition) (italics mine). Let us mention two important occurrences of *image*: "et ces ellipses, ces *images* bousculées et instinctives avaient toujours été étrangères à Dietrich Berger" (and these ellipses, these shaken-up and instinctive images had always been foreign to Dietrich Berger) (97-98), and "Le plus grand mystère n'est pas que nous soyons jetés au hasard entre la profusion de la matière et celle des astres; c'est que, de cette prison, nous tirions de nous-mêmes des *images* assez puissantes pour nier notre néant." (The greatest mystery is not that we are thrown haphazardly between a profusion of matter and a profusion of stars; it is that, in this prison, we extract from ourselves images powerful enough to deny our nothingness.) (98-99; this text echoes Pascal's fragment on the Two Infinites). In these excerpts *image* denotes and connotes all the styles characterizing man's works of art or any form of creativity. Malraux here is not concerned with a struggle between being and nothingness, a struggle belonging to the domain of blind metamorphoses, of cosmic becoming. Instead, he is exploring man's fight against destruction and death, which has become a cultural confrontation between the Imaginary and the constant threat of annihilation. The Western tradition has defined the dilemma of man's destiny by balancing two verbs: to be or not to be. Malraux does not pretend to replace the Parmenidean formula or Hamlet's version. Instead, he enriches it with an antithesis made of two nouns. He does not say: to imagine or not to be, but rather *Imaginary or nothingness;* thus, man has two options: he can live in either the world of the Imaginary, or the world of death.

Another typical use of *image* in *Les Noyers de l'Altenburg* is connected with remarks Malraux makes about ancient Egypt. He is speaking of the *double* as *image sculptée* (sculpted image) (137): "le double est au cadavre ce que l'esprit qui rêve est au corps endormi" (The double [that is, sculpted image] is to the corpse what the dreaming mind is to the sleeping body) (137). Then, when man invents the judgment of God, the *double* is replaced by the soul (*l'âme*): "Les *images* des doubles disparaissent des tombeaux" (The images of the doubles disappear from the tombs) (137). In a very significant progression of synonymy Malraux establishes a system of equivalences between *double-âme-image-sculpture* so that the two signifiers *double* and *âme* are both images, but in different cultures, and both belong to man's imaginary world; *images* are *sculptures*, so that *image* is no longer a reproduction or deformation of perceptions, but a creation of signs and symbols.

The Books on Art

With Malraux's next book, *Les Voix du silence* (1951), we find a most important change in vocabulary and subject matter. This is not signaled by the occurrence of new words, or even of new topics—all critics agree that Malraux's themes and style show a certain permanence throughout his work. Rather, the change is a matter of semantic distribution and emphasis. Superficially, the subjects seem new: the novelist has become an art critic or a philosopher. However, a closer look shows that, though the genres are different, underneath Malraux retains the same profound purpose. The novels proposed images of revolutionary conquest, whereas the books on art recount stories of artistic conquest. What is really new is the primacy given the word *imaginaire* in its dual and ambiguous function as adjective and noun. The epistemological trend, which we have observed in even the very first works, reaches full force when, thanks to his study of individual artistic creations, Malraux succeeds in identifying consciousness of the world and the world of consciousness. *Le Musée imaginaire* is both consciousness and world: "le plus vaste domaine de connaissances artistiques que l'homme ait jamais connu" (the most immense domain of artistic knowledge that man has ever known) (44).[8] "*Musée imaginaire*" designates a collection of artistic creations, the museum, metamorphosed into a new state of existence: the Imaginary. We can participate in forming this new world through a new cultural imagination in which we see those mental structures we call cultures as modes of the Imaginary.

In *Les Voix du silence* we witness a lexical reorganization and the achievement of a new and powerful coherence of meanings and references. The word *imaginaire* now stands at the center of the Malraucian linguistic universe. The hive of words has found—or, if one prefers, elected—its queen, a sort of grammatically neutral signifier, at the same time subject and complement, noun and adjective, substance and quality. *Imaginaire* becomes a subject for any possible sentence, so that a succession of propositions can be reduced to the syntagmatic chain: the Imaginary is $p_1, p_2,$

p3. ... (p for predicate). Subject of any proposition, the Imaginary has also become, in what logicians call "the universe of discourse,"[9] the ultimate complement for any other word. It possesses unrestricted ubiquity. It replaces the Being of traditional ontology; the Cartesian God, guarantor for the laws of the mind and the world; the *Nature* of the Enlightenment; the Hegelian *Begriff* (concept), ...

This new linguistic order implies a radical modification in the philosophy of the sign. In Derrida's terms, one could ask: does substituting the Imaginary for Being or the God-guarantor of our "intelligible sky" permit Malraux to avoid the "logocentrism" dominating Western languages? We can guess Malraux's answer: "One should not confuse my overt and obviously deep agnosticism with traditional forms of skepticism or even with more recent manifestations of positivism or relativism. I reject the logical order of our grammars and their ontological preconceptions. Furthermore, in putting the Imaginary at the center of man's linguistic universe, I show that my agnosticism is not a simple confession of epistemological limitation and ignorance but a new philosophy of the sign, without which any attempt to escape our cultural jails is futile. By admitting the triangular system of the signifier, the signified, and the referent, philosophers and linguists remain realists even when they bracket the problem of the referent. I do not go back to an idealistic interpretation of the sign. The true issue for the writer is to take the sign out of the domain of realism. It does not suffice to state that the referent is unknown or unknowable, as do ancient and modern agnosticisms. One should understand that the referent—or the domain of references, as I prefer to put it—is neither the Universal Being nor any regional being. Such entities do not exist. The only reality through which the sign makes sense in its three dimensions of signifier, signified, and referent is the Imaginary. Thanks to my linguistic conversion, our languages can stay outside the ontological scheme: essence/accident, substance/phenomenon. It is more difficult to avoid the grammatical laws of the syntagmatic order, which use ontological preconceptions for the sake of efficient communication. This is why my agnosticism has turned into a rhetoric of interrogation. I do not use the old trick of suspending or neutralizing judgment (what the Skeptics called aporetic and ephectic). For me, affirmations and negations are constantly reanimated by the interrogative dynamism of the Imaginary. This is why in the end my agnosticism is a Gnosis of the Imaginary, a Gnosis of the world where answers are questions, and truth, style. I do not see any other way to fight logocentrism and its realist or idealist conveniences!"

Let us look now at the lexical situation in the four parts of *Les Voix du silence: Le Musée imaginaire, Les Métamorphoses d'Apollon, La Création artistique*, and *La Monnaie de l'absolu*.

In *Le Musée imaginaire* the dominant words are *métamorphose, culture, conscience, style, stylisation, formes, rêves, représentation, annexion, suggestion* (or *suggérer*). Needless to say, this lexical series forms a synonymic lattice, with nuances, at times coming close to opposition (for instance, the passage from *rêves* to *formes* to *style*). Compared to this set, the imag-paradigm remains in its former modest position, but, although it occurs infrequently, little by little it takes possession of the text.[10]

We rarely find *imaginer* and *imagination* in *Le Musée imaginaire*. Some examples are: "La reproduction a créé des arts fictifs (ainsi le roman met-il la réalité au service de l'*imagination*)" (Reproduction has created some fictitious arts [thus does the novel put reality at the service of the imagination]) (22); "son art—même sa technique—servait son *imagination* autant que celle-ci servait son art" (his art—even his technique—served his imagination as much as his imagination served his art) (70; the art of the draughtsman; *imagination* refers to the artist's talent and creativity as well as to his power of imagining, that is of representing an ideal being); "un monde créé pour le plaisir de l'*imagination*" (a world created for the pleasure of the imagination) (85); "Lorsque la peinture avait été un moyen de transfiguration, cette transfiguration . . . avait reconnu à l'*imagination* des droits royaux, s'était liée à une profonde coulée de fiction" (When painting had been a means of transfiguration, this transfiguration . . . had recognized that the imagination had royal rights, was linked to a deep flow of fiction) (118); here the key word is *reconnaître* (to recognize)—it indicates that imagination needs an act of recognition, a kind of artistic awareness, if it is to be part of the world of art and culture and to be promoted to a new universe of discourse.

Because in this book Malraux prefers the word *forme*, he uses *image* no more frequently than *imagination*. *Image* refers mainly to paintings or other works of art seen and understood as images. Here is a typical example: "L'art était subordonné à beaucoup de ces *images*, et nous les subordonnons toutes à l'art" (Art was made subordinate to many of these images, and we made them all subordinate to art) (64). At the end of the book, however, in describing the cinema, Malraux gives *image* its usual meaning (note that in English when the cinema is spoken of, *image* is translated as "frame"): "Ce qu'appellent les gestes de noyés du monde baroque n'est pas une modification de l'*image*, c'est une succession d'*images*" (That which the drowned's gestures in the Baroque world call forth, is not a modification of the image, it is a succession of images) (120); "Le problem n'était pas dans le mouvement d'un personnage à l'intérieur d'une *image*, mais dans la succession des plans" (The problem was not in the movement of a character within a frame, but in the sequence of the shots) (120-121); "Il put chercher ensuite la succession d'*images significatives*" (Then he could try to find the sequence of significant frames) (122; "he" refers to the film-maker); "La suggestion du mouvement, telle qu'elle naît des *captures d'images* de Degas ou des abstractions scythes . . ." (The suggestion of movement, as it is born of Degas' images-captures or of Scythic abstractions) (123).

For the first time *imaginaire* becomes the key lexeme in the imag-paradigm; it has a dual use, nominal and adjectival. The title itself—*Le Musée imaginaire*—stands for the text in its entirety, as signifier and referent. The all-enveloping consciousness of past and present works of art, the Imaginary Museum contains them unique and whole. It is a sort of Hegelian Concrete Universal, comprising all particular and historical universals. The world of art has achieved awareness of itself and, in so doing, has become a world of awareness. This reversibility of the noun and its adjectival or nominal complement is the most important law of Malraux's linguistic universe: as the word refers to the world, it itself forms a new world that integrates the old one, the one we call reality. The adjectival or nominal supplement is the dominant power here: "Imaginary Museum" does not signify "a museum with the property of being imaginary" but "the new type of museum, a *museum of the Imaginary*," which retrieves past forms of art and past cultures under the cupola of the Imaginary; thus it is the *Imaginary of the Museum.* Do not scorn such grammatical playfulness simply because it has become a facile game in some recent literature and criticism. For Malraux, reversal is the universal act of human consciousness; it fuses subject and object, mind and world, cosmos and culture; it is the act by which man, in his unique victory over destiny, changes the real into the Imaginary and the Imaginary into the real. At the level of grammar, reversal makes the adjective or the nominal complement more than simply information added to the noun; instead, it subordinates the noun to its complement. True nominalization is achieved by the adjective or the complement. The dual status of the signifier *imaginaire*, adjective or noun, is the best example of this new linguistic awareness. Finally, let us note that for Malraux the universal nature of reversal allows literature devoted to the arts ultimately to attain a victorious achievement: knowledge of the arts, which is actually the awareness of art as something integral, self-sufficient, permits a fusion of art and knowledge of what art is so that knowledge of the arts becomes *the art of knowledge.* It is our civilization that fuses these two parameters, artistic and epistemological, of any culture. Such is Malraux's linguistic Utopia under the roof of the Imaginary Museum.

Later we shall see how we can live under this roof and enjoy a linguistic architecture that remodels the modern museum according to the plans of Rabelais's abbey or of the City of Sun. For the moment let us look at a few examples of how *imaginaire* conquers the text. *Imaginaire*, as adjective, is associated with *monde* (world) (52, 89), with *spectacles* (shows) (54, 85), with *peinture* (painting) (104). Two expressions deserve a closer look: "comme si un *imaginaire esprit de l'art* . . . poussait . . . une même conquête . . ." (as if an imaginary spirit of art . . . pushed . . . a same conquest . . .) (44) and "Ainsi entrent dans l'art ces *sur-artistes imaginaires* . . . qui s'appellent des styles" (Thus enter into art these imaginary superartists . . . which are called styles) (44). The neologism *sur-artistes* suggests the passage from the real world, to which the artists belong, to an imaginary world, where they are transmuted into styles. The syntagm *imaginaire esprit* is curious because Malraux rarely puts the adjective *imaginaire* before the noun. Normally, this sentence would have called for the usual order: *esprit imaginaire*. It would be too easy to assume that Malraux here is simply trying to vary the placement of the adjective. It is as if the expression were suggesting a double noun: a mind or spirit that is imaginary, and an Imaginary that has the quality of the mind or of the spiritual life. Here we can observe Malraux's use of apposition at the level of the microtext, an apposition that helps us to follow when he equates style with *sur-artiste*. Style, as a quality of the actual work of art, is the true spirit of art. Malraux concludes: "Ce domaine—qui s'intellectualise tandis que l'inventaire et sa diffusion se poursuivent . . . c'est, pour la première fois, l'héritage de toute l'histoire." (This domain—which intellectualizes itself while the inventory and its diffusion continue . . . for the first time it is the inheritance of all history) (44). The verb *s'intellectualiser* (to intellectualize itself) emphasizes the epistemological value of the Imaginary and contrasts it with the real world of human dreams and reveries. Does this not prove that under the surface Malraux means "un imaginaire esprit de l'art" to express the underlying equivalence of three nouns even though on the surface grammatical rules require him to retain the formula adjective, noun, complement?

Here is a short list of significant uses of *imaginaire* as noun: "*ce réalisme de l'imaginaire*" (this realism of the imaginary) (54); "l'expression . . . de l'*imaginaire harmonieux*" (the expression . . . of harmonious imaginary) (70), "un autre puissant *domaine de l'imaginaire*: le théâtre" (another powerful domain of the imaginary: the theater) (89); "la fin de *l'imaginaire*" (the end of the imaginary) (118). One sentence contains a typical grouping of words around *imaginaire*: "L'idée même de beauté, en particulier dans une civilisation qui fait du corps humain l'objet privilégié de l'art, est liée à *l'imaginaire* et au désir, unit les formes qui seraient 'belles' à celles qui le sont; c'est une idée-fiction" (The very idea of beauty, particularly in a civilization that makes a privileged art object of the human body, is linked to the imaginary and to desire, unites forms that would be "beautiful" and those that are; it's a conceptual fiction) (85). One wonders if Malraux is not referring implicitly to Croce's *Logic* when he coins the expression *idée-fiction*, which would serve to translate those conceptual fictions Croce contrasts with fictional concepts.[11] However this may be, the sentence uses an important semantic constellation in explaining the place of beauty as the *idée-fiction* of a civilization where the human body is at the same time imaginary object and object of human libido.[12] One would wish and expect more comments on this connection between *imaginaire* and *désir*. To my knowledge, Malraux never gathered together and elaborated his ideas on eroticism and on the relation between the Imaginary and the dream within our culture. But there is an evident link: erotic experiences, artistic experiences, cultural participations are various expressions of a similar effort to imagine oneself and the world. The Imaginary is the "intelligible world," which makes those experiences possible and which renders intelligible the existence of beauty as *idée-fiction* for our culture. Without being facetious, I might suggest that the

Imaginary Museum shelters the existence of the Imaginary Brothel.

To sum up these comments on *Le Musée imaginaire,* I quote a sentence from its last paragraph: "C'est selon un ordre mondial que se classent, confusément encore, les vagues successives de la résurrection mondiale qui emplit *le premier musée imaginaire*" (It's according to a world order that are ranked, still confusedly, the successive waves of the worldwide resurrection that fills the first imaginary museum) (125). Here Malraux juxtaposes *ordre mondial, résurrection mondiale, musée imaginaire.* More specifically, the Imaginary constitutes a new universal order, which replaces divine order and challenges the natural order: *the order of the Imaginary*, which is resurrection as a new form of knowledge, the episteme of the Imaginary, the only resurrection and immortality possible. At the lexical level, *imaginaire* has suddenly passed from an obscure and rarely used word to the forefront of the semantic stage; it becomes the strongest organizer of Malraux's lexicon. The other elements of the imag-paradigm are now its implicit servants, even if Malraux does not clearly specify their respective functions.

In the other three parts of *Les Voix du silence* we find a similar situation: primacy of *imaginaire* in the imag-paradigm. In a significant reversal, *image* serves to qualify the Imaginary in its universality or subspecies. The adjective *imaginaire* has definitely become *the* signifier, the term of reference for all sorts of nouns, although *image* continues to compete in the text with *rêve* and *forme*.

Here are a few pertinent excerpts from *Les Métamorphoses d'Apollon:* "pour la première fois apparaît une *fenêtre imaginaire* qui découpe la scène" (for the first time appears an imaginary window that outlines the scene) (261; referring to Giotto's invention of the frame); "objectivité *imaginaire*" (imaginary objectivity) (220; about medieval sculptures representing the Virgin, Christ, the Saints); "Ses plus hautes figures étaient une *cour imaginaire* de ce Beau dieu" (His most exalted figures constituted an imaginary court for this handsome god) (266; about Giotto).

In *La Création artistique* we find: "*Voir* veut vite dire pour nous: imaginer sous forme d'oeuvre d'art. Toute *imagination* de cet ordre relie la forme réelle à une forme déjà élaborée . . ." (For us *to see* quickly means: to imagine as a work of art. All imagination of this kind couples the actual form with one already worked out . . .) (272; Malraux italicizes the word *voir*). This text allows us to grasp the new status of *imaginer* and *imagination*. Both relate to man's capacity for seeing through the intermediary of "telling": to imagine is to see within a speech act, and imagination denotes the action of seeing thanks to language. Also, this text shows the epistemological intent of Malraux's language, the ultimate end of which seems to be to make the real world into a world that is intelligible to man, which suggests that what is intelligible is the Imaginary.

Finally, in *La Monnaie de l'absolu* we find these examples: "*la prise de l'imaginaire* sur les hommes . . . *l'Imaginaire* avait cessé de s'incarner

"Human reality belongs to the imaginary"

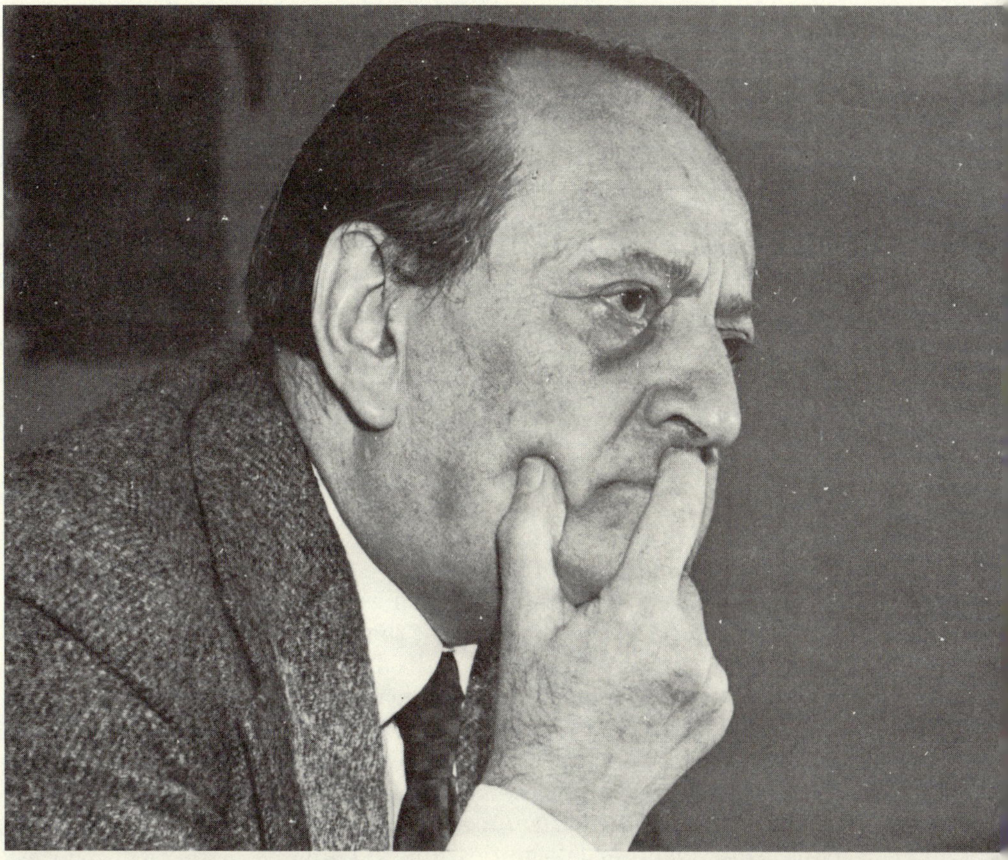

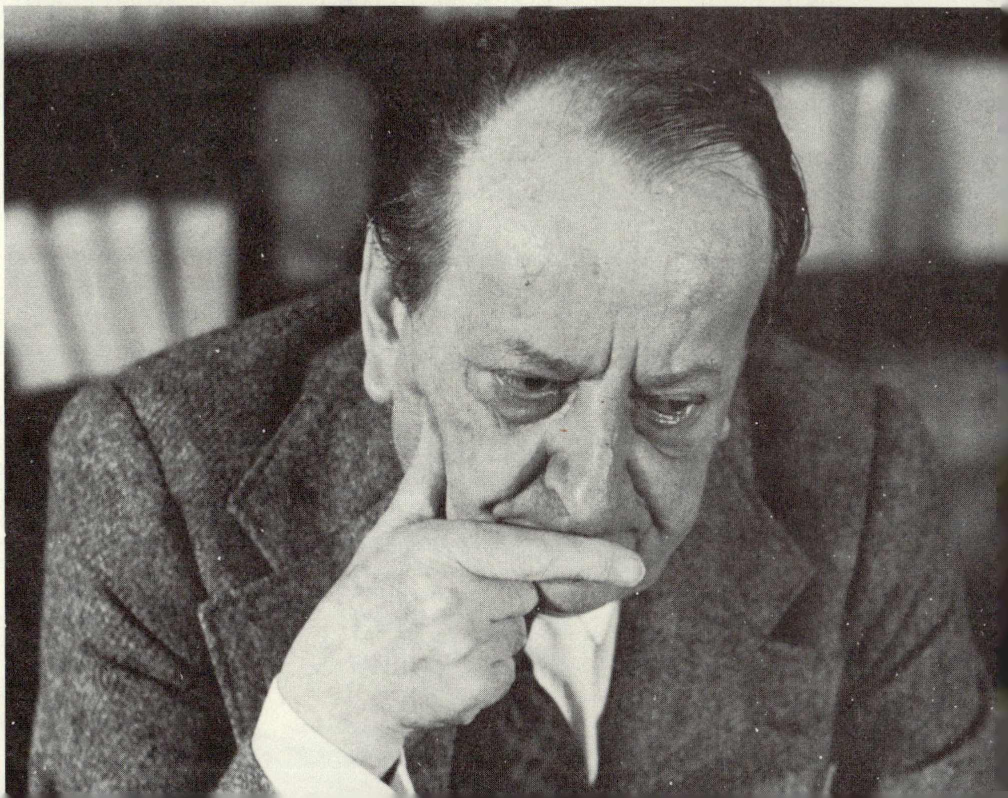

dans l'histoire vécue" (the hold the Imaginary has over men . . . the Imaginary had ceased to become embodied in real history) (485); "un imaginaire qui la nie" (an imaginary that denies it) (486; "it" stands for *bourgeoisie*); "aux pays de *l'imaginaire*" (to the land of the imaginary) (493).

We must, however, wait for *La Métamorphose des dieux* (1957)[13] to observe the imag-paradigm in full bloom. In this work *imaginaire* and *image* appear very often. *Imagination*, instead, almost disappears, and *imaginer* is used only as a synonym for *prise de conscience*, often with *on* (one) or *nous* (we): *on imagine* (one imagines) or *Imaginons* (let us imagine) (for instance, 2, 50, 66, 92, 149, 244, 270, 308, 382). Let us also note the quasi synonymy of "avec tant de lucidité et *d'imagination*" (with so much lucidity and imagination) (187), which echoes the last paragraph of the first part of *La Métamorphose des dieux*, where the author intervenes in his text with the first-person statement: "Je tente ici de rendre intelligible ce monde . . ." (I try here to make this world intelligible . . .) (35); the deictic play between *je, ici,* and *ce* contrasts the particularity of the attempt with the universality of its achievement. This is why the imag-paradigm is from now on limited to the couple *imaginaire/image*, though from time to time Malraux uses *imaginer* and its noun *imagination* to remind us that the author of a text that promotes, projects, brings to consciousness the Imaginary must himself make a constant effort to imagine the Imaginary.

After describing an act of intellectual faith, Malraux stresses the nature of his book (35): it is not a history of art or of aesthetics. It is a *signification* (in its etymological meaning: production of signs) becoming aware of itself. Such a *signification* appears with "la première civilisation consciente d'ignorer la signification de l'homme" (the first civilization aware of not knowing the meaning of man). Thus, awareness of a state of ignorance leads to awareness of a *signification;* to signify is to imagine the Imaginary. The title of the book gives a name to this operation of signifying: metamorphosis. Thus, the process of signifying is assimilated to the most universal action in the real world, which is the passage from form to form. In using the preposition *de* between *metamorphosis* and *gods* in the title, Malraux goes beyond simply playing skillfully with one of the most common ambiguities of French grammar. Does he mean the act by which gods are themselves metamorphosed or the act by which gods organize man's world of illusion? It would be naïve to accept the first hypothesis. What Malraux is saying is more complex. The act by which we become conscious of man's significance gives birth to the man of significance and the world of significance, so that the word *gods* in its alliance with *metamorphosis* changes an apparent metaphor (the gods being metaphors for the works of art by means of which man discovers and creates his own significance) into a reversing synecdoche: the gods are part of the Imaginary, and the various imaginaries get their "part d'éternité" (35). The metaphoric gods symbolize a diachronic play of infinite metonymies, which, in their succession and juxtaposition, constitute the Imaginary.

Now let us look at how Malraux uses *imaginaire* and *image* in the great trilogy containing *La Métamorphose des dieux*, *L'Irréel*, and *L'Intemporel*. In writing *imaginaire*, he explores all of the word's grammatical possibilities: as an absolute subject or complement, with an adjective, with the preposition *de* (of) and its object or itself as the object (*imaginaire de . . .*, or *. . . de l'imaginaire*), or as an adjective after a noun. He tries all these grammatical variations, not systematically, but with a sure instinct for the appropriateness of each, sometimes with capitalization, sometimes not, although rarely, with dashes between the lexemes, and always with a prolific punctuation. This driving originality results in the formation of new syntagmatic units that intervene in complex phrases, sentences, and paragraphs, imposing upon them new patterns of meaning. Under the surface of a formal grammatical coherence, they convey the profound and permanent significance of man's artistic creations salvaged through the ultimate style of the writer who writes about the Imaginary. The Imaginary is more than the signifier of signifiers; it is also a style that transforms artistic and linguistic forms into a unique and intelligible discourse: the style of the Imaginary. Each scientific language looks for a specific logic to discipline its symbols; the language of the Imaginary would be destroyed if the writer using it tried to organize its symbols within the pattern of a logic. Though there is no possibility of a logic of the Imaginary, there *is* room for an appropriate style. To repeat a formula I have already used: here style is the imagining of the Imaginary; its forms are images. Finally, this style constitutes the only language through which man succeeds in changing the Imaginary of his consciousness into the consciousness of his Imaginary. Is this the ultimate victory of literature over art? The *Musée imaginaire* is the work of the word; happy rival of the work of art, does it have the last word?

In this trilogy Malraux uses *images* to represent or, more precisely, to re-present, the life and history of the Imaginary, the various manifestations of its metamorphosis. The way he situates the imag-paradigm within the three parts of this immense panorama and superb synthetic vision does not vary in important ways. Here are a few examples; I prefer simply listing them to attempting to classify them according to their meaning because each time the word occurs it implies and sends us back to previous occurrences. In *La Métamorphose des dieux:* "les *images* de vérité" (images of truth) (25); "exécuter des *images* qui sont des oeuvres d'art" (to make pictures that are works of art) (26); "*images* de l'homme éternel" (images of eternal man) (25); "accession des *images* à un monde immortel" (accession of the images to an immortal world) (28); "*images* d'un miroir" (a mirror's reflections) (31); "le monde des *images* que la création humaine oppose au temps" (the world of the images that human creation contrasts with time) (34); "les *images* sacrées comme figures exemplaires" (sacred images as exemplary forms) (90); "*image* divine"

(divine image) (91); "*images* distinctes de l'apparence" (images distinct from appearance) (127); "les images des basiliques" (the images of the basilicas) (135); "les *images* qu'appelle l'Église" (the images the Church calls for) (156); "le langage naturel des *images*" (the natural language of images) (198); "la valeur pédagogique des *images*" (the pedagogical value of images) (199); "*l'image* de Jésus (the image of Jesus) (219); "faire rivaliser les *images* de son rêve avec celles du monde de Dieu" (to make the images of his dream compete with those of God's world) (379).

In *L'Irréel*: "*écart* entre l'apparence et le monde des *images*" (distance between appearance and the world of images) (39; Malraux italicizes *écart*); "non des imitations, mais des *images*" (not imitations but images) (39; Malraux's italics); "dans le monde des *images* chrétiennes" (in the world of Christian images) (150); "les *images* sculptées" (sculpted images) (168); "*images* que l'on peut tenir pour des allégories, symboles de forces fondamentales" (images that one can consider allegories, symbols of fundamental forces) (176).

In *L'Intemporel:* "des *images* d'Épinal" (33); "voici des *images* amputées de l'irréel comme du sacré" (here are images cut off from the unreal as from the sacred) (91); "une très haute *image* de l'homme" (a very lofty image of man) (117); "l'invention des *images*" (the invention of images) (301); "*l'image* de Garbo sur le pont d'un paquebot" (the picture of Garbo on the deck of a liner) (381); "des *images* de tous les musées" (images/pictures of all the museums) (387); "le filtrage des *images* du monde" (the filtration of the world's images) (389); "le metteur en scène tourne ses *images* narratives ou documentaires en fonction de ses *images* significatives" (the [film] director shoots his narrative or documentary images/frames in terms of his significant images/frames) (395); "les grandes *images* du fantastique" (404); "celles du Musée imaginaire" (those of the imaginary museum) (404); "ces poubelles d'*images*" (these garbage cans for images) (412); "cette foison d'*images*" (this abundance of images) (412); "conscients du pullulement d'*images* qui recouvre et recouvrit la terre" (aware of the rapid multiplication of images that covers and covered the earth) (412).

The continuous line of the signifier *image* is closely interwoven with the no less continuous chain of *imaginaire*. Let us identify a few links or stones along this linguistic way. In *La Métamorphose des dieux: "La promotion de l'imaginaire"* (the promotion of the imaginary) (58); "cette Victoire *imaginaire*" (this imaginary Victory) (98); "des canevas *imaginaires*" (imaginary canvases) (211); "un domaine plus profond que *l'imaginaire*" (a domain deeper than the imaginary) (239); "un pouvoir *imaginaire*" (an imaginary power) (240); "*l'imaginaire* lié à la fiction" (the imaginary linked to fiction) (240); "un *imaginaire* de Vérité" (an imaginary of Truth) (240); "métamorphoser le sacré en *imaginaire*" (to change the sacred into imaginary) (243); "*l'imaginaire* chrétien" (Christian imaginary) (243); "formes qui expriment *l'imaginaire*" (forms that express the imaginary) (244); "*l'imaginaire* est un monde de valeurs humaines" (the imaginary is a world of human values) (246); "l'art apporte à *l'imaginaire* ses formes les plus hautes" (art brings to the imaginary its highest forms) (250); "ils ignorent *l'imaginaire* de Vérité, mais pressentent *l'imaginaire* de fiction" (they do not know the imaginary of Truth, but guess at the imaginary of fiction) (274); "l'architecture de *l'imaginaire*" (the architecture of the imaginary) (308); "le théâtre *imaginaire* de l'Italie" (the imaginary theater of Italy) (358); "le divin incarné dans l'imaginaire rencontre la réalité promue à *l'imaginaire* (the divine incarnated in the imaginary meets reality raised to the imaginary) (364).

In *L'Irréel*: "la métamorphose de *l'imaginaire*" (the metamorphosis of the imaginary) (104); "la profondeur de *l'imaginaire* n'est pas faite de ce que les hommes imaginent, mais de ce qui s'imagine en eux" (the depth of the imaginary is not made of what men imagine, but of that which imagines itself in them) (115); "*l'imaginaire* invente sa tradition" (the imaginary invents its tradition) (124); "le peintre ne transcrit pas *un imaginaire* que les rêveurs (voire lui-même) posséderaient" (the painter does not transcribe an imaginary that dreamers [even he himself] would possess) (131); "la fiction dans laquelle *l'imaginaire* commence à échapper au Créateur" (the fiction in which the imaginary starts escaping from the Creator) (132); "ils sont des hommes de *l'imaginaire*" (they are men of the imaginary) (162); "les galeries *imaginaires*" (the imaginary galeries) (156); "apporter à *l'imaginaire* le prolongement du surnaturel" (bring to the imaginary the extension of the supernatural) (278).

In *L'Intemporel*, where *imaginaire* abounds: "unis par *l'imaginaire* culturel" (united by the cultural imaginary) (5); "*l'imaginaire* pictural" (the pictorial imaginary) (23); "toutes les figures de *l'imaginaire*" (all the forms of the imaginary) (56); "lorsque l'apparence devient le réel, *imaginaire* et foi subissent la transformation la plus profonde depuis l'époque où l'irréel devint le rival du sacré" (when appearance becomes the real, imaginary and faith undergo the most profound transformation since the age when the unreal became the rival of the sacred) (80); "Par qui *l'imaginaire* avait-il pris forme jusque-là sinon par la peinture?" (By whom did the imaginary take shape up to then if not by painting?) (91); "le fait pictural que Delacroix a mis au service de *l'imaginaire*" (the pictorial act that Delacroix put at the service of the imaginary) (107); "en face de ce tableau imaginaire" (in front of this imaginary picture) (207). Here are some interesting uses of *musée imaginaire* in *L'Intemporel:* "le *musée imaginaire* va remplacer le musée de l'imagination" (the imaginary museum is going to replace the museum of the imagination) (113); "le *musée imaginaire* n'est pas une anthologie" (the imaginary museum is not an anthology) (149); "le monde de l'art et le *Musée Imaginaire* sont nés ensemble" (the world of art and the Imaginary Museum were born together) (160); "le *Musée Imaginaire* de la Chine" (the Imaginary Museum of China) (192); "Le *Musée Imaginaire* occidental" (the Imaginary Museum of the West) (196, 238); "le *Musée Imaginaire* des peintres" (the Imaginary Museum of the painters) (263); "la culture picturale, c'est-à-dire le

Musée Imaginaire" (pictorial cultural, that is, the Imaginary Museum) (297); "le jury du *Musée Imaginaire*" (the jury of the Imaginary Museum) (304, 333); "la Bibliothèque de la Pléiade, *musée imaginaire* de la littérature" (the *Bibliothèque de la Pléiade*, imaginary museum of literature) (337); "il (l'audiovisuel) sera au *musée imaginaire* ce que celui-ci fut au Louvre" (it [audiovisual technique] will be to the imaginary museum what this last was to the Louvre) (345); "le *musée imaginaire* de l'audiovisuel" (the imaginary museum of the audiovisual) (360); "ce que le prochain *musée imaginaire* ne sera pas" (what the next imaginary museum will not be) (366); "notre *musée imaginaire* comme un zoo" (our imaginary museum like a zoo) (368); "le *musée imaginaire* exerce dans l'imaginaire des pouvoirs différents" (the imaginary museum exerts different powers in the imaginary) (374-375; that is, different from those of audiovisual creation); "le *musée imaginaire* motorisé" (the motorized imaginary museum) (375). Finally, let us note two very rare synonyms for *musée imaginaire*: "prendre conscience de notre *musée intérieur*" (to become aware of our interior museum) (367, also 164); and, at the end of the tenth section of *L'Intemporel*, Malraux alludes to Jung's archetypes and prefers the expression *formes primordiales* (primordial forms) to designate "les cauchemars ancestraux" (ancestral nightmares). He seems to suggest that the new spirit of the museum is interrogative (311).

Malraux's Gnosis of the Imaginary

Placing these examples—a concordance would give many others—in direct confrontation with each other immediately shows why, as I have already said, we cannot, as Malraux could not, construct a logic of the Imaginary. If we tried, we would enter a vicious circle in which we would have to call for other lexemes to qualify *imaginaire*, when any other word we might use would depend on *imaginaire* for its sense. This situation arises from the grammatical ambivalence of the word as Malraux uses it; it also explains the subordination of the related verbs and the virtual elimination of *imaginer* and *imagination*. We arrive in a universe of discourse where all possible discourses have only one universal modality—one that replaces the traditional logical distinction between the possible, the real, and the necessary—*the modality of the Imaginary*. In other words, the Imaginary is the universal modality of the semeiotic (artistic and literary) world.[14]

As such, it is also man's world. Past and present cultures incarnate the Imaginary, constitute its forms. The Imaginary is also a criterion of man's presence in the cosmos and his biological metamorphosis. Aristotle said—and Western civilizations repeated after him—that man is a rational animal. Malraux says, "Yes, if we consider rationality part of the Imaginary." The true Malraucian motto would be: "Man is the only animal that converts Being, not into nothingness, as Sartre believes, but into the Imaginary." This is man's way of adding culture to nature, awareness to existence, art to fate, the metamorphosis of truth to the metamorphosis of illusion, Imaginary to Maia. Thus, the Imaginary possesses a double dimension, cosmic and semantic; it converts worlds into signifiers and signifiers into worlds. It plays the role that the word *Being* plays in the classical and modern ontologies: individuals exist within the Imaginary, which for them is the virtual power giving significance to their lives and actions.

This view sees the Imaginary as an infinite force of formalization. In a sort of challenge to the Hegelian or Marxist visions of history, Malraux describes, and makes us conscious of, the successive incarnations of the Imaginary, incarnations that are different universals, categories, phases of the human world. Among these are the supernatural, the sacred, the divine, the unreal, the intemporal. Let us not expect Malraux to describe a logical process within a dialectic of the Imaginary, in which phases obey an implacable order of formation and decline; he follows neither Hegel nor Marx—not even Spengler!

Thus the Imaginary has taken the successive forms-phases of the supernatural, the sacred, the divine, the unreal, the intemporal, and finally the Imaginary itself. Each one challenges its predecessors, especially its immediate predecessor, not because of the dialectic exploding power of the negation of negation, but because each brings about a deeper and larger degree of consciousness. More precisely, in each new form-phase a specific form of the Imaginary achieves consciousness and, in so doing, is metamorphosed into a new cultural reality. For example, man's awareness of the gods as the dominant element of a religious culture promotes a new culture that is no longer the culture of the sacred, but that of the divine. Artistic creations are not presented and explained according to the technical procedures of composition and expression they exemplify, but according to their *place* and *significance* in the category to which they belong and in reference to the Imaginary. I say place and significance because the Imaginary is at the same time sense and world: a mental space and an order, governed by the laws of reflection and reversibility, which define the constant effort of constructing a whole through which the mind projects itself into a culture. This is why I speak of Malraux's opus in its entirety as a Gnosis of the Imaginary: it goes beyond history, beyond scientific research, beyond aesthetics as a normative science in quest of laws controlling the artistic world. Malraux's text shows the significance of every moment of human creativity; categories of the Imaginary have replaced the eons and daimons of the old Manichean Gnosis, but they remain irreducible dualities or differences.[15]

The world of the Imaginary, being simultaneously the imagination of the world, is formed by the immediate two-way conversion of reality into the Imaginary and the Imaginary into reality. There is also a similar reversibility between the conscious and the unconscious, but not in the Freudian sense. Malraux's Imaginary entertains neither feeling of guilt nor instinct of regression; on the contrary, it is made of an affirmation of dignity and of progression. No phase of the Imaginary is self-aware. When it starts to become self-aware, it begins to change into another new phase: for instance, to believe in the sacred is to be unaware of the sacred as a category of the Imaginary. When the artist is conscious of belonging to the sacred, he or she enters the divine, and so on.

The Imaginary is the world of the *artist* as opposed to that of the *conqueror.* The conqueror dreams of the Imaginary, but his dreams are never converted into works of art. He participates in the Imaginary, whereas the artist metamorphoses conquests into artistic creations. Malraux has not systematically explored the duality artist/conqueror, which is inherent in his text and which could help explain the mysterious route of his diachronic progression from the novels to the books on art. Both explore the Imaginary worlds: In the novels Malraux presents various Imaginaries, various conquerors, different kinds of dooms and doomsdays; the irreversible destiny of his conqureors always obeys the fatality of death. For the artist, instead, death becomes the reality to be challenged, and the artist's work, successfully or not, claims the right to enter eternity.

We can find indirect, but important, suggestions on the duality conquest/art in the antinomy *rêves/images.* I have already mentioned the lexical hesitation between the imag-paradigm and the rêv-paradigm in Malraux's works before *La Métamorphose des dieux.* In his last works Malraux seems to see a radical contrast between the works of the artist and the dreams of the conqueror or of the masses. These last works also provide brief indications of the existence of good and bad Imaginaries, even of a pathology of the Imaginary. Many reasons can be given for Malraux's reluctance to explore systematically the problem of negative values or forces in the imaginary world. In any case, we should not accuse him of having completely ignored this difficult question, which is the weakest spot of all Western philosophies.[16]

Fundamentally, the Imaginary is constituted in terms of its confrontation with reality. Many synonyms connote this *prise de conscience*, which is at the same time action and reflection. Malraux starts the semantic exploration of the Imaginary with the usual opposition at the level of perception of the external world: what is not perceived is imaginary, that is, what does not correspond to a real object exists only in our imagination. Then he faces the inescapable question all epistemologies come up against: what is that "real" on behalf of which we say that the Imaginary is Imaginary? Malraux's answer is: death. This affirmation, simple as it seems, arises out of a deep metaphysical option: the moral and psychological aspects of man's death take on meaning only in reference to the cosmic and biological dimensions of death. Most of Malraux's readers are understandably fascinated with the last pages of *La Voie royale* and give to Perken's death and to his statements on death an exemplary value. They forget that Malraux's novelistic universe is full of deaths, all of them different from Perken's, which is the death of the conqueror. Quite apart from his, there are the varied deaths of the revolutionaries: compare

Tchen's, Kyo's, and Katow's deaths, for example. Think of the heroic and anonymous deaths in *L'Espoir*. *Man brings style to death* and transposes it into an artistic revelation; he gives value to death, which is the antivalue and, paradoxically, reality itself. In Malraux's vision, the real is the Becoming of Greek thought, the Illusion of Oriental philosophies. Death is the law of continuous metamorphosis, the law of the degradation of reality. The thermodynamic principle of the degradation of energy, known as the Carnot-Clausius principle, is its physical interpretation: to be born again is to decay again, in an endless combination and dissociation of forms, with no progress and no decline. It is impossible to detect in Malraux's work any sort of Bergsonian resonance: his vision of the vegetal and animal worlds is never inspired by faith in creative evolution. Under the immobile repetition of the Cosmos, life repeats itself in its absurd mobility. Human history participates in the same repetition: everywhere the same adventures where conquests are dreams and where death is the only end!

One understands why and how the Imaginary appears as antidestiny, that is, antinature, antideath. One understands also the deep significance of the struggle against death, the challenge to death, and the synonymy between artist and medieval knight, both contrasted with the conqueror. This struggle is the ultimate consequence of the truth that man is the being who knows he will die: consciousness of death transforms the realm of death into the world of the Imaginary. At this point of profound understanding, Malraux leads us far from the modern epistemologies, as Sartre analyzes them in the first chapter of *L'Imagination*.[17] The Imaginary is consciousness itself, metamorphosis that paradoxically negates metamorphosis. Consciousness of death neutralizes, disembodies the reality of death; it closes the world of perpetual decay, rebirth, and decay; and it opens the new, absolute world of the Imaginary, the true reality. Again, in Malraux's last texts, a basic antinomy derives its meaning and power from a synonymic identification, where synonymy goes beyond its superficial function of accumulating signifiers. Man lives and experiences the dramatic opposition of the real and the Imaginary through the opposition of death and consciousness, which are both principles of two contrasting universes:

$$\frac{\text{Real}}{\text{Imaginary}} \equiv \frac{\text{Death}}{\text{Consciousness}}$$

so that the consciousness of the real is the Imaginary of death.

Such an epistemology does not take us back to the classic dualism of space and mind. It does not pretend to interpret the passage of man from nature to culture, nor does it transpose the old duality of the sublunar and supralunar worlds that postulates the Platonic distinction between the world of ideal forms and the corrupted world of sensations and images. The Imaginary is not a substitute for the real world or an addition to it.

The cosmic and biological metamorphosis will go on infinitely: there is no possible victory over death in the real world, because death *is* the real. Conversely, metamorphosis cannot destroy the Imaginary. Furthermore, in an analogical play typical of Malraux, the Imaginary possesses its own becoming, its law of metamorphosis; but the metamorphosis of styles does not entail the destruction of preceding styles; far from it, it confers upon them new meanings: for instance, the culture of the intemporal does not destroy the medieval cathedral; it finds a place for representations of the gods in the Imaginary Museum. Death is illusion and dissolution, the ceaseless movement of infinite differences. On the contrary, art, through its reflective power, changes differences into styles; it challenges the destructive effect of time. The Imaginary is the real becoming eternal. In other words, one could say that Malraux calls for analogies in order to understand differences and basic oppositions. In the grammatical awareness of the text, he establishes a synonymic circularity between the two poles of his universe of discourse—the real and the Imaginary.

Thus we arrive at this paradox: does not the duality of the real and the Imaginary repeat itself within the imaginary world? Is not the Imaginary Museum, like the book on the Imaginary Museum, the Imaginary of the real worlds of art? Or *is not art the real, when literature is the Imaginary?* In the last analysis, the Imaginary Museum is nothing else than the book itself. Are we witnessing a metamorphosis of the world of art into the world of literature? Does this mean, consequently, that literature "rivals" art and that its retrieval of art through linguistic symbols reflects the challenge the writer throws at the artist? I feel that at the end of his life Malraux was aware of this problem:[18] This is probably the profound question posed in his last book, *L'Homme précaire et la littérature*, which is a secret dialogue between the various Imaginaries of art and the Imaginary of literature. In attempting to interpret the movement of Malraux's works from his first texts to this book, we can say that for him the function of literary creations is to give a new dimension of consciousness, that is, a reflective degree of Imaginary, to the works of art and the historical cultures they incarnate. This is why the last contrast Malraux envisioned brings face to face the Imaginary and the aleatory: the Imaginaries are threatened by the statistic dispersion of the aleatory, when they are not saved and resuscitated by the word of the writer. That famous enigma, In the beginning was the Word, should be reformulated: In the beginning was Art/In the end will be the Word!

The Imaginary in Twentieth-Century French Literature

I would like to enlarge the field of analysis presented above from a new perspective and raise the following problem, which seems to me the natural extension of our study of Malraux's Imaginary: Has the word *imaginaire* taken on a significant and powerful role in French literature of the twentieth century? The answer to this question will indirectly reinforce the originality of Malraux's writings. My question brings up the problem of the use of the imag-paradigm in texts by other French authors; the works I choose to examine are Jean-Paul Sartre's *L'Imagination* (1936) and *L'Imaginaire* (1940)[19] and Jacques Lacan's *Ecrits* (1966). I am not raising a problem of intertextuality between these writers and Malraux. The dim view Malraux took of psychoanalytic semantics is well known. In the case of Sartre, one can guess that more than once Malraux thought himself a precursor of existentialism, but *L'Imaginaire* was published in 1940, and Malraux's wide use of the lexeme *imaginaire* begins after 1945. Nor do I suggest that Malraux got from Sartre the idea of making *imaginaire* a powerful signifier. What is more important, I believe, is that authors of different texts of the same period, texts having parallel problematics, felt the need to use that lexeme as a semantic and stylistic organizer.

I will begin this comparative research in the use of *imaginaire* with a reference to the study published at the beginning of the century by one of the founders of scientific psychology in France. The *Essai sur l'imagination créatrice* by Th. Ribot is a work well known to any student in psychology before 1940 (Sartre refers to it in *L'Imagination*).[20] I take this essay as representative of the use of the imag-paradigm before the new uses we find in the middle of the century. For Ribot the semantic play within the imag-paradigm concentrates itself on the triangle *imaginatif-imaginaire-image*. He gives the lexeme *imaginatif* (imaginative) (which will almost disappear in the texts of Malraux, Sartre, and Lacan) a considerable nominal and adjectival power, with a few important qualifications: "les grands imaginatifs" (the great imaginatives) (266), "les imaginatifs purs" (pure imaginatives) (253), "les vrais imaginatifs" (real/true imaginatives) (140), "la création imaginative" (imaginative creation, numerous references), "la vie imaginative" (imaginative life) (271), "le travail imaginatif" (imaginative work) (275), and so on. *Imagination* is not directly contrasted with any other psychological function; Ribot's text implies the opposition *imaginer/raisonner* (to imagine/to reason), which is synonymous with the duality *inventer/démontrer* (to invent/to demonstrate). *Imagination* is defined as the "tendance naturelle des images à s'objectiver" (natural tendency of images to become objective/make themselves into objects) (VI), which means that the image has an "élément moteur," a tendency to move. Thus, human imagination is the source of any sort of action that does not arise from pure mechanical instinct or habit. Ribot rarely uses the lexeme *imaginaire* as adjective and never as noun. For him, *imaginaire* designates the negative aspect of the imagination and refers to the mystical or artistic imaginations. Here is a significant phrase: "fictif et imaginaire comme dans l'art" (fictitious and imaginary as in art) (211).

Malraux and Sartre

In Sartre's works a new semantic triangle appears throughout: *imagination-imaginer-imaginaire*, where *imaginaire* denotes the totality of images. *Imagination* remains the most powerful organizer of the vocabulary. Sartre's most interesting lexical decision concerns the present participle *imageant* (imaging) used as adjective: "la conscience . . . se constitue en elle-même comme imageante" (consciousness constitutes itself in itself as imaging) (362), so that one could say: imagination-imaging-imaginary. The passage of *imaginaire* from the adjectival form to nominal status connotes the transfer to a specific order, to a world. Furthermore, the Sartrian imag-paradigm is based upon a profound semantic system: the antinomy real/unreal, the synonymy unreal/imaginary; the identification between imagination, imaging, consciousness. That system entails the secret opposition of art and knowledge and also the lexical solidarity of the following lexemes: imagination, unreal, nothingness, liberty, antiworld. This last word, *anti-monde*, refers to the most original part of Sartre's theory: the imagination involves evasion from the real world, rejection of the human condition as being-in-the-world, and what it builds is an antiworld (261). For example, "dans le rêve, chaque image s'entoure d'une atmosphère de monde" (in the dream, each image surrounds itself with an atmosphere of world) (324). Sartre proposes this definition of the dream: "le rêve n'est point la fiction prise pour la réalité, c'est l'odyssée d'une conscience vouée par elle-même, et en dépit d'elle-même, à ne constituer qu'un monde irréel" (the dream is not fiction taken for reality, it is the odyssey of a consciousness destined by itself, and in spite of itself, to constituting only an unreal world) (340).

The Sartrian relation between real and unreal is ambiguous. It has a negative and a positive value: "toute situation concrète et réelle de la conscience dans le monde est grosse d'imaginaire en tant qu'elle se présente toujours comme un dépassement du réel" (every concrete and real situation of consciousness in the world is heavy with imaginary in so far as it always presents itself as an overstepping of the real) (358). He goes on: "L'irréel est produit hors du monde par une conscience qui *reste dans le monde* et c'est parce qu'il est transcendantalement libre que l'homme imagine" (the unreal is produced outside the world by a consciousness that *stays in the world* and it is because he is transcendentally free that man imagines) (358; Sartre's italics). Sartre's essay ends with a theory of the work of art as the most important product of the "imaging consciousness." The work of art is an "unreal" (362): "l'objet esthétique est un *irréel*" (the aesthetic object is an *unreal*) (363; Sartre's italics); this means that it takes its aesthetic value from the unreal, which is at the same time a world and a mode of existence. He concludes: "La contemplation esthétique est un rêve provoqué et *le passage au réel est un authentique réveil*" (aesthetic contemplation is an induced dream and *the passage to the real is an authentic awakening*) (371; italics mine). The last paragraph of the book is devoted to the qualification of beauty as the value of the imaginary. This implies the "néantisation" (nihilation) of the real world. Then Sartre makes the revealing statement: "Dire que l'on 'prend' devant le vie une attitude esthétique, c'est confondre constamment le réel et l'imaginaire" (to say that one "assumes" an aesthetic attitude in the face of life is constantly to confuse the real and the imaginary) (372). That statement is followed by a perplexing remark: "l'extrême beauté d'un femme tue le désir qu'on a d'elle" (a woman's extreme beauty kills the desire one has for her) (372). Why? ". . . car le désir est une plongée au coeur de l'existence dans ce qu'elle a de plus contingent et de plus absurde" (for desire is a plunge/dive into the heart of existence at its most contingent and most absurd) (373). Let us not comment on the metaphor of "plunge into the heart of existence" but simply observe that, on the eve of imagining his first great synthesis, *L'Etre et le Néant* ("*Being and Nothingness*"), Sartre puts his reader at the border between the real and the unreal. He will try again and again to bring the reader back to this belief: the real is the only value worth searching for, and finding it is our only aim. In Freudian terms, Sartre unites the two principles of reality and pleasure: to desire is to desire reality, and the possession of reality bursts into authentic pleasure. The "authentic awakening" is an escape in reverse—an escape from the Imaginary. At this point we can understand the profound significance of Sartre's *littérature engagée*, his interpretation of the duality prose/poetry, and his constant effort to make of literature the critical language of truth, the critical mirror of reality.

A comparison of how Malraux and Sartre use the imag-paradigm shows similarities and differences. Both accept the same basic antinomic pattern: real/unreal, and the synonymic chain: unreal, imaginary, consciousness. Sartre's elaborated theory of consciousness could help to interpret Malraux's rather vague metaphoric view of the struggle between reality and the Imaginary. Thus one can speak of a formal similarity between the texts of these two writers. There is, however, a radical difference, which explains why the surfaces of their texts are finally so unlike: where Sartre devalues, Malraux overvalues. For Sartre, the world of the Imaginary is an antiworld; for Malraux, it is the world of human culture, the awareness of artistic creation. The word *culture* is absent from Sartre's text, even when he analyzes the essence of the work of art. Malraux does not invite us to return to reality, but rather to attain a new and superior reality by converting reality into the Imaginary. It is clear that Sartre's Imaginary is afflicted with a guilt complex, something that is totally absent from Malraux's Imaginary. Sartre accepts the Biblical *image* of the Fall: reality is the paradise we have lost and strive to regain; in its true function, consciousness brings us back to the world—it should never offer us the opportunity to escape. Malraux's text is free of the Biblical condemnation. The explanation for this may lie in the fact that his writings implicitly refer to an eschatology of metamorphosis, a doctrine that is not Biblical, but Oriental. We could also say that Malraux rejects the

Biblical image because his work refuses it. In contrast, Sartre uses the reference to reality as the promise of redemption: human consciousness can and should redeem itself and return to the paradise of reality. *L'Etre et le Néant* is the opposite of *Le Musée imaginaire*: the first is the *Odyssey* of liberty, in which man is threatened by the temptation of the Imaginary but finally returns to the Ithaca of reality; the second is the *Iliad* of the Imaginary, in which the threats are lack of talent, the power, exerted by popular masses and madness.

Malraux and Lacan

The reader may be surprised that I have not confronted Malraux and Sartre with Bachelard, who also promoted a phenomenology of the Imaginary. For my purposes, and in spite of the great merit of Bachelard's analysis, such books as *L'Eau et les rêves* (1942), *La Psychanalyse du feu* (1938), *La Poétique de l'espace* (1957), and *La Poétique de la rêverie* (1961) add no new notions to those developed by Sartre and Malraux. I think that a comparison with Jacques Lacan's concepts of the Imaginary and the Symbolic should help us better understand the importance of the imag-paradigm in our time and especially Malraux's way of organizing our languages and our cultural behaviors. Lacan's *Écrits* was published in 1966, but some of the texts in this work date from the early thirties. It is clear that there are many parallels between the works of Malraux, Sartre, and Lacan. These works converge and diverge as they express, examine, and provide models for our immediate intellectual present and future.

If the comparison with Sartre helps emphasize the true originality of Malraux's vision and of his use of the imag-paradigm, an examination of the thought of Jacques Lacan can help point out the profound significance of Malraux's language. Let us begin with a quotation that seems to answer the basic question of *La Condition humaine.* Lacan is referring to that "lambeau de discours plus vivant que sa vie même" (scrap of discourse even more alive than his life)[21] to which each of us is deeply attached; then he immediately continues: "C'est aussi que ce lambeau de discours, faute d'avoir pu le proférer par la gorge, chacun de nous est condamné, pour en tracer la ligne fatale, à s'en faire l'alphabet vivant" (It is also this scrap of discourse, for want of being able to utter it through the throat, each of us is condemned to make himself its living alphabet, in order to trace its fatal line). The *écrit*, entitled "La psychanalyse et son enseignement" ("Psychoanalysis and its teaching") (1957), from which these quotations come, ends with the following statement, which is another echo of Malraux's aesthetics: "Tout retour à Freud qui donne matière à un enseignement digne de ce nom, ne se produira que par la voie par où la vérité la plus cachée se manifeste dans *les révolutions de la culture. Cette voie est la seule formation que nous puissions prétendre à transmettre à ceux qui nous suivent. Elle s'appelle un style.*" (Every return to Freud providing material for an instruction worthy of the name will take place only through the route/way that allows the most hidden truth to manifest itself in cultural revolutions. This route/way is the only education we can claim to transmit to those who follow us. It is called a style.)[22]

Despite such similarities, we can find, even on the surface of these discourses, lexical and semantic divergences of some importance. Lacan's use of the imag-paradigm is limited to the lexemes *image-imaginaire.* Although in Malraux *image* denotes any cultural product, for Lacan *image* is a synonym of phantasm, and its forms are regrouped under the signifier *imago.* The word *imagination* is replaced by *identification*, denoting a circular movement between the subject and the Other.[23] Malraux's consciousness, with its power of progressive *dépassement* (overcoming/transcending), becomes Lacan's concept of intersubjectivity in which One and the Other play their games on each side of the mirror: "Quand l'homme cherchant le vide de sa pensée s'avance dans la lueur sans ombre de l'espace imaginaire en s'abstenant même d'attendre ce qui va en surgir, un miroir sans éclat lui montre une surface où ne se reflète rien" (When man in search of the emptiness/void of his thought goes forward in the shadowless gleam of imaginary space without even waiting for what will loom up out of it, a tarnished mirror shows him a surface in which nothing is reflected).[24] The dream of unity achieved through successive and recovered unifications, as envisioned by Malraux, would be, in Lacan's eyes, pure phantasm, and the Imaginary Museum, a collection of phantasms promoted to the rank of works of art. In a joking way Lacan transforms the word *ennui* (boredom) into *unien* (one-ian), the boring identification of the Other with the One. Then he calls for the Aristophanes of Plato's *Symposium:* "Aristophane . . . nous donne le cru équivalent de la bête-à-deux-dos dont il impute à Jupiter qui n'en peut mais, la bisection: c'est très vilain, j'ai déjà dit que ça ne se fait pas, on ne commet pas le Père réel dans de telles inconvenances"[25] (Aristophanes . . . gives us the obscene equivalent of the beast-with-two-backs, the division of which he attributes to Jupiter who really has nothing to do with it: it is very naughty, I have already said that this isn't done, one should not commit the real Father to such improprieties). He concludes superbly and comically: "j'Autrifiais l'Un"[26] ("I made the One become the Other" literally Lacan writes: I otherfied the One).

Lacan's dialectic interpretation of human consciousness situated between the polarities of the One and the Other involves a total revision of the duality imaginary/real. We have seen that Malraux and Sartre found their texts on the traditional antinomy real/unreal, which in Western philosophies has been the source of conflicts between realism and idealism. Sartre advocates a return of human consciousness to the real,

de la pain éclose. Stephendoff..... Ah! bon sang St Vingueur d'Illing, nous obtiendrons l'avoir
Il réfléchit.

"Hem! Lounq'on est tré bien renseigné, on a il est qu'à choisir. Je voudrais le savoir
savoir — : "Il n'est vraiment pour rien dans ce que je viens frapper Tang St Cochon
à rond ouah...."

Il donne un interrogateur, il répond, avec un ton à la fois ironique et amer:
" — Nous sommes sains et saufs arrivés à un meilleur moment...
— Il est où a Tang ?
— Un vague général...
— De le connais ?
— Comme ça, comme beaucoup d'autres. C'est Tang — il fait d'importance. Il préfère un
coup d'État. Bien. Il vous nous offrez celle au nez. Ça l'regarde. Mais lui, en l'occurrence, me
compte pas. Il n'est qu'un hasard nécessaire, qui a supposément à. C'est oublié, c'est à quitter
la L'ang Shom, d'abord, comme s'il convient. Sa ce moment, le
nous Kouomin derrière lui. L'Hug Shom, d'abord, comme nous l'attend. Chopen
cinq anglais s'ouvent l'argement devant ceux qui se proposent de nous d'attend. Chopen
nous anglais s'ouvent l'argement devant ceux qui se proposent de l'intelligence servir
homme du regiment de Tang lui est entièrement fait par le geste de l'Intelligence service
un bon prix. mallerveusement— Hongkong n'en fera bien. a qui feront à Tang aussi
— mallerveusement— qu'il soit Bettan. Et il y a aussi Telang. Oui, "l'honnête Telang. Oui", y a-t-en
de file en leur air, qu'il soit Bettan. Et il y a aussi Tang. a-t-il était singulier— ne il m l'idia la — li
m tout à d'houes. Je suis sûr que Tang, a-t-il était singulier— un peut mettre Telang. Oui à la place de
Comité d'État. Il m'a poub'mettre Telang qui lui. Le société publique et vicole l'chnifianant comme
officiait à Pouwn. a pet à me peut mettre acheter par le l'beaux appels empipe du monde " comme
Comité d'État. Il a aufracement notre achite par lui Pouvel out défende. C'est beau
c'est certain. Il s'employant avec le Pou.la ncan l'amore de ma chandri a anglais,
"J'irai de quelle l'amer étranger! [mellé]— nétour de ma chandri a anglais,
alvé qu'] riel de complicité. Tamirnet. Ce jellette, ici, c'est nuit.
L'âge de papier! Je vois cela d'ici: complicité! Le juliette ici, vieux d'en
Impar à cigars sur l'oreil, dérvolité m'a de tout ce qui m'a vom fait. filam ne vieux d'en
b... - Il plonge sont moche comme des médecins j'attend. Il attend de nouveaux rapports..."

Manuscript page of *Les Conquérants*

whereas Malraux promotes the Imaginary to the rank of a superior reality. I think Lacan goes deeper than either of them in dealing with this traditional conflict. He changes the duality real/unreal into the triad real/imaginary/symbolic, a triad that, in fact, combines two dualities—real/imaginary and imaginary/symbolic.

Malraux and Sartre do take into account the Symbolic, but both see it as a product of the Imaginary. For Lacan, instead, the Imaginary and the Symbolic together constitute the deepest contradiction in human experience. Next, Lacan gives the word *real* two new meanings in addition to the meaning "that which is exterior to the subject." First, "real" is what is real for the subject; thus, reality is nothing more than perceptions and images. Second, this system is identified with the Mother: the word *mother* becomes the signifier for reality. Finally, Lacan adds a third meaning: the subject discovers another reality through the intermediary of the symbolic order of language. The function of psychoanalysis is understood as "une relation dialectique où le non-agir de l'analyste guide le discours du sujet vers la réalisation de sa vérité" (a dialectical relation in which the non-act of the analyst guides the subject's discourse towards the achievement of its truth).[27] In the following paragraph Lacan makes an antirealist statement, which illuminates his epistemology of the Imaginary and the Symbolic: "En fait, cette illusion qui pousse à chercher la réalité au-delà du mur du langage est la même par laquelle le sujet croit que sa vérité nous est déjà donnée, que nous la connaissons à l'avance, et c'est aussi bien par là qu'il est béant à notre intervention objectivante" (In fact, this illusion that induces one to look for reality beyond the wall of language is the same by which the subject believes that his truth is already ours, that we know it in advance, and it's due to it as well that he is wide-open for our objectifying intervention).[28]

Thus, the only access "the subject" has to reality is through language representing the order of the Symbolic. Language is the product of the symbolic function that belongs to living things, animals as well as men. It forms the space of discursive and symbolic action, within which man's intersubjectivity is organized. Such is the role of the Symbolic Father, figure of the law and master of the signifiers; the symbolic phallus is the centrifugal power of signifying. Lacan develops these fundamental concepts into a rich and complex theory of language, especially of the relation between signifier and signified, the double metonymic and metaphoric aspects of the signifier and its connection with the dialectic of the One and the Other. For our present purpose it is sufficient to become aware of these theoretical extensions and to observe how they may be applied to Malraux's writings.

One point is clear in this linguistic comparison: neither Sartre nor Malraux has put the problematic of language at the center of his discourse. Neither ignores it, but Sartre is obsessed by the return to reality, and Malraux never succeeds in shaking off a constant fascination with the world of artistic creation. Malraux once said that the artist is the rival of reality, but all his life he faced another, and maybe more disturbing, rivalry, that between the writer and the artist. This is why I have a twofold reaction to the Malraux-Lacan confrontation. First, I find it undeniable that, theoretically speaking, Lacan achieves more richness and depth from his handling of the imag-paradigm and his transposing of the duality real/imaginary into the triad real/imaginary/symbolic than do Sartre and Malraux in their explorations of the Imaginary. The main merit of Lacan's effort lies in the organizing of a new problematic, whereas Malraux and Sartre fail to transcend common and traditional ideas about the real and the unreal. Furthermore, Lacan's interpretations of neurotic and psychotic behavior could help in dealing with some of the questions Malraux leaves unanswered, particularly those concerning axiology and the pathology of the Imaginary. Today the duality of the Imaginary and the Symbolic should be an epistemological requirement.

However, and this is the second part of my reaction, is it fair or even pertinent to apply a Lacanian model to Malraux's text? It is one thing to call on Lacan for a deeper understanding of Malraux and another to reproach Malraux for not being Lacan! Malraux never claimed to be an epistemologist, a psychologist (far from it!), or a psychoanalyst, just as he never claimed to be an historian of art. We are, of course, free to add our own theoretical chapters to *La Métamorphose des dieux*.

Evaluation of Malraux's Work

I then come to the question that has been in the back of my mind since the beginning of this study: if Malraux's work does not belong to the world of scientific language, where does it belong? Is it a new form of novel? An imaginary discourse on the imaginary world? How can such an imaginary discourse exist without affirming the truth of what it says and thus falling back into the category of scientific language?

Malraux does not answer this problem directly or indirectly. I can envisage a solution by using the complementarity real/truth, which Lacan considered through the psychoanalytic relation between the patient and the analyst. The analyst's challenge is to bring his patient from a realistic language that is, in fact, illusory to a language of truth thanks to which he—the patient—finds his rightful place within the symbolic order of discourse. I wonder if Malraux does not present us with a similar situation. His text has the *appearance* of a language of truth; most readers adopt, often unconsciously, a realistic attitude toward it, as if the text were reflecting a reality of which it is the faithful mirror. (Sartre deliberately fell into this trap; even his novels and plays hang their imaginary costumes upon the hook of reality.) Nonetheless, refusing to be confused with the philosopher or scientist, Malraux rejects the proposal that truth is the mirror of reality and his language, the mirror of art. In that perspective, he accepts Lacan's view that language is truly a chain of signifiers. The value of signifiers is not truth, but linguistic power; this power gives the universe of art, not its truth, but its awareness, that is, its intersubjective and linguistic reality. This is why for Malraux works of art are finally transposed into the texts of the Imaginary Museum, which is not really a museum or a collection of photographs, but an assembly of linguistic signs. *Artistic expression finds its completeness in the form of the signifier.* The historical conquests of man are subjected to a similar condition: the conqueror expects consecration through the work of art and/or the text; he is not master of this consecration, this last conquest, any more than the artist can decide by himself his place in the linguistic universe. Lacan himself remains silent in front of this problem. Perhaps we should take the imaginary/symbolic a step further, to the level of the symbol/word within the symbolic order.

The following diagram sums up this semantic condition.

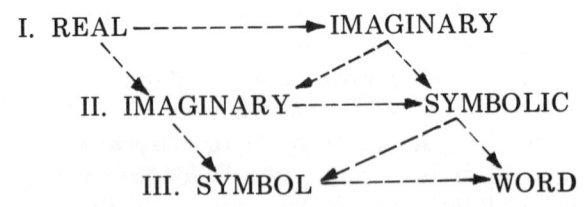

```
I. REAL --------→ IMAGINARY
        ╲      ╱
   II. IMAGINARY ------→ SYMBOLIC
              ╲       ╱
        III. SYMBOL ←------→ WORD
```

Sartre's text remains at level I, Lacan makes of level II the pattern for human psychology; and Malraux, who seems to ignore level II, experiences level III. But one may wonder if Malraux shows in his writings an awareness of the double role of the Symbolic as it stands between symbol and word. My answer to this question, given without any hesitation, is yes. Half of Malraux's work is devoted to the linguistic resurrection of silent symbols—the Voices of silence! I already mentioned that, for me, the great challenge of Malraux's work is not a presentation of the rivalry with the real, but of the rivalry between the artist and the writer, between the symbol and the word, or, if one prefers to use Malraux's vocabulary, between the artistic image and literature. Here Malraux is close to Derrida's denunciation of the perversion of graphs by articulated sounds, but with two differences: there is no denunciation, no culpability, but rather divine (in Malraux's meaning) competition between the symbol and the word. Malraux extends the conflict of "la parole et l'écriture" (the spoken word and writing) to the most profound duality of art and literature. The nostalgia of the text is not another text; it is a painting or a sculpture. The Malraucian text does not tend to destroy itself, especially because it has nothing in common—at least it tries to have nothing in common—with the logocentrism of Western philosophies and literatures. Malraux hopes to avoid the autodestruction of his texts thanks to the substitution of a rhetoric of interrogation for a logic of true affirmative or negative propositions.[29] However, his verbal triumph—what Lacan calls superbly "l'assomption jubilatoire de son image spéculaire par l'être encore plongé dans l'impuissance motrice et la dépendance du nourrissage

Malraux at the Ministry of Cultural Affairs, about 1961

qu'est le petit homme à ce stade *infans*"[30] (the jubilant assumption of his specular image by the little man at the *infans* stage still immersed in his motor incapacity and nutritive dependance)—hides a secret awareness of impotence: not a feeling of reason and culpability in remembrance of the lost "trace", but the lucid sentiment that, even though the linguistic mirror may accumulate ingenious ornaments, it will always remain mirror; it can deceive the reader for a few moments; it never deceives itself. At the very end, Clappique in front of his mirror, half tragedian, half humorist, refuses to be the curator and manager of human consciousness, but he does finally consent to become the linguistic architect of the Imaginary Pantheon!

Notes

1. See my article "André Malraux's Aesthetics: The Problematic of Universals," in *Twentieth Century Literature*, Vol. 24, No. 3 (Fall 1978).
2. Especially in his works on art, Malraux frequently uses the expression *domaine de références* to connect a person or a work with the cultural world to which he or it belongs or should be attached if the reader is fully to understand his or its place and spirit.
3. The phrase "stylistic coherence" designates more than the formal arrangement of the text. It implies Malraux's theory of style as the original value of a work of art or a culture.
4. Quotations from *Lunes en papier, La Tentation de l'Occident, Les Conquérants, Royaume-Farfelu* are from André Malraux, *Oeuvres* (Paris: Gallimard, 1970), Vol. I; quotations from *La Voie royale* and *La Condition humaine* are from the same edition (Vol. II).
5. Italics in all quotations from Malraux's works are mine except where otherwise indicated.
6. Quotations from *Le Temps du mépris* and *L'Espoir* are from André Malraux, *Romans* (Paris: Gallimard, 1951).
7. Quotations from *Les Noyers de l'Altenburg* are from André Malraux, *Les Noyers de l'Altenburg* (Paris: Gallimard, 1948).
8. Quotations from *Les Voix du silence* are from André Malraux, *Les Voix du silence* (La Galerie de la Pléiade, Paris: Gallimard, 1951).
9. André Lalande, in his *Vocabulaire technique et critique de la philosophie* (7th edition in one volume, Presses Universitaires de France, 1956), gives two definitions of the universe of discourse: "A. Ensemble d'idées, ou plus exactement des éléments et des classes logiques qui sont pris en considération dans un jugement ou un raisonnement . . . B. Se dit aussi maintenant, en un sens plus large, de l'ensemble de toutes les présuppositions qu'implique un jugement ou une question" (1167) (A. Set of ideas, or more exactly, set of the logical elements and classes which are taken into consideration in a judgment or a reasoning . . . B. Today it is used also, in a larger meaning, to designate the set of all the presuppositions which a judgment or a question implies.) Thus the Imaginary becomes for Malraux, after 1950, the permanent reference of his own discourse. Each text presupposes an implicit reference to the Imaginary's omnipresence.
10. For me, "dominant semantic power" and high frequency of occurrence in a text are not the same. Even words not present in the text can have this kind of dominance. I freely confess that my judgments in such cases are based on my general and detailed understanding of the texts, on what Malraux would call "my imagination of the text," that is, on a synthetic intuition resulting from many readings and comparisons. This intuition is also similar to the inevitable and indispensable intuition that Spitzer recognizes as the point of departure for stylistic analysis.

11. See *Logic as the Science of the Pure Concept,* translated from the Italian of Benedetto Croce by Douglas Ainslie (London: Macmillan and Co., 1917), p. XII. Croce defines the character of his logic as follows: to affirm the concrete universals and to affirm the concrete individual, as proof of the Aristotelian *Scientia est de Universalibus* ("Science Is about Universals"), and proof of Campanella's *Scientia est de Singularibus* ("Science Is about Particulars"). On p. 23 he analyzes the distinction between *fictional concepts* (for example, house, hat, cat) and *conceptual fictions* (for example, triangle, free motion).

12. The expression *imaginary object* refers to the Pascalian "objets imaginaires" in the famous fragment against painting. Malraux quotes it (*Le Musée imaginaire,* 70). My use of the word *libido* to interpret Malraux's word *désir* can be criticized because of Malraux's well-known opposition to psychoanalysis. I agree that Malraux would never have accepted all the implications Freud found in the word *libido*. It is, however, clear that in this sentence the word *désir* has sexual overtones even if it has no direct Freudian connotations. The question remains: does the discreet and almost modest word *désir* allow us to avoid Freudian views on the formation of human cultures and to discard their demystifying and disintegrating power?

13. References to *La Métamorphose des dieux* are from André Malraux, *La Métamorphose des dieux* (La Galerie de la Pléiade, Paris: Gallimard, 1957; to *L'Irréel* from André Malraux, *La Métamorphose des dieux, L'Irréel* (Paris: Gallimard, 1974); to *L'Intemporel,* from André Malraux, *La Métamorphose des dieux, L'Intemporel* (Paris: Gallimard, 1976).

14. Malraux speaks of an Imaginary of truth, which designates medieval culture, and we can go further in considering that the scientific conquests of recent centuries belong to a specific Imaginary: sciences are theoretical imaginaries that lead to the vision of "l'homme aléatoire" (the aleatory man): does this mean that the Imaginary reaches a point at which it destroys itself?

15. I have used this expression to qualify Malraux's aesthetics: art is affirmation of differences, and differences are essences structuring the artistic worlds. See my article cited in note 1.

16. Here are two texts, which clearly reveal Malraux to be conscious of the problem of positive and negative values in the Imaginary worlds. First, an extract from the address he delivered in New York, on May 15, 1963: "Prenons garde que cette industrialisation du rêve est sans commune mesure avec ce que fut l'action du roman ou du théâtre . . . Notre civilisation fait naître autant de rêves chaque semaine, que de machines en un an. Ainsi s'établit un romanesque que le monde n'avait jamais connu, et dont la présence dans la vie de centaines de millions d'êtres humains est fort différente des présences romanesques ou légendaires de jadis: il ne peut être comparé qu'à ce qui fut l'obsédante présence de l'imaginaire religieux" (Let us notice that this industrialization of dream has no common measure with the action of the novel or the theater in the past . . . Our civilization gives rise to as many dreams every week as machines in one year. Thus is established today a romanesque that the world has never known, and whose presence in the life of hundreds of millions of human beings is very different from the romanesque or legendary presences of old: it can be compared to the obsessing presence of the religious imaginary in the past.) Then, referring to the recent creation of Ministries of Culture, Malraux adds: ". . . toute civilisation est menacée par la prolifération de son imaginaire, si cet imaginaire n'est pas orienté par des valeurs" (. . . all civilizations are threatened by the proliferation of their imaginaries, if these imaginaries are not directed by values). In a very typical stylistic fusion, he passes from man's expression of hope to an interrogation without an answer: "Dans le plus trouble déferlement de rêve qu'ait connu l'humanité, nous savons confusément que nous devons trouver nous aussi notre chevalerie. Mais quelles valeurs peuvent orienter ce rêve, qui semble ignorer toutes les valeurs?" (In the most troubled unfurling of dream that Humanity has ever experienced, we confusedly know that we should also find our knighthood. But what are the values that can direct this dream which seems to ignore any sort of values?)

Second, in "Le Mythe de la science et le destin de l'homme," published in February 1975, in *La Revue des Deux Mondes,* Malraux states that biology is a new genesis or, which is the same thing, an antidestiny, an effort to make our species intelligible. Then he considers the state of our civilization, where Man has become master and ruler of the universe, but is still in need of universal values. He refers to our culture as "un imaginaire devenu fou" (an imaginary gone mad). Ironically he concludes: "Ne constatera-t-on pas avec stupéfaction que le temps qui découvrit la physique nucléaire et la vraie génétique s'est satisfait de concevoir l'homme entre le marxisme et la psychanalyse?" (Will we not observe with astonishment that the epoch which discovered nuclear physics and genetics satisfied itself with seeing Man as between marxism and psychoanalysis?) Maybe scientific research will succeed in giving a new foundation to man, "sinon il nous restera l'honneur d'avoir conquis la lune, pour aller nous y suicider" (if not, all that will be left is the honor of having conquered the moon in order to go there to commit suicide). I am tempted to see in this reference to the moon more than an allusion to the American astronauts. Could the moon be the symbol of the Imaginary? If so, Malraux was evoking the apocalyptic vision of our Imaginary going berserk, out of the reach of our consciousness, and leading to the death of man. Neither Marx nor Freud can save us!

17. Jean-Paul Sartre, *L'Imagination*, 1st ed. (Presses Universitaires de France, 1936). This book analyzes the preliminary steps to *L'Imaginaire* (1940). Its purpose is to show prejudices and weaknesses of Western epistemologies since Descartes. Sartre concludes: "Mais l'image *est un certain type de conscience.* L'image est un acte et non une chose. L'image est conscience *de* quelque chose" (162, Sartre's italics) (However, the image is a certain type of consciousness. The image is an act, not a thing. The image is consciousness of something.)

18. André Malraux, *L'Homme précaire et la littérature* (Gallimard, 1977). The last lines propose two reciprocal interrogations: "Nous résignerons-nous à voir dans l'homme l'animal qui *ne peut pas* ne pas vouloir penser un monde qui échappe par nature à son esprit? Ou nous souviendrons-nous que les événements spirituels capitaux ont récusé toute prévision?" (331, Malraux's italics) (Shall we resign ourselves to seeing in man the animal that cannot not want to think a world which by nature escapes from its mind? Or shall we remember that the capital spiritual events have denied any sort of prediction?)

19. Quotations from *L'Imaginaire* are from Jean-Paul Sartre, *L'Imaginaire* (Idées, Paris: Gallimard, 1940).

20. Th. Ribot, *Essai sur l'imagination créatrice* (Paris: Librairie Felix Alcan, 1900).

21. Jacques Lacan, *Ecrits* (Paris: Editions du Seuil, 1966), p. 446.

22. *Ecrits*, p. 458. Italics mine.

23. *Ecrits*, p. 53, with the famous *schéma L*.

24. *Ecrits*, p. 188.

25. Jacques Lacan, *Télévision* (Paris: Editions du Seuil, 1974), p. 41.

26. *Télévision*, p. 42.

27. *Ecrits*, p. 308.

28. *Ecrits*, p. 308.

29. See my article cited in note 1.

30. *Ecrits*, p. 94. I know that Lacan's extract refers to the domain of the Imaginary as opposed to the order of the Symbolic. However, access to the order of the Symbolic does not eliminate the phantasms of preverbal human experience. One may wonder if the artist or the writer doesn't have the vocation and mission to organize the Imaginary and its phantasms within the network of the signifiers. Lacan's phrase seems to express adequately, that is, ironically, the situation of the writer in this motory impotence and his need for a wet nurse, that is, a Mother-culture.

10

Framing Malraux

TOM CONLEY

In the context of a new literary forum that rejects themes and origins of texts and that elucidates obscurities with a lack of faith in some dream of pedagogical virtue, that may even distort the author of which it speaks—at stake is the bypassing of the tepid propriety of so much current writing—Malraux emerges as a problematic figure. The more we batter his work, the better it stands. Many essays (apart from those of documentation) fall into topoi of commemoration and hagiography that either speak, in other words, of a new Saint André or reinstitute the novels and essays from standpoints of Biblical typology. Because Malraux seems to invite and refuse imitation and adulation, we should like to entertain an alternative "reading" of the fragments on art. They appear more successful than the other texts because the images destroy the grandiloquence or univocality of a master's voice; quite cannily, *La Métamorphose des dieux* emerges as the variant of a comic strip, a *bande dessinée* whose effect is to inauthenticate the originality of every picture the book places in profile. A retrieval of the books on art, in view of the most percussive paintings we know—of New York origin, notably, at first distressingly absent from the work—can begin at its most innocuous beginning, the *Mona Lisa*, and proceed to her mutations in Flanders and Manhattan.

The only possible recuperation, Malraux suggests, of *La Gioconda* is by way of serialization. She must be flattened into two dimensions of lithographic reproduction. Not the least remarkable of her appearances in *L'Irréel* is the unfamiliar squaring of the landscape to the right of two versions of the portrait.[1] One is by Leonardo; the other, by a Flemish copyist over a century later. Emerging from the book as two forms of abstraction, his comparison of the details shows how the Northern imitator put a less illusionistic landscape into the background. Emphasis is on the planes and valleys illuminated with broad strokes of amber pigment. Leonardo's painting tells what shall later be modern in Rembrandt and Goya, as the woman's face is set beside a painterly abstraction and the colors of her physiognomy translate chromatic reduction: which herald abstraction of things unknown to the Italian Renaissance. The process of the *Mona Lisa* undoes the work of art as cult-object that she at once embodies, represents, and puts in question. Malraux insists on how, for Leonardo, the source of light becomes all the clearer when we turn the page and see two versions in stereotype: the dumb matron on the right, "correctly" portrayed, "unveils the secret" (p. 207) of the rich greens and pastelled indistinction of the original. A more truly rendered landscape does not allow a play of darker tones (that otherwise only Piero di Cosimo could put in dialogue with his Simonetta, as the next plates indicate), which makes *La Gioconda* so unique.

Less unique than our seizure of the *secret* of abstraction is a rhetorical—almost comical—ploy in his presentation. Its unfolding literally informs the image and proceeds to replicate it less distantly from Duchamp than we are wont to think, for Malraux first presents two of Leonardo's drawings—one of a warrior, another of a chimera—dating to 1480 so as to underline the rather farcical adolescent (recalling the *farfelu*) aspect, one with a rigorous mastery. These were not, the text adds, simple pieces of fantasy: as biographers have

> *L'accent d'adolescence, et parfois d'enfantillage, qui fait si bon ménage dans les cartes de Léonard avec "l'opiniâtre rigueur d'esprit," venait souvent de la recherche d'une féerie mineure. [206-207]*
> (The trait of adolescence and sometimes of childishness, which in Leonardo's plans lives so well with the stubborn rigor of the mind, often came from search for a lesser fairyland.)

shown, Leonardo had to please the courts of Milan and Paris with machinery for festivals, plan surprises and sketch pieces of circumstance. Without citing him, Malraux quotes Vasari's account of Leonardo's lizard, which was adorned with wings filled with quicksilver and masqueraded with a beard and horns and then was tamed and carried in a box with which he could terrify friends. That such an acute observer of nature could indulge in such frivolity is a sign less of a beacon of the West than a genius who determines how the *irréel* is born of the very perversions of cult-values.

Of importance for Malraux's comic strip of masterpieces is immediate contiguity with Freud, another "hero" who cites the same source in the penultimate chapter of "A Childhood Memory of Leonardo da Vinci." Where Malraux appeals to trompe l'oeil and nascent kitsch—like paper moons—to undo the illusionism of Western cultural perspective, Freud, also, appeals to juvenilia for serialization of grandiloquent "enigmas."

Convergence of Freud and Malraux

Here the possibility of a convergence of Freud and Malraux is crucial, for both perform an analytical comic stripping in nearly the same way. In

Freud's essay the lizard-in-the-box buttresses the patient and seemingly excessive attention that early chapters pay to the vulture-fantasy and its proof via sources like that of Horapollo's *Hieroglyphica*. Yet Freud's evocation of the parlor piece turns into a prototypical *camera obscura* or portative camera (a Kodak with a literally caudal shape, the tongue and tail of the lizard anointed in chemicals not dissimilar to those used in early photography) and is congruent with the overbearing scheme of the likeness (in Freud's idiom, *Gleichnis*) of eyes and genitals. Freud's text opens onto a circular system of interruptions and gaps between an eye-breast-penis-clitoris-tail-mouth-etc., of two versions of the same, a vulture, a *Geier* gliding over the child *in culla*, establishing how the incunabular volume of Leonardo's bookish birth can be no more than lithographical versions of a *Traumdeutung*.[2] Leonardo's box fits the scope of Freud's intent: now Malraux's functions somewhat similarly to the extent that the trivial pieces herald the masterworks in the profile of images (plates 137-143 in *L'Irréel*): the playfulness of chimera makes of mystery a superficial form—which the extreme, extravagant enlargement of the real and fake *Gioconda* proves in the middle of the volume.

What the borders cut out of the multiple comparison is keynote since, in looking for the serpentine road, alpine lake, and iridescent horizon that we have learned to know as the background to "La Gioconda," we do not find anywhere. After scrutiny the viaduct behind the neck can be discerned below a mottling of brown within an abstract patch of green and amber, ostensibly an impressionistic scene unlike the clarity of the Flemish copy on the right-hand side (p. 208). This uncanny modernity of a landscape *flatter* yet more deeply abstract than what we imagine is what Malraux underscores via recourse to all subsequent

La vallée du coin supérieur droit s'enfonce dans un espace tout différent de celui des plans étagés qu'elle surmonte. Sur l'eau, un léger effet de lumière, peu conciliable avec un ciel sans nuages, permet l'établissement d'une large zone d'ombre (à la hauteur du nez) qui donne à la vallée sa

persuasive irréalité, et ne détache pas la figure sur l'immensité, mais la relie à l'infini. La comparaison de la Joconde avec sa copie de Rome, où le peintre a cru remplacer le fond de Léonard par un "vrai paysage," en dévoile le secret. [p. 207]

(The valley of the upper right corner is buried in a space entirely different from that of the staged plans it surmounts. On the water, a light play of light, hardly reconcilable with a sky without clouds, allows the setting of a wide zone of shadow (at the height of the nose), which gives to the valley its persuasive irreality and does not detach the face from the immensity but draws it to infinity. The comparison of the Gioconda *with her Roman copy, where the painter believed he replaced Leonardo's background with a "real landscape," unveils the secret of it.*

representation of landscape; we can visualize how the "*Gioconda* is the first famous portrait where a background envelops a figure" (p. 213). But does it? As if the text were denying the series of images it put in profile, our return to the two close-ups shows how the same, at least in terms of envelopment, is likely to be reversed. In the very lower left margin of Leonardo's version, three painterly lines of amber disappear in the dark brown mass (*La Gioconda*'s shoulder) and then lead the trajectory toward the minuscule aqueduct in the background. Yet the detail of which one reading begins with the margin of the frame blends, thanks to the sway of the lines and their curve, front and back into abstraction. Such a presentation, particularly when the sharp edge of the cape in the Flemish copy distinguishes fore- from background to the right, tells us how, with Leonardo, one space "envelops" another. The figure also envelops the landscape.

But the allusive suggestion leads us directly back to Freud, for the chiaroscuro of the detail allows not just an imaginary emergence of mimetic shape from the indistinction of the background in play with the craquelures of the oil paint, but, more importantly, access from the portrayed figure back to *il primo motore* that both Freud and Malraux seem to draw from the same detail. Here Malraux illustrates and defends Freud's concern for the stream of amniotic waters from the life of Leonardo and his works. The comparison might demonstrate how a glaucous water forms an alpine line distinct from the horizon in a manner the Flemish master did not render it; and the patches of earth in the zigzag of a stream are not of verisimilar to the contours of river that the copyist put in his landscape. So the soupy melange of green and brown cross-hatchings indicates on the one hand how Freud saw the indistinct flow of a primary matter whose representation, by extension, could only be of the abstraction Leonardo masters. But on the other, Malraux's choice of the detail, followed by the reproduction of the portraits side by side, disengages what is uncannily evident in Freud's quasi-lithographic study.

Complementary bends of road and river to the left and right of the *Mona Lisa* are such that the bust screens the logical joining of the two. As we have noted, the aqueduct leads into the folds of garment on the left shoulder, which disappear, first diaphanously and then transparently, into the flesh of the chest. The detail also leads to comparison with the rapport of landscape-as-envelope on the other side of the portrait, where the road flows in and out of the veil as if to mark either its translucency or, in Malraux's words, the folding of landscape over the body. A patch of amber provides the viewer with much more than will be made explicit by *L'Irréel*, since the path seems to lead directly to the nipple of the *Mona Lisa*'s right breast.

For Freud and Malraux the effect, if not comical, is necessarily extravagant. At the point where the psychoanalyst had praised Leonardo's energy, the *Irréel* serves as frame, ground, and border for her passage of imaginative energy. We read throughout Freud's text praise couched in a

*In reality Leonardo was not devoid of passion; he did not lack the divine spark which is directly or indirectly the driving force—*il primo motore*—behind all human activity. He had merely converted his passion into a thirst for knowledge; he*

> *then applied himself to investigation with the persistence, constancy and penetration which is derived from passion, and at the climax of intellectual labour, when knowledge had been won, he allowed the long restrained affect to break loose and to flow away freely, as a stream of water drawn from a river is allowed to flow away when its work is done.*[3]

melange of half-electrical and half-amniotic figures. It is as if Freud were fixed on the very details that Malraux bodies forth in the pictural comparison. By superimposition we discover that Freud sees the road and stream emanating from—and flowing into—the breast of the radiant *Gioconda*. Because she is on the verge of laughing, she is ready to commutate the spark of light that follows the course of the observer's eye in the daylight outside of the painting to the landscape within its borders.

Such a travail of the limits of the painting, wherein the force accumulates in attention to the irridescently zigzagged folds of the left sleeve or the cascade of watery streams of light over the edge of the bodice, depends on the figural indistinction of fore- and background, which the pictorial sequence of *L'Irréel* proposes in its rectangular sequence. If Freud's reading of Leonardo can be seen as literally *depending* (the verb being Malraux's) on the hypothesis of the visible modernity or "irreality" of the *Mona Lisa*,[4] so much the better. Nipples or buttons, similar erogenous points, can be seen as any or all of a series of beaks, caudal tips, broken lines, pupils, brushstrokes or ridges; they mark an interval in which the viewer must smile by virtue of his or her detachment from it. In terms of the *Memory of Childhood*, we appreciate *La Gioconda* only when we leave her or find her image obliterated by the reflection of fluorescent light on the glass surface over the tableau in the Louvre: this precipitates a smile for the reader of *L'Irréel*, as the absence of the real picture forces the flow of water through the breast to congeal difference of world and body in such a way that the turning up of her lips is a transfer of our smile; and, of course, as viewers having just looked up at the painting—in the manner the infant Leonardo had seen his mother-bird's beak and feathery genitals in his mouth in the report of the dream *in culla*—we detach ourselves from dependence on it in the fashion of the baby Freud uses to arrive at the concept of *Mundwinkelverziehung*, when that infantile instance in each of us is "satisfied and lets go of the breast" when we fall asleep, that is, when we leave the four, maternally determined, borders of the painting.

Malraux's operation uses more photographic than conceptual apparatus to reach the same points, for the juxtaposition of *La Gioconda* with her Flemish twin in adequate detail and close-up indicates that, in facing the set of pictures, we have been erected on prosthetic tripods and displaced into an imaginary scene of Flanders abutting Italy. We "unveil the secret" of the painting by paradoxically "detaching ourselves to it" through the spoils of photoduplication, which might be figured as a stereoscopy of stereoscopy. And consequently the reading of original and copy (plates 141 and 142) promotes the mise-en-scène of a replicated going and coming of the lady-in-the-landscape in the field of our perception. All the devotional remanence of an imaginary trip through the open doors of the "Louvre" in a search of the Mother of modern painting is forestalled in seriality for which only Duchamp's moustache and subscription provide an outcome adequate to Freud and Malraux.

All of these convergences, so evident in the ploy of text and image, force us to visualize the blur of background and foreground of the *Mona Lisa* as analogue of creation and transcription, original and copy. In the case of the former, we must interpret Malraux's epigraph to *L'Intemporel*

L'artiste n'est pas le transcripteur du monde,
  il en est le rival.

(The artist is not the transcriptor of the world,
  he is the rival.)

as less than Hegelian residue. In the re-edition of *La Métamorphose des dieux*[5] the notion of a contemporary "transcriptor" would no doubt include

Malraux at home in Boulogne, 1948

the variant meanings of transcription as a process of translating a piece of music for an instrument *other* than the original, as would be the instance for words into pictures and vice-versa. Since the books are likened to an "imaginary museum," the author is excluded from the ranks of artists: as transcriptor, the author-reader-writer need not be in some archaic rivalry with the world,[6] which the multiple tension of borders, what we term the eloquence of Malraux's "comic stripping" of edges, in the montage of the picture books, serves to undo. We must, therefore, see the epigraph less as an echo of the heroic dialectic of the artist-in-the-world than as the happily reproductive sham that can be made of it in a composition juxtaposing the *Gioconda* against her mirror-image of another time and space. All this is to say, if the risk can be run of allusion to the figure with whom Malraux converses at the end of *L'Intemporel*,

> Comme l'a dit un jour Picasso, au grand scandale des gens qui l'entouraient—*Je ne cherche pas, je trouve.*[7]

> (As Picasso said one day, scandalizing those who surrounded him—*I don't search, I find.*)

The findings of comparative essays, set in a pre-given mimesis of the history of art (from cult-value to the sense of expositional or arbitrary values), put forward the occasion to find the same overriding tension that a breakdown of difference succeeds, if not in problematizing, at least in displacing onto every artifact attaching itself to—and hence halfway defining as—history. The graphics of Malraux's exergue serves the point, for *rival* and *transcriptor* are in the same vertical field of reference, one substantive always undone in a borderline of the other. A process of autoimplication gives to the *Metamorphoses* an incestuous mode of generation, as the play of pictures in the simulacrum of an art-history (let us say, à la *Story of Art* by a Gombrich) allows space enough for the writing of a *texte*. The result is enough to promote reading and viewing as a mode of page-flipping. The shuffle and cavalcade of pictures generate a transpicuous novel whose continuities are not where we seek them but, rather, everywhere they can be found.

Mona Lisa and the Wicker-Screen Madonna

For this reason Malraux's praise of Leonardo's monumental conflation of planes, reduction of chromatics, and use of short, painterly strokes can be attached to a complementary moment in *L'Intemporel*, in an aside on the Flemish realism whose play of image and text provides more than an opposition of Northern and Southern values. Below a plate of the Master of Flémalle's *Wicker-Screen Madonna* (1425) and adjacent to the detail of its window giving onto a bourgeois landscape (the scene of a roof being repaired along a street of brick and wooden buildings that would become in the next two centuries the subject of Vermeer's cityscapes), Malraux remarks how the cadre—including that of his book—overdetermines Occi-

> *Nous tenons pour banal qu'une oeuvre s'inscrive à l'intérieur de notre champ visuel. Si elle le déborde, nous la fragmentons. Tendance que le Musée Imaginaire n'a pas affaiblie, mais renforcée, parce que les photos des oeuvres, même sans marges, sont cadrées! Il s'agit de plus que du champ visuel: de notre perspective, de "la petite fenêtre" qui délimite les primitifs flamands, de notre lecture des sonnets et non des épopées, et même des statues érigées au centre de nos places (inconnues hors du monde romain et de l'Europe), de tout ce qui faisait dire à mon camarade indien: "Vous allez sur la lune, mais vous n'êtes capables de peindre que des carrés."*
>
> *(We consider as banal a work inscribed inside our visual field. If it goes overboard, we fragment it. A tendency that the Imaginary Museum has not reduced, but rather reinforced, because photographs of works, even those without margins, are enframed. More is at stake than the visual field: our perspective, our "little window" which delimits the Flemish primitives, our reading of sonnets and not of epics, and even of statues erected*

in the center of our squares (unknown outside of the Roman world and Europe), all that made my Indian friend say, "You go off to the moon, but you can paint nothing but squares.")

dental space. In turn, Chinese cylinders have a background so unknown to the time and space of Lascaux and Oriental grottoes that even the thought of rolling up a Cézanne is almost impossible. Frame, tympanum, metope, the window, the Flemish square: all these perpendiculars disavow the possibility of what Malraux calls *le parcours de l'oeil* (p. 359).

Should Malraux allow for the possibility in his own text for the disavowal of the disavowal of fixed space, it would be within the borders of the reproduction of the *Wicker-Screen Madonna* in respect to the breast of the *Mona Lisa*: between the Madonna offering the breast to the child and the window in the upper right corner of the frame is a book seated—yet floating—on the red pillow of the wooden frame of the divan. Oriented toward the sky beyond, one of its pages turning between left and right (following the iconography of the Immaculate Conception and the tropology of the *Novum Speculum Salvationis*) and beneath two lions that cannot but recall (which the text does twenty-three pages later) a montage of *October*, the book serves as shifter between inside and out. Yet for Malraux its oppositional sense between a highly iconized "Old" and "New" order would be less significant than the way the image of movement undoes, as it maintains, the stricture of the frame. The tip of the breast would be the Occidental lure of the center of commerce and growth of "bourgeois realism," a fixation as innocuous as that of the vanishing point in all the Oedipal dimension that the Master of Flémalle's Madonna, only when contiguous to Leonardo and the Indian's remarks, serves to undo.

Even more is at stake in light of Malraux's praise of the loss of illusion among the great masters of representation (Leonardo, Rembrandt, Goya) because the imaginary freedom of the open book, whose flipped pages unbind the cadre within its

Malraux with some statues he brought back from Afghanistan about 1933

borders, *depends* once again on a maternal recurrence as a lure: the choice of Robert Campin reveals a cylindroelliptical configuration in the oval portrait of the Virgin Mary against the circular matting set in front of the opaque rectangle that is the fireplace. Square, circle, ellipse, oval, and pupil contrary to the *Mona Lisa*, the *Wicker-Screen Madonna* does not blend various spaces of illusion, yet only threatens to do so in a progression of geometrical oppositions. Behind the screen and over part of the Madonna's hair, emerges a wisp of flame that will burn the whole representation. The wind from the window, turning the pages and reminding the viewer of the Annunciation, will kindle the fire and char the figures. Here the precarious moment of devotion marked by the book between life and death has its vanishing point at the Madonna's nipple. We can only deduce because of incompatibility of breast and frame that the picture is figured so tardively in *L'Intemporel*.

Humanist residue? A lure of the square? The obliteration of the real by access to a sacred space (which the nails of the open shutter prefigure along with other signs of Campin's "saturated realism") finds its analogue in Malraux's transcription of the volume beyond, in background, as another foreground in his detail (on p. 359). The rose window of the church in the distance, behind the roof under repair, translates the nipple; another road unwinds in the back, as does the light on the folds of drapery of the pillow-cover in the foreground. Hence, again, the landscape represents its undoing in the flow of force that can be likened, as the text almost proposes, to the weening of the Middle Ages and all that they denote as the economic underpinning of the *Réel*. It is this continuous passage of discontinuous forms that tends to work against—and within—the borders of Malraux's text and to lend to the images a renewed instance of force. Here the *parcours de l'oeil* will figure as an impossible and utopian passage of visibles, or of a *parcours d'idées*. This freedom is evanescent only in the passage across paintings and in the radical repositioning of their perspective.

The sense of unbinding of the square depends again on the contiguity of other plates. Their order in a series of multiplied borders assures the virtuality of their readings. By entertaining the notion of an archaic book—an elegant broadsheet of sorts—that regresses to an indistinction within the distinctions it uses, the illustrated texts, like comics in the domain of ideas, have no easy generic description. It can be maintained that the course of reading *L'Irréel* and *L'Intemporel* is so specular that pairing of the Master of Flémalle's and Da Vinci's ladies does no more than identify the viewer's taste or, in a more Freudian optic, the spectator's severing from the paintings by way of the breast. If so, the method revealing the scopics of desire functions not so much to indicate what we have chosen to fetishize through lithography as to display Malraux's own complicity in promoting the appeal; that is, a convergence of masquerade and parade of indeterminate icons that puts the pictures between the phantasm of art as at once a rivalry and heroic upheaval at their resemblance to the arbitrary signs deployed by the media—whether of power, of sex, of nostalgia, or of death.

Set against the tableaux of magazines whose lavish visuals display careful iconiziation of death, *La Métamorphose des dieux* might be displayed in newspaper stands. For its grand quarto format and glossy pages are the areas where the work may well have its greatest reader appeal, in the comic strip and *feuilleton* of modern art. That a work which aims so high can be visualized in places so pulpy may well, like *La Gioconda*, be the sign of its finest destiny.

Hypothetical bordering of Leonardo or Campin in the space of comic strips can lead us back to many of the conclusions put forward in the texts above, but with a miniscule difference. When Malraux deals with cavalcades of images, he approaches the inverse of those heroic confrontations that have attracted many readers of various generations to his writing. Hence the dilemma younger readers face before Malraux, for often the restitution of sacred forms seems obverse to the platitude of mythologies he presents. Because of an absence of the most "appropriate" art, for his enterprise, produced in New York after the Second World War, we deduce a hostility toward what is most resemblant of Malraux, in the work of a De Kooning, Rothko, or even a painter like Brice Marden.[8] It would be better to account for the overstepping of modern art of New York in terms of the imaginary rivalry Malraux puts in epigraph, rivalry that the images serve to undo and square away in the illusion of sacred forms. And so, rather than asking why, today, read a writer so silently aggravated by the mock-heroic forms of modern art—why Malraux is so blind to the great swath or flat surface of color of "Women," "Squares," "Annunciations"—better simply for us to generalize issues of pictorial passage.

Notes

1. In *La Métamorphose des dieux: l'irréel* (Paris: Gallimard, 1974), pp. 208-211.
2. This has been the subject of our "Leonardo Da Vinci à la queue-leu-leu," appearing in the proceedings of "De l'art . . . les bords," *Colloque international de la sèmiotique et de la psychanalyse* (Milan, 1978).
3. *Leonardo Da Vinci and a Memory of His Childhood* (New York: Norton, 1964), pp. 24-25.
4. By dependence we also suggest a mutual sense of hanging, as *La Gioconda* "hangs" in the Louvre in a state of demideath. Its most appropriate Franco-Latin sense might be found in several lines by one of Leonardo's aptly named contemporaries, Maurice Scève:

> O Belle Gorge, O précieuse ymage
> Devant laquelle ay mis pour tesmoignage
> De mes travaux ceste despouille mienne,
> Qui me resta depuis ma playe ancienne.
> Et devant toy *pendu dé*mourra
> Jusques à tant que ma dame mourra.

In the blason of the breast, such fetishization of the lady is, of course, dependent on the slippage (hence the polishing effect) of the penultimate line, which can be read in echo of

> Et devant toy *dépendu* mourra.

5. *L'Intemporel* (Paris: Gallimard, 1976), p. v.
6. Malraux deflates all the mythology of an "originary violence" by visualizing it repeatedly. Hence the effect undoes all that has, as such, a terrorist value in the tenets of a "new philosophy."
7. Quoted by Lacan, *Le Séminaire: Livre XI* (Paris: Seuil, 1964), p. 12.
8. The similarity of intent between Malraux and Marden bodies forth in Jean-Claude Lebensztejn, "From," preface to catalog of Marden's "Recent Paintings and Drawings, September 23-21 October 1978," *The Pace Gallery* (New York, 1978), pp.1-5.

ically reading each line?

PART 4

FANTASY AND IMAGINATION

11

Poetics and Passion

MARY ANN CAWS

Ce que je tiens le plus à dire n'est pas, il s'en faut, ce que je dis le mieux.

Breton, La Clé des champs

(What I most care to say is far from being what I say best.)

To the question, "What is art?" Malraux replies, in *Les Voix du silence:* "That by means of which forms become style." And to a parallel question about poetry or even poetics, we might give this partial answer: "That art of making by means of which thought conveys passion." How may we address ourselves simultaneously to style, to thought, and to passion except by our insistence on the presence of the text, whether it be that of the page or the painting? The journey of each reader through the ways of a living thought must find the passage and passages befitting that presence as it must also find its own frame. Malraux's intensity demands always our own commitment and our passion.

The Nature of Art

Art—and in that we may include poetry, in the sense we are using it here—is that which triumphs over accident as the universal finally wins out over the particular, at once redeeming it and imbuing it with irony. For it is in the individual and the accidental that we suffer what is called "man's fate," of which André Breton says that our way of accepting the unacceptable human condition, even as we refuse it, makes of us what we are. And the smallest perceptions of all writers who are poets bear the weight of the universal concept without betraying individual eye or heart. If Malraux constantly describes evil as pitted against fraternity in the grimmest battlefields of the First World War, marked with the ubiquitous traces of poison gas, our eye is held along with that of the narrator, in *Lazare* and before that in *Les Noyers de l'Altenburg (The Walnut Tress of Altenburg)*, not only by the rotted grass, the gigantic vegetation of slime, the spiderwebs sparkling with poisoned dew in the meadows thus "abjectly ornamented," but also by the single ray of the setting sun catching in its glow the cross of Lorraine on the chest of a fallen soldier. Even when the emotional charge that Malraux plainly feels is emptied from the image, the aesthetic detail sustains the text, as we tend to compare it with a ray of light in a Rembrandt or a Caravaggio, an oblique grace redeeming the darkness in these two painters who will guide us also at the conclusion of our brief remarks. To be sure, after this passage by death and horror, Lazarus is raised, whether from the war field or the bed of sickness, and, like Lazarus, sometimes a Colonel Berger and sometimes a Capitaine Alexandre, so that poets of the stature of André Malraux and of René Char may bear witness to the resurrection by the written word. We remember now the early morning scene of *Les Noyers*, the brilliant green after the fog and gray of the world marked by war, when the multicolored washing hung out on the line had all the freshness of renascence and of simple human miracle.

Repeatedly, in all the works of Malraux, the unforgettable moments that balance against the great dialogues are, objectively seen, the smallest ones, as if the eye had to be trained to perceive them. The huge red hand on the glove maker's signboard in *Lazare* could be taken, for instance, as an image of pointing toward what we might not have seen before. No reader can overlook the separations experienced throughout Malraux's long passage by art and poetry, for the hand is again and again unrecognized by the man possessing it, and the voice is repeatedly unrecognized by the ears because it is known in the throat, so that the outer and the inner are rent apart. But what the uncaring or hasty eye might not have seen is precisely the convergence operated by art in spite of such separation and because of it. Now when we look back at the whole span of Malraux's work as only his death permits us to, which its closure thus opens, certain images cluster unexpectedly in relation to each other, and we are unashamedly touched by their gathering.

The play of lamps and of shadows in *La Condition humaine* with its Chinese lighting sets up its own profundity of black and white against the gray death and green renascence of the France to which Malraux returned. The images of Nietzsche's mad laughter in a train passing through a tunnel and of the peasant woman on her way to market, ramming the chicken's head back into the basket, two images already juxtaposed in *Les Noyers*, form part of the scene now in our mind with an image from *Lazare*, where exhausted refugee children sleep under the rain as it beats down on the cardboard cartoon figures brought to divert them in the terrible hours of the Spanish Civil War. Our political and historical memories may differ, not necessarily our perceptions. This is to say that in the long run of art, both geography and events, whether terrible or touching, become part of the value we choose to make for ourselves as a second human condition, no less profound for its rethinking. We know, of course, that art finds its own sense in and through the absurd; that the answer to Sartre's question and ours, "What is literature?" may differ; that what Malraux calls the "irrational of caverns" is essential both to fraternity and to the sacred, that is, also to poetry. We know that the taste of bitter almonds of which he speaks may have its final importance on the same scale as the whispered question, "Why?" pondered by generations before the human corpse beside the caves of Lascaux and Les Ezies, asked by Malraux once more, explicitly and implicitly. Corpse and cavern, "cadavre et caverne"—the sound of the words casts its own spell. When the word *convulsion* haunts Malraux, or the expression "possession foudroyante," it is the word itself also and not only the abstract concept that convulses and possesses him. The poetic prose of René Char on his own illness like a lightning stroke closely resembles that of Malraux: "convulsion, foudroyante": the hero is struck down from the sky, in a sense, but he survives by words and by the smallest details perceived, gathered, expressed, and thus illuminated. Each poet is his own phoenix.

The word against the concept, as Yves Bonnefoy would say, and the imperfection of a human tongue against the perfected form of an idea only: that then is poetry. Or listen to Wallace Stevens (in "The Poems of Our Climate"):

> Note that, in this bitterness, delight,
> Since the imperfect is so hot in us,
> Lies in flawed words and stubborn sounds.

In the mines, Malraux tells us, the word *lamp* is said with the magic respect due to it, is pronounced as befits the darkness, in solemnity. And only a poet would notice.

The Nature of Poetry

The *Voix du silence* are then the voices of poetry. In one of the illustrations to this volume, Caravaggio's St. Jerome stretches out his right hand and the pen it holds beyond the book. His eyes—which our own can never meet, since they are turned away and perhaps even closed—are directed toward his left hand rather than his text. The painting, singled out by Malraux, is neither that of a reading nor of a creation, but rather of an interior concentration, its verticality hidden by its nature, in opposition to the clearly visible horizontal line of book and table and writing hand. This line would lead us to another scene, whose lighting Malraux draws in correspondence with this one, that in which Georges de La Tour's Magdalen—or rather Madeleine, as Char points out, before her sainthood—gazes past what we shall all become, so that our human fate is read into the canvas. "Skulls have never laughed so much as they do for us," says the doctor in *Lazare*.

"I have seen," begins a sentence on the next-to-the-last page of *Les Voix du silence;* and, separated by other voices and other visions, its continuation is implied: "In the evening where Rembrandt is drawing still, all the illustrious Shadows, and those of the cavemen artists, follow with their gaze the hesitating hand that prepares their new survival or their new sleep" (p. 640)." The meditation concludes with the "song of constellations" triumphant in and against man's most ironic fate whereas the artist's hand, like the poet's, trembles with all the paradoxical privilege of being human, this action drawing its strength from its extreme human fragility. In the force of the contradiction we recognize a Pascalian quivering of contraries, a vibration in style as in thought, rendering all the more intense the unique resonance of Malraux's discourse. And this night of stars, too, like this flame and this cave at the conclusion, for Malraux eternally dialogues with his stars and ours, as his caves and constellations echo those of Plato and of Pascal, dark and light hurled together. "L'éclat des flammes vient aussi de la profondeur de la nuit." (The flash of flames comes also from the very depth of the night.) From the baroque artists and poets to Char's Talismanic night of contemporary vision, the haunting contrast of obscurity and luminosity holds us present to the scene, which we cannot now perceive as other than mortal.

A black sun haunting a tragic and lucid sky: Malraux takes for his guide the same image as his contemporary René Char, who finally chooses as his only clarity the horrendous and yet splendid *Flayed Ox* of Rembrandt. It is not, after all, extraordinary that the human condition should take on the very color of its suffering from cruelty, for that, too, is the color of its passion. It is rather to be marveled at—in the face of all natural elements and all logic—that the artist, whom we would always identify with the poet, should continue endlessly to ask the same questions when contemplating a flowering May meadow, as Nietzsche does, or a field of wheat, like Braque and then Breton. "Can art hold firm when confronted with a meadow and with human mortality beside it?" asks Nietzsche. "Can it hold its own in the face of a wheat field?" asks Braque. "And," asks Breton more tragically, "can it hold in the face of starvation?" It must, or must not *be*. These concerns haunt the long history of Malraux's speculations on art and on life: his answers, partial of necessity, are ethical as they are aesthetic, philosophic as they are poetic.

Poetry, like life, like art, consists of a series of these answers to what Malraux calls "the invincible question" (p. 629), answers perhaps ephemeral, possibly eternal, held forever in a work of art. And as we interrogate or respond, the gaze we turn—whether to a smiling angel or a reading saint or a flayed beast—is already the stuff of our own making. "I have seen," Malraux continues, for his sight and ours, and he spares no aid to vision, turning Giotto—precisely the *Raising of Lazarus*—upside down to detect the sculptured forms and even printing it in that manner, examining a negative of a Caravaggio or a Rubens, enlarging, reducing, meditating. All of this so as to see or to bestow sight, as on a Lazarus newly arisen. "Voir/To see" as Eluard called a series of poems, and elsewhere: "Donner avoir/To give to have," or then "To give to see." For in the act of offering, the seer sees more richly. Again, each permitted resonance increases the field of hearing, as Malraux's own *Voix du silence* are also "voies" or ways of keeping silent and then again paths for a language supremely visible.

If we too follow these paths now, in his steps and with his eyes, it is to be taken as an homage to the vision, to the courage of presenting a museum without walls of separation but also without the comfort of categories, an early example of intertextuality, of interreadings and wide communions.

Now the underlying question is itself invincible, as we are not, and the voice also: "L'invincible voix intérieure" is not just the voice we hear through our own throat, anguished in its alienation from the ear, but also an interior path we choose to follow in spite of its ending, that place marked by the death skull upon the reader's table, by his candle and his mirror.

If poetry is linked, as Malraux reiterates of art, to that which lies beyond appearance and yet is tied to matter and to form, it bears witness also to the anguish of that trembling hand. "What does Rembrandt matter in the flow of nebulae? But it is mankind that the stars deny and to mankind that Rembrandt speaks" (p. 639). That language is the language of poets, of the great voyagers whom Malraux calls the great navigators for their passage across the trackless domains of the heart as of the mind. *Poieisis*, after all, meant the constructing of ships and the making of perfume, for the senses were not to be isolated from the mental venture.

Finally, we can only be lit by the torch we carry in our own hand, Malraux reminds us, and that torch may well singe the hand bearing it. The flame on which we meditate and the illumination of art are far from being mere consolations. The poet, according to Yves Bonnefoy, is the one who burns. Seeing, in the framework of *Man's Hope*, the place of possible convergence for the world and art, we may well discover in reality only the place of actual loss, that loss intensified by what might once have been hoped. Bonnefoy maintains, and we with him, that "the anguish of the true place is the condition of poetry." Which of us is to say whether that anguish is nostalgia or prediction, or where our place might finally be? Poetry, like all art, is made of presence, and we would celebrate, in spite of all our open contradictions and our own half-ridden anguish, the ways of those silent but speaking voices, *Les Voix du silence*, as they lead us paradoxically, now, toward the sustained presence of André Malraux.

Chapter Four

One of Malraux's sketches decorating "Chapter Four" of a book

12

Archetypes: Dissolution as Creation

BETTINA KNAPP

From whence does the creative factor emerge? What drives men to seek new forms, to attempt to confront and to dominate their destiny through the work of art to gain eternity? *The Voices of Silence (Les Voix du Silence)* poses these questions in a volume that is not only a philosophical work, but a metaphysical probing, a book reflecting Malraux's own anguish and his perpetual tension and energy.

For Malraux the artist-creator is a *hero*, a *conqueror* of a past that no longer fulfills his needs. Because the artist-creator is more sensitive than the ordinary man or woman, he or she is able to delve more profoundly, to make contact with Jung's collective unconscious, a primordial past devoid of linear or rational time. This descent into Self enables the artist to confront the creative impulse within, to perceive cataclysms, to foresee abysses. Such an exploration reaches beyond conventional or traditional norms—into *prima materia* (primal matter). Like Mallarmé's *Igitur*, the artist "descends the stairs of the human mind and goes into the depths of things" and first perceives the archetypal image (or images) from which a creation will be molded in this inexpressible world, in this penumbra.

Energy is implicit in the archetypal image and is interwoven into its very substance, creating a "magnetic field," an "energy center," comparable to a volcano. If the energy (or archetypal image) remains repressed within the unconscious, it may explode, not only influencing but also deforming the vision.

The energy that emanates from the collective unconscious as an archetypal image becomes a force powerful enough to affect the rational mind. The work of art synthesizes the dialectic between conscious and unconscious. The more powerful the archetypal image, the more it dominates him or her who may ascribe to it magical powers and divine force so that it may become comparable to the Greek *daemon*. Picasso, for example, was its victim during his Blue Period or his Bull Fighting series, as were Henry Moore with his perpetual mother-child motifs, Chagall and his Jewish mysticism, and Yves Tanguy and his mangled forms and empty skies.

The artist's creation translates a numinous experience—that is, it is the embodiment of the archetypal images that live inchoate within. The form the artistic endeavor takes—a painting, a statue, a tapestry, a cathedral, a literary work—becomes the specific language (or the symbol) expressing the artist's inscape. Once the work of art has been perfected by rational discipline, it no longer belongs to his or her absolute or ideal world of abstraction and lives on its own in the collective domain.

According to Malraux, the artist is a psychopomp, a guide who renders the amorphous palpable and who transforms by limiting. Like the mystic, he or she is a visionary who can go across the material domain to unmanifested lands. At times, life may go on in harmony with the world; and at other times, in disorder and *chaos*. The painting becomes the visible sign or symbol of a transpersonal reality—and the revealer of infinite mysteries.

To analyze a painting—which we may define as symbol of the unknown—too explicitly is to deprive it of its mystery, to divest it of its creative impulse, and to *irritate* the energy buried in the collective unconscious, which the artist will fashion into archetypal images. By acting as a "psychic transformer," the symbol renders visible that which drowses in man's depths. As long as the symbol does not become overly rational, this source of dynamism, this catalyst will continue to stir and to activate the energy of the archetypal image that compels its rise to consciousness. But once the mystery has been revealed and the symbol has become too rational (and this is the destiny of religions as well), it becomes sterile and disintegrates. Its components are absorbed by the artist, who slowly blends the more vital elements into the collective unconscious until they can again be revivified into consciousness.

As the artist makes contact with his or her collective unconscious, he or she precedes his or her era; he or she lives in two realms—the temporal and the atemporal. The artist possesses a unique talent and is the precursor, the prototype, the prophet of the future. How many times has it been said about a philosopher, a painter, a sculptor, or a scientist that he lived before his time, that he saw into the future. The message of a

Cézanne, of a Van Gogh, or of a Piero della Francesca rejects the false conventional attitudes of the time and surpasses them.

All important artistic, religious, philosophical, and scientific movements have had their prophet-founders. With lucidity, the artist fashions and colors the disparate elements within his or her being and then exteriorizes these as paintings, statues, poetry, musical compositions, films, and so on. Nations, peoples, societies, wrote Erich Neumann, "are conditioned by the power of an inner psychic reality which often enough appears in the first place as fantasies in the mind of an individual." Works such as the canvases of El Greco, Goya, and Delacroix emerge from the collective unconscious and are Janus-faced because they point to the past and to the future.

This process was also expressed by medieval Hebrew Cabalists by two words whose meaning is altered by simply changing the place of one letter: *ain*, which means "nothing" becomes *ani*, which means "I"—thus *nothing* becomes *Something*. The amorphous potential forces embedded within the unconscious become something in the artistic object with an alteration or transformation of energy.

Once the energy implicit in the new form diminishes, the vision withers, what might be called ossification sets in, and the art form in question begins to decline. Malraux, however, does not view such "decline" as a death or degeneration of an aesthetic expression. In the second part of *The Voices of Silence*, "The Metamorphoses of Apollo," the anti-Spenglerian Malraux considers differences in artistic ways—such as the so-called "Barbaric" art as opposed to "Hellenic art"—not as a dissolution or degeneration of an artistic vision, but rather as a break, *un arrachement*, a cleavage, which underscores the differences between each civilization in the incessant cosmic flow. Malraux regards what we erroneously consider to be the end or decline of an artistic vision as the manifestation of new cultural values—a *renovatio* (renewal) or *innovatio* (innovation). "An art lives on what it *brings*," wrote Malraux, "and not on what it abandons." It is judged inferior or regressive only in comparison with another technique or aesthetic, for example, Gothic art when contrasted to the spectacle of Renaissance art or the Greek vision juxtaposed to the Barbarian view. "Regression is a form of art, as widespread, as *significant*, as that which begins with the Acropolis at Delphi and terminates with Constantine," explained Malraux (*Les Voix du Silence*, p. 129). Regression or decline is actually an alteration or transformation of cultural and psychological values, a response to new needs of an evolving society. To prove his theory, Malraux uses the *stater* coined for Philip II of Macedonia on which the Hellenic god Hermes was stamped.

The Greek Hermes was the incarnation of beauty, of perfection, and of harmony. This same face seen by the "Barbarians"—in the Greek sense of the word—lacks inner balance. It is said to be *fragmented* and *disfigured*. But is such a judgment sound? Is it valid, questioned Malraux, to denigrate the product of one culture while praising the manifestations of another? For Malraux, the answer is, of course, no. The money coined by the Barbarians showed that their lives were difficult and crude. These so-called Barbarians saw Hermes as sun, lion, circles, geometrical figures that, as Malraux notes, may be compared to certain modern designs.

Malraux is unequivocal: transformation in art or any other concrete manifestation of human psyche must not be envisaged as a degeneration of human aptitudes, but rather as an expression of altering unconscious factors. In India, he notes, the Hellenic Apollo was transformed into a Buddha. In Afghanistan, the most ancient Buddhas were Apollos endowed with "signs of wisdom." The Gandhara statues of Buddhas and bodhisattvas (fourth century B.C.) are Apollos with slanting eyes. Malraux underscores the resemblance between the "Smile at Rheims" and the Gandhara Buddha heads: both are endowed with the characteristics of Hellenic Apollos: their smile, their inner wisdom, and their serenity (*Les Voix du Silence*, p.159). Christianity transformed the Greco-Roman Hermes into a Christ figure: the "Shepherd Christ," the "Good Pastor."

The question remains as to why Malraux chose the gods Apollo-Hermes to underscore his thesis that art is a process of transformation and not of periodic degeneration.

Hermes was a terrestrial god. Clever and versatile, he guided the dead to Hades; he was the patron of tradesmen, miners—those questing for buried treasures, a fertilizing agent. Psychologically, he represented the *earth archetype*, which centers on matter. "Barbarians" chose Hermes to represent the contents of their unconscious because he incarnated the terrestrial side of man. Their forms of Hermes were in direct rapport with their own psyche. Their lives were *visceral*, not *cerebral*.

Apollo, conversely, was the god of the sun, light, and the mind and the enemy of all that was somber, dirty, or profane. He protected the harvest against vermin and rot, propagated health and happiness in man, and was a healer. God of mental and moral purity, of order, and of justice, Apollo incorporated mental attitudes and was the *archetype of spirituality*. Hindus, for example, reproduced Apollolike Buddhas before creating their own style.

The intense struggle of the artist during transitional periods is evident in the paintings of Bosch, for example, an artist divided between the spirit of the Middle Ages and that of the Renaissance. His paintings, *The Temptation of St. Anthony* or *The Garden of Worldly Delights* or *Christ Carrying the Cross*, depict the schism between asceticism (favored by the scholastic doctors with their obsessions about temptation, chastisement, and pain, which Bosch translated by means of an infestation of demonic faces on his canvases) and feelings of growth, flowering, richness, and joy emerging with the Renaissance. This appreciation of the earth principle became visible in Bosch's brilliant color tones.

The artist is a *medium* through whom the forces of the universe are manifested. For Malraux, the dissolution of an aesthetic form is the expression of a creative factor and the exteriorization of an archetype. It is

The sculpture Malraux "acquired" in Indochina and which figures in *La Voie royale*

perhaps less ebullient, less dazzling than earlier artistic visions; perhaps it is even distorted, mangled, and macerated. Nevertheless, it is a human being's way of expressing feelings, disenchantment or meditations on life. As Malraux wrote, "Art lives on what it *brings* and not on what it *abandons.*"

MELANGES
MALRAUX
MISCELLANY

One of Malraux's sketches on a title page

13

The Artist as Exemplar of Humanity

MICHELINE TISON-BRAUN

Malraux began the *Psychology of Art* by noting that it was meant neither as a history of art nor as a treatise of aesthetics. There was to be no effort at discovering the origin of art. Malraux had already given up ascertaining the origin of anything at all: everything had always already begun. "As far back as we can go in art, we find conventions and forms" (203).[1] A phenomenologist without being aware of it (before the word had gained wide acceptance), he limits himself to an attempt at understanding the nature of the creative process. But the scope of his investigation is much broader than his stated objective: the artist, like the hero, is the "exemplar," the epitome of man's possibilities, for Malraux finds the essence of life in the creative process. Is the expression "cultural anthropology" appropriate in a discussion of Malraux's works? Vuillemin,[2] for example, uses it when he compares Malraux's and Cassirer's endeavors (to the advantage of the latter). Would "psychology"—the category Malraux chose for his initial title—seem more suitable? The book is, indeed, about psychology if the term is taken to mean study of the spirit (or Spirit). Not the individual limited psyche, but the Spirit served by man, its witness, and by great men, its messengers, whose irreducible presence extends beyond all human acts and creations. Although Malraux does not believe in a personal God, a creator and legislator of the world, his entire work is an acknowledgment, at first implicit, then more and more clearly formulated, of a Spirit, immanent to humanity and transcending history, civilizations, and individual works. A man's worth can be estimated as he partakes of this Spirit, which confers upon him, in his life, his "share of immortality."

Yet psychology does not seem to be an adequate label. *Psycho*, yes, but *logy*? Not insofar as this suffix implies coherent discourse. Most of the articles devoted to Malraux's essays on art, even the most flattering, find the lack of formal composition of these writings confusing. They underscore the difficulty experienced in following such eruptive thinking. But Joseph Hoffman, one of Malraux's admirers who can penetrate the inner logic of his writing, speaks of a "three-dimensional style": while analyzing a fact or an event, Malraux always restores the work to its dialectical context—painting and sculpture, East and West, past and present. He adds that Malraux's thought is clear if one accepts that a "symphonic composition" in the essays on art and in the novels follows the movement of a "deeper questioning."[3] Such is, indeed, the movement of Malraux's thinking. Other critics reveal contradictions in the thoughts themselves. Having asserted that art and history are independent, Malraux then sketches the historical evolution of art. Having first defined art as the highest expression of freedom and a revolt against man's fate and then modern art as the logical end of this freedom, he next shows that the unconscious determinism of modern artists impelled them to admire as symbols of freedom fetischist art, that is, art most strictly subject to tradition. Still another critic observes the equivocal meaning of the word *metamorphosis*.[4] On a certain level, all these objections are justified, but just not on the plane where Malraux places himself: to bind him to a system would be to ignore his main intention.

Inasmuch as the suffix *logy* implies a system, Malraux has written not a psychology, but a psychophany, a manifestation of the spirit in art. And this psychophany is superimposed on two registers. It is on one level a partly chronological presentation of great works of art. Influences and conflicts, however, are drawn not as history but as epic. As in the *Iliad*, where one is witness only to personal combats, conflicts, and alliances, a general strategy organizing Malraux's work is missing. Unity comes from an identical thrust manifested in hundreds of works and suggesting unexpected relationships between time, styles, and places.

On another level, the level of interpretation, Malraux wants to express this drive that he sees and experiences. Aware of contradictions in his theory, he, too, sometimes adopts a systematic approach and strives for order and logic. Example: Realistic art is a myth; all great art is creation, refusal of reality. But what about Chardin? What about Vermeer? Did they eternalize a moment of reality? Is applying the word *illusion* both to an idealization full of love for the substance of things and to the horror of *Guernica* an overplay? Here again, criticizing is easy. But it is more important to understand how Malraux, while striving towards intellectual coherence, achieves a new epiphany and reveals his own spirit as it vibrates to artistic reality. Does it matter whether realistic art exists? Chardin's painting *The Housewife* includes a loaf of bread not for the family's nourishment, but because a certain fuzzy blue required a somber crackling gold. And that is what matters. Malraux's spirit lights up, soars, falters, sometimes disperses, but usually rekindles itself. His thought erupts. Those who judge it intricate unwittingly speak the truth, because it emerges spinning its own web; or to use another simile, his thought bursts forth like the branches of a tree, not a tree perhaps but a forest, a baobab forest in which branches take root through intertwining lines and counterlines, resembling the animal plaques of Steppe art. The relationships between the characters of his novels can be illustrated in the same way. In *L'Espoir*, characters grow side by side like plants issued from the same compost heap; and their intentions, however contradictory, intersect in a network of common wills. This is the inner logic of Malraux's works, a logic that expresses the creative exchanges between artists scattered throughout various civilizations.

Peace reigns between works of art in Malraux's museum without walls. Conflict exists only between the museum and the real world. This terrestrial world exhausts itself in ferocious, sordid combats that the heroes try to transcend. The world of limited and unshareable objects is one of fanaticism and fear. But art escapes these misfortunes by its very lack of reality, by creating another autonomous world, a world open to the unlimited expanses of the Spirit. Malraux certainly knows that artists, like politicians, tear each other to pieces; nevertheless, their works enter into unexpected alliances, a thousand leagues and a thousand years away. Epic of human creation, epiphany of the spirit, such is art.

The Role of the Artist

What is the artist actually trying to do? In *The Walnut Trees of Altenburg*, Malraux writes, "I call an intellectual someone whose life is directed by an idea." He adds, "Intellectuals are a race." In the case of the artist, creative process is directed not by an idea, but by what Malraux calls a *schème*. The term suggests a simplified image, a sort of sketch. But Malraux uses it in a much broader sense, going beyond the realm of the plastic arts. Certainly, *schème* is form, line, volume, configuration of sounds and colors; also composition of a work, a novel, or a poem (335 ff). The word comes closer to what we call today, in the broadest sense of the term, structure. Malraux distinguishes the *schème* from what he calls *écriture* (idioms, mannerisms)—a word that he, unlike Barthes, applies specifically to artistic techniques. The *écriture* of an artist can be imitated; it lends itself to forgery and to pastiche. The *schème*, on the other hand, cannot be imitated; it is not only form—although the presence of form is necessary—but above all the expression of the "artist's deepest emotions vis-à-vis the universe of which he is part" (414). "Every great painter has his secret, that is to say the means of expression of which his genius usually avails itself" (385). The *schème* is the "artist's answer to a question," an "appeal to give the world new meaning." It is indeed form, but form filled with meaning. The *schème* is inimitable because it is rooted in the artist's experience, in his presence to the world. It is tempting to call it his incarnation, for although the creative act is the essence of the world, the *schème* is the essence of the artist. The *schème* can evolve, can change in the course of an artist's life; it can define itself in harmony or in conflict with other *schèmes*, but a constant always remains, a sort of quintessence of a vision of the world: "that vision of the mind's eye, whose light endures when the body's eyes are failing" (280).

A masterly analysis of the *Last Judgment* (324 ff) shows aging Michelangelo's *schème*: sacred terror in front of a god of vengeance—born of St. Augustine and Savonarola—could only be expressed through the harmony of ochre tints and "Biblical blue" and by the space separating this Christ of malediction from the falling crowd of Damned. Under the stigmata of terror and sin, as fatal as those of Oedipus, their faces retain the tragic dignity of Man's condition. Although religious art of the Renaissance often degenerated into fairy tales, here the terrifying and complex vision of the world led contemporaries to condemn the fresco for fear of having to condemn themselves.

For the artist, the *schème* is a vocation, a fascination; even before he becomes conscious of it, the *schème*'s latent imperious presence forbids him to copy even his most venerated masters. Unlike the forger, he will even modify a technique in order to follow his *schème*. This is illustrated by the comparison of two copies with their originals: Cézanne's copy of Sebastiano del Piombo's *Christ in Limbo* loses its mellowness and is decomposed into contrasting planes; Delacroix's *Pietà*, imitated by Van Gogh, adopts the undulating lines of the wheat fields to come. So tyrannical is the *schème* that if the artist, like Rembrandt, is not accepted by his contemporaries, he will sacrifice his life, his comfort, his happiness, even his glory to it; he prefers to be forgotten than to betray his essence.

Except for some more examples that illustrate but do not explain, Malraux devotes the rest of the text to stating what art lacks. He carefully isolates the creative act from all other mental operations: perception, natural association of images, personal experience, and desire. Art is not a copy of reality: Malraux's analysis of the naturalistic illusion and his assertion of the inexistence of realistic art are well enough known so that review is not needed. More interesting, in view of Malraux's early association with surrealism, is his disbelief in an artist's subjective experience as a key to his work. The case of Kassner, the prisoner in *Time of Contempt* devoured by mental images, shows that creation does not depend on a spontaneous merry-go-round, but on the artist's ability to hold back. "Artistic creation does not spring from a surrender to the unconscious, but from the ability to tap and channel it" (306).

Malraux attacks subjective theories of creation with the same passion with which he denies *mimesis*. Of course, the artist's experience of both the inner and outer worlds influences creation provided that a dialectic rather than a linear causality is assumed: The artist's psyche, his experience in the world, his unconscious drives all influence the creative process, but these, in turn, model the creator's own psyche. Of greater importance, however, than any direct or indirect influence is the autonomy of creation. The artist may be master or slave or rebel, Don Juan or the *Mal-aimé*; but he must create an *oeuvre* that seeks not to express his experience but to transcend it.

Malraux's disbelief in the creative ability of the unconscious applies to the collective unconscious as well. There are no spontaneous, anonymous creations of the national spirit. Malraux is not ready to extend to any collective the reverence he refuses to the individual. The *we* in his eyes is as hateful as the *I*. The collective creates nothing. It occasionally (rarely) recognizes its own guiding images in the work of a great artist, most often a mediocre one who supplies stereotypes. Indeed, with technical development, the production of stereotypes has become an industry that Malraux names with sarcasm "art d'assouvissement" (an art aimed at vulgar self-gratification).

In opposition to all these forms of the *ego* (with a small *e*), Malraux defines creative man as a spirit seeking to transcend itself and aware of its place at the center of a cosmos. These concepts must be rigorously defined. What Malraux calls transcendence is not an athletic will struggling against the weaknesses of the flesh and of the heart. What must be transcended and what Malraux calls destiny is life as it is: facts, events, feelings, and even models, including the most precious heritage of the past and of the masters ("Nathanaël, throw my book away . . ." as Gide would say). *Transcended* does not mean destroyed, renegated, or even abandoned, but implies a going beyond. The break that initiates all creation is not a manifestation of hostility. It is true that Malraux celebrates the creative value of the "Spirit of discontent" (339); but discontent is reprobation not of the masters but of the self who lacked the courage, or perhaps the same power for liberation as these masters. Masters should no more be imitated than nature; the oft repeated quote might be paraphrased: "Not to imitate the masters, but to create like them."

The autonomous quality of the creative vision is disturbing. The concept is not less perplexing if we suppose, as did traditional idealism, that the creator's mind contains a preformed vision that needs only to be "expressed," that is, forced out. The obstetrical metaphor only sets the problem one step back. Why should the Muse intervene between the artist and his creation? Minerva emerges fully armed from Jupiter's head. Vision is nothing until the appearance of a form. Vision and form are the same reality. To distinguish one from the other is only a view of the mind, a useless dichotomy, a threat of regression *ad infinitum.* Such explanations are foreign to Malraux, who is so convinced of the complete autonomy of artistic creation that he sees in it a sort of *actus purus* (pure act), a creation *ex nihilo.*

But the enigma cannot be gotten rid of so easily. When Malraux avoids runaway rhetoric or does not indulge in his taste for paradox, he perceives the real nature of the miracle: the mind's ability to assemble and to fix in a coherent and communicable structure the unformed imitations of the world—a world that appears to him as "scattered and ephemeral" and as much "in need of man in order not to repeat but to renew itself" (466).

It is here that the artist is the exemplar. Everything that Malraux says about the *oeuvre* could be applied *mutatis mutandis* to the formation of personality, which is not a substance but a power. Man is not what he hides, as one of the characters in the *Altenburg* indicates, for there is nothing to hide. There is no essential Ego to discover, any more than there is a preexisting vision to express. Tchen's personality, for example, was not contained either in his genes or in his Sino-Christian upbringing. From these, he retained at most an uneasiness, which predisposed him to tragedy. But the initial act that instituted his personality was an invention whose "logic" he recognized only later. In the same way, though Leonardo could be expected to create great masterpieces, the *Mona Lisa* could not be predicted. By considering creation—of a work as well as of the self—not as the discovery of a preexisting reality, but as the exercise of a will to transform, Malraux escapes false antinomies: form and content, vision and structure, intention and act. Without knowing it, he thus agrees with the philosophers of freedom (Heidegger and, less obviously, Sartre), who dominate the postwar period.

If the creative act, as an expression of freedom, cannot be reduced to its origins, could it then be better defined by its aim? Of course, this aim cannot be reduced to any of the known and classified purposes of human conduct. Art is not utilitarian. "The artist's forest is not the hunter's." It goes without saying that it has nothing to do with ethics. Not even with metaphysics: Metaphysics explains the world; art explains nothing; it points to a mystery. Finally, art is not even necessarily related to beauty. Its action is of a different order, which is cosmic: Man is the being through whom the world "renews itself instead of being repeated" (464). This explains why the artist can never clearly state his aims, the reason for his endeavor: He is not "expressing something he has experienced, he is responding to a call" (412). He is called to nothing else but to create a universe of signifying forms, but signifying what? Art rewards its devotee with the feeling of having found the only secret; and by the same token bestows upon him, beyond misfortune and even indignity, a "joy equal to certainty"—this joy, thanks to which, as Proust said, "death is less demeaning, may be less probable." It is in this way that the artist is akin, but on an higher level, to the founder of empires or religions and to

Malraux with Albert Beuret and Jacques Vandier, curator of Egyptian antiquities at the Louvre, 1947

all compelling vocations, which are heroic and magnificently useless. Such a passion, both unreasonable and sacred (for the one who experiences it), should shed light on the human enigma. This is indeed why Malraux addresses himself to the imaginary, in an attempt, once more, to penetrate the secret of Man and of Being.

The shadows of Heidegger and of Merleau-Ponty, whose meditations on art were still to come, again glide over the horizon. For these philosophers, the poet or the artist is a hierophant, who unveils to man his true mission. Hölderlin on the one hand and Cézanne on the other established landmarks on the road that leads to the discovery of Being. These creators intuited the powers of art long before philosophers formulated a systematic phenomenology of it. Through his meditation Malraux similarly attains the confines of the imaginary, where everything remains to be discovered.

The Artist and Humanizing the World

Outside him in the chaos of the world, within him, in the unformed teaming mass of desires and images, man feels himself invested by another universe, his mission being to humanize it.

Humanize means first to render intelligible, communicable, by creating a form that fixes the elusive. The form, whether it be visual, musical, verbal, rhythmic, or even ritual, is the indispensable mediation that shakes off original lethargy. Creation is not abandonment to reverie, but its incarnation. Otherwise, the artist himself would remain ignorant of his genius and a stranger to the world within his mind. This incarnation, no doubt, implies some "reduction." "Every style is the scaling down to our human perspective of that eternal flux on whose mysterious rhythms we are borne ineluctably in a never ceasing drift of stars" (323). This is, in fact, the ambiguity of all creation. If creation is not incarnated, it remains buried in limbo among unrealized possibilities unknown to the very one who could have conceived them. On the other hand, vision, incarnated in a form, vulgarized, rationalized, accessible to the senses and to common sense, may become conventional and not worth preserving. The miracle of genius, as well as the guarantor of its permanence, is allowing imagination to guess at something else beyond the form. To adapt vision to human limits does not mean to imprison it within these limits.

Thus, to humanize, in the full meaning of the word, is to invent a form that suggests more than it manifests and retains for the spirit the possibility of transcendence. "Amidst man's dwellings"—precarious and forlorn as they are—the artist of genius is able to suggest expanses of vacant darkness. The adventure of mankind is never completed. The end of art, conceived as an unsurpassable perfection by the Classics, is only a mirage, as is the end of history in Marx or the end of dialectic in Hegel. Art is an eternal wandering, a series of interrupted revelations, each one revealing a more profound mystery. To humanize, in its full meaning, implies the discovery of a form, strong and firm enough to impose itself and yet open to metamorphosis. Again, such an "opening on being" excludes the very possibility of art as a copy of reality. According to an example twice used by Malraux, man, searching for a new lever, does not invent an artificial arm but the wheelbarrow. While creating a homologue of reality, the artist learns how to leave out enough to evoke a feeling and a desire for unrealized possibilities. By a strange about-face, the work can also illustrate this very aspiration—sometimes in a comic manner as the "little man of the Cyclades" that for Picasso symbolized an endless question. More often the symbol is in the form of drama or of a dream; and sometimes it can be purely formal, as in the case of the aforementioned prisoner in *Time of Contempt*, whose hallucinations are symbolizing their own rhythm of panic.

To humanize brute reality is then to subjugate it to the laws of the spirit at its zenith; to structure this reality, substituting order and meaning for mechanical association of images.

Once thus humanized, the *schème* becomes the real essence of a work of art; it acquires a life of its own largely independent of time and enters the realm of metamorphosis. As a striking example, Malraux mentions the variants of the *Idiot*, in which the *schème* conceived by Dostoyevsky remains, even when the roles of the characters are changed (333). Reciprocally, a form emptied of all content by the effects of time, remains long after the vision of the world it incarnated has vanished. (Here, mourning statues by Giovanni da Pisaro are given as examples.) A new vision cannot find its form immediately; early Christian art contented itself for centuries with the artistic forms bequeathed by its persecutors (282). At the same time, the new creed was hollowing these forms out to such an extent that they eventually collapsed, making way for an entirely new style. Creation is a "skeleton in search of its flesh" besides surviving indefinitely the once living body.

Such is the autonomy of form, and yet Malraux does not believe in pure formalism. Indeed the structure creates the work, but this structure must be meaningful. The form prevails in the mind only because form appears to be the best carrier of meaning. We now come to the crucial question: What is this meaning that is man's mission to bring out into the world? What does meaning mean? Can the word be defined? Although every philosopher worthy of the name must attempt thus to define the undefinable, it is only in modern times that the paradox has been fully recognized as such. Malraux has not read Heidegger, but is familiar with Nietzsche and Dostoyevsky and their contradictory answers to the related question: "Does the world have a meaning?" This does not mean: Does the world correspond to my desires or to my conception of justice? But it means: What compensates for so much injustice and adversity? Here again the answer is less important to Malraux than the tone of the voice that formulates the question and the expanses it must cross to reach us. Even if a generation has lost all faith in the principle ordering the world, a principle that would explain and justify the indignity of man's condition and of man's inhumanity, the artist retains a subjective certainty that he can compensate for the gods' indifference by his ability to create a parallel universe that is coherent and filled with meaning. As Valéry's Méphisto observes: "There is another world than the other world." This other world of art has to be made or uncovered, but may not be a product of chance. Malraux has no respect for painters who splatter their canvases with a donkey's tail or their long hair dipped into paint pots. He admires Picasso, the least realistic of painters, because Picasso does not surrender himself to chance, but uses it. He would gather that which chance offers him—pebbles, bolts—asking: "What can I do with these?" In other words, how can I extract meaning out of them? What meaning? Malraux is pursued by the sphinxlike gaze of this immutable question. Heidegger leaves it in suspense because it does not really belong to the realm of philosophy. What meaning? Where does meaning come from, and what guarantees its validity? Malraux's interrogation has not yet attained its greatest depth. In spite of the lyrical beauty of his themes, a gap is perceived at the heart of his thought. Not Artaud's void in which the thought of so many of his contemporaries is engulfed, but a void at the center of a vertigo, with thought spinning in circles at the edge. Over and over again, Malraux repeats that "genius is power of autonomy." He refuses to recognize any point of departure in the subjective, in the concrete, in tradition, in personal experience; he objects to any explicit end. Quotes can be multiplied, as can examples of lyrical or aphoristic formulas . . . yet we will not increase our knowledge of the secret. We understand how creation comes about, what makes it possible, but not what makes it necessary. It was left for Malraux's latest works not to elucidate the nature of the voice that whispers to the hero and to the artist, but to perceive it at a deeper level.

Notes

1. The number in parentheses refers to pages in the *Voices of Silence*, trans. by Stuart Gilbert (Princeton University Press, 1978).
2. *Les temps modernes* (January 1951).
3. Joseph Hoffman, *L'Humanisme de Malraux* ("The Humanism of Malraux") (Klincksieck, 1963), p. 302.
4. Joseph Frank, *The Widening Gyre* (Indiana University Press, 1977).

PART 5

THE SEMIOSIS OF HISTORY

14

Malraux and Medellin

WALTER LANGLOIS

[Je crois que le romancier] doit créer un monde cohérent et particulier, comme tout autre artiste. Non faire concurrence à l'état-civil, mais faire concurrence à la réalité qui lui est imposée, celle de 'la vie', tantôt en semblant s'y soumettre et tantôt en la transformant.

André Malraux in Malraux par lui-même

([I believe that the novelist] must create a coherent and special world, just like any other artist. Not to rival the factual world, but to rival the reality imposed on him, that of 'life', sometimes by seeming to submit to it and sometimes by transforming it.)

The relationship between Malraux's novels and the facts of his real life has been a subject of controversy ever since the publication of his first serious work, *The Conquerors*, in 1928. When that book appeared, certain critics immediately attacked it for being more of an autobiographical and ideologically slanted "documentary" than a truly creative novel. In a revealing

1929 speech, Malraux readily admitted that his story was indeed deeply rooted in a historical and personal reality, but he emphasized that in his fiction he had made a *selective* use of that reality in order to convey a series of truths about the human condition in contemporary terms.[1] This explanation did not satisfy some readers, and when subsequent Malraux novels appeared, they reiterated accusations that the works were primarily autobiographical or political rather than genuinely creative. This kind of criticism became particularly vehement when *Man's Hope* was published because Malraux's leadership of an international group of fliers in Spain—one of the central elements in the novel—was widely known. We have shown elsewhere how Malraux combined and transformed two actual events from the life of his squadron to create the famous Descent from the Mountain, the striking incident that highlights the final section of the novel.[2] Now, in order to show this writer's creative imagination at work in another context, we would like to make a similar examination of a second important passage from the book: the attack against Medellin, the squadron's first major engagement and the beginning of its existence as a military entity.

The Medellin raid is described in chapters II and III of the concluding third section of "Careless Rapture" ("L'Illusion lyrique"), the first of the three major divisions of the novel.[3] Precisely dated August 14, the chapter opens as three French Potez bombers from Magnin's International Squadron, together with three American-made Douglas planes of the Spanish commercial airline, LAPE—hastily converted from civilian use—take off without fighter escort for an important late-afternoon bombing mission. Their objective is "a column of Moors engaged in the Estremadura offensive" (*MH*, 96) and which—after taking the important city of Merida several days earlier—was now proceeding from Merida toward Medellin. The head of Air Operations in Madrid had telephoned Sembrano and Magnin (a character closely modeled after Malraux) to report that Franco was personally in command of this "strong motorized force . . . believed to contain the pick of the fascist army." This made it an even more important target.

After a fairly short flight southwestward above the arid plain, shimmering in the heat of the late afternoon of an August day, the six Republican planes pass over the city of Badajoz on the Portuguese border, "with its Alcazar and deserted bull-rings." Several of the men in Magnin's formation wave their handkerchiefs, while the Spanish bombardiers in the Douglases "let fall scarves patterned in the Republican colors" (*MH*, 97). The planes then turn southeastward to Merida and, finally, Medellin, with its "open square." There being no sign of troops in that town, the squadron turns back westward, following a highway leading toward the enemy lines at Merida. Because it is five o'clock in the afternoon, they are flying into a sun that is rather low in the sky, and it is difficult to see anything except blank whiteness beneath them. However as the lead plane, piloted by Darras and carrying Magnin as observer, turns out of the direct sunlight to follow another highway, the fliers suddenly see "the straight road in front studded with little red dots at regular intervals . . . They were too small to be cars, yet moving too mechanically to be men. It looked as if the roadway itself was in motion. Suddenly Darras understood . . . The road was a solid mass of lorries covered with drab tarpaulins, yellow with dust, and the red dots were the hoods painted in red oxide; there had been no attempt at camouflage" (*MH*, 98-99). The planes begin dropping their 10-kilo bombs. However, the first load explodes harmlessly on each side of the road or in the nearby fields. Then, "suddenly one section of the road stopped vibrating. The column had halted. Unnoticed by Darras, a bomb had hit one of the lorries, overturning it across the road." The forward part of the column races onward toward Medellin, while the segment behind the wrecked vehicle tries to squeeze around it on either side "like a river flowing round a rock." The bombs continue to fall, and when the smoke starts to dissipate, "Darras had a glimpse of a welter of lorries sprawling bottom upmost [and] . . . saw only little specks of khaki dotted with white turbans flying for their lives, like panicked ants carrying away their eggs" (*MH*, 100).

Leaving the blazing trucks behind, the six aircraft of the squadron turn toward Medellin to try and destroy the fleeing head of the column before the arrival of enemy fighter planes. The pilots quickly locate the trucks in the town; they are grouped "in the shadows of the city square. As the populace was hostile they had not dared to scatter" (*MH*, 101-102). A few of the vehicles are hidden alongside the walls of houses on nearby streets. The Republican fliers drop their remaining explosives, several 50-kilo bombs, which burst in the middle of the Medellin square. At the same time, they suddenly become aware of the arrival of six aircraft whose silhouette resembles the LAPE Douglases; they are the feared Junkers, recently sent to Franco's air force by Hitler. The inadequately armed but rapid Douglases turn and flee toward the safety of the Madrid airport, leaving the three Potez, whose armament matches that of the Junkers, to protect their rear. The French military planes rapidly outdistance the Germans, who seem unable to focus the fire of their chattering machine guns, and all of the Republicans are able to reach the base at Barajas without serious damage.

The Medellin incident as recounted in *Man's Hope* ends late the same day when Magnin goes to the Air Ministry in Madrid to complete the report he had made by telephone immediately after landing. There, Garcia, the chief of military intelligence, congratulates him warmly on the raid: "You've pulled off our first victory in the war," he says (*MH*, 109). Magnin demurs: "It wasn't a big show, of course, more like a frontier raid. Six machines. Still we managed to do in some of their lorries on the road." Garcia replies: "It wasn't the bombs you dropped on the road that did them the most damage, but the ones in Medellin itself. Several heavies landed plumb in the market square. Don't forget it's the first taste the Moors have had of what a serious air-attack can mean. The column has gone back to its base [at Merida]. Our first victory" (*MH*, 110). As we shall see, for this account in his novel Malraux made a very selective and imaginative use of the real incidents of the actual Medellin raid in which he had personally participated.

Historically speaking, the Medellin skirmish was only one incident in the advance of General Yagüe's African army, composed primarily of Foreign Legionnaires and Moors, northward from Andalusia along the Portuguese border. Yagüe's objective was the Tagus Valley, where, as French Ambassador Jean Herbette had astutely surmised at the very outset of the rebellion, he intended to join up with General Mola's Burgos army from the north before moving eastward to relieve Toledo and attack Madrid.[4] This African force, which a number of radio broadcasts erroneously reported to be under the personal command of Franco himself (he was actually still in Seville), had left Andalusia about August 7.[5] On August 10, just as Malraux and his squadron of French Potez-54 bombers were arriving at the Barajas airport near Madrid, Yagüe's troops had captured the important rail and road center at Merida.[6]

According to contemporary accounts, in an effort to retake this city, the Republican Air Ministry temporarily relocated a contingent of planes, probably several light observation craft and at least one of the three LAPE Douglases under the command of the seasoned civilian pilot Novarro, from Barajas to a small airfield at Don Benito, a town about 60 kilometers east of Merida on the Trujillo-Medellin road.[7] From Don Benito these planes were able to support the Republican forces in their counterattack against Merida during the next few days. The purpose of the aerial raids was not only to help the Republican People's Militia but also to try and disrupt the functioning of Yagüe's headquarters, set up in one of the hotels of the city. The Republican command felt that it was essential to prevent what would obviously be the General's next tactical move: an assault on the vitally important rail and communications center at Badajoz, some 65 kilometers to the west of Merida on the Portuguese frontier. Unfortunately, the bombing and ground attacks did not interfere with Yagüe's plans, and he promptly dispatched to Badajoz a motorized column of about 3,000 Legionnaires and Moorish troops, reinforced with artillery, under the command of Colonels Castejon and Asensio. As Castejon later recounted,[8] he reached the border city in the late afternoon of August 13 and by nightfall had succeeded in taking the buildings oustide its walls. At 5:00 A.M. on the fourteenth, aided by elements of Asensio's column, he launched his assault against the Republican Colonel Puigdendolas and his 5,000 government troops and quickly took the fort of San Cristobal in the suburbs. There he placed his artillery, which kept up a steady bombardment of the Republican positions during most of the rest of the day.

By 10:30 A.M. Castejon had forced his way into the city with his tanks and infantry, and the battle raged bitterly for over five hours.[9]

News of the assault on Badajoz had reached Madrid shortly after dawn on the fourteenth, and at numerous times during the day bombers were dispatched from Barajas and Don Benito to try and stop it. However, the Republican soldiers and People's Militia were hopelessly outclassed in training and weaponry (they had few machine guns and no artillery or tanks), and by late afternoon the Moors had gained the initiative. In spite of fierce resistance, after a few more hours the Fascists controlled the city. Then in the bullring there began the infamous massacre of men, women, and children subsequently described with horror by a number of foreign reporters who arrived on the spot not long afterwards.[10] This slaughter continued throughout the next day. As a Republican minister, Indalecio Prieto, later indignantly described the event, the Republican prisoners were "forced to go out into the arena while the spectators seated in the bleachers machine-gunned them. These atrocities surpass in horror those of Nero's time, when those who went out into the circus for combat only fought against wild beasts, and not against the spectators."[11]

During the following day, August 15, as reported by Franco's headquarters in Seville, the Nationalists continued their cleanup operations along the Hispano-Portuguese frontier until all of the "Marxists" had been eliminated and the rebels were in firm control of the whole area.[12] On August 16, Castejon, confident that Badajoz was secured, took a major part of his force and returned to Merida.[13] In an interview that the Colonel gave to a reporter there on that very evening, he noted that the air and ground attacks by the Republicans were not enough of a threat to prevent his resuming his advance toward Madrid almost immediately. Indeed, he revealed that he planned to proceed the next day along the highway that led northeastward from Merida toward Trujillo, the Tagus Valley, and ultimately the capital: "My column, reinforced by a 'bandera' of the Foreign Legion [about 600 men] and three 'tabores' of Moors [about 225 men] is leaving for the purpose of taking Don Benito where the Republicans have an air base . . . I am taking some batteries of artillery and some aircraft to help in the attack. Before taking Don Benito, I intend to pass through Medellin and Santa Amalia where there are strong concentrations of fleeing Communists and others who are arriving from Madrid."[14] Most of the other units of Yagüe's African army under Colonel Tella were ordered to move along the road leading due north, paralleling the Portuguese border, to take the city of Caceres, before turning eastward toward Trujillo. From there it was planned that the whole reunited Yagüe force would move against Navalmoral de la Mata in the Tagus Valley and thence to Talavera de la Reina on the way to Toledo and Madrid.

The *carretera* or main road along which Castejon moved his motorized column on the morning of Monday, August 17, runs almost due east from Merida for about 25 kilometers before angling northward toward Trujillo. About seven kilometers beyond this turn a country road branches off to the southeast. It leads to the towns of Medellin and—eight kilometers farther on—Don Benito. If these two places remained in Republican hands, they would constitute a threat to the rear of the advancing column's right flank, particularly from the Republican aircraft reportedly stationed at the Don Benito field. (The Franquistes did not know that these planes had apparently already been withdrawn to Madrid.) Therefore, when Castejon reached the Medellin turnoff, he halted his column and dispatched an initial force of some seven truckloads of troops to begin the assault on these two towns. If he expected a rapid easy victory, he was sadly mistaken.

Shortly after leaving the main highway, the Medellin-Don Benito road winds between two small wooded hills and passes through the hamlet of Santa Amalia before continuing directly into the center of Medellin, crossing the Guadiana River bordering the town by a stone bridge that is more than half a kilometer long. The Nationalists obviously expected this bridge to be cut, for the first two of the seven trucks detached from Castejon's column, later captured by the Republicans, carried special equipment to repair it.[15] When the attackers did not foresee was the fierce resistance that the defenders of Medellin would put up at their forward positions in Santa Amalia and at the bridgehead itself and the major impact that the intervention of the Republican aircraft would have on the whole operation.

According to various reports published in the Spanish press at the time, it was at about 5:00 A.M. that Monday, August 17, that one of the early observation and patrol flights of the Republicans discovered the Castejon column just as it was beginning to leave Merida.[16] Madrid was immediately informed that there appeared to be at least 300 trucks and a number of other lighter vehicles in the convoy. The ground battle on the road leading to Medellin did not actually begin until about an hour and a half later. According to the detailed account of Federico Angulo, a newspaperman for *El Socialista* who was in charge of part of the defense of the town, the initial assault by the seven truckloads of enemy troops (numberplates indicated that four of these vehicles had been captured at Badajoz) soon obliged the Medellin Republicans to withdraw from their outposts in Santa Amalia to positions just before the Guadiana Bridge. There, with the help of several artillery pieces and two tanks, they were able temporarily to halt the enemy advance.[17]

Meantime, given the importance of the column and the rumors that Franco himself was leading it, Madrid had decided to send out two big bombers from Barajas, each loaded with about a hundred 10- and 50-kilo bombs, to destroy it. "The moment was critical," as the *El Socialista* reporter put it in his subsequent account, "because if the defenders of Medellin could not hold out against the power of those who were attacking, the aircraft would not have enough time to intervene, and the capture of Don Benito would become inevitable." Fortunately, however, Republican artillery fire on the Santa Amalia road prevented the arrival of reinforcements from the main Fascist column, and the Republican militia was able to maintain its position at the bridgehead. This immobilized the rest of Castejon's forces waiting on the Trujillo highway until the first two bombers arrived from Madrid at about 9:30 A.M. Castejon's main column was, of course, the primary target of the attacking aircraft, and it evidently began to move as soon as the Republican planes approached. Angulo's eyewitness account, subsequently published in a number of Spanish newspapers, provides a vivid firsthand description of the aerial attacks by the planes from Barajas.[18]

After a preliminary pass, the two bombers released their explosives from an altitude of between 600 and 1,000 meters; the rebels began to flee, abandoning their trucks on the road. Soon a number of the vehicles were ablaze, and the wooded hills on each side of the road leading to Santa Amalia were also on fire, sending thick clouds of black smoke up into the sky. All along both the major column and the Medellin detachment, the Republican pilots could see small vehicles moving about rapidly. They assumed that these contained rebel officers who were vainly trying to regroup their men and prevent further panic and flight. Two artillery pieces in the main Castejon column began firing at the Republican planes, but they were not antiaircraft guns and were totally ineffective.

Meantime the Republican artillery near the bridge continued to shell the road leading to Santa Amalia, thus preventing the arrival of reinforcements from the rebel column on the highway, which would have aided in a breakthrough to Medellin itself. Then two more planes arrived from Barajas with a fresh load of explosives to carry on the attack. More trucks blew up amid dense clouds of dust and smoke. In the column there reigned an "indescribable panic," according to one report, as the enemy fled in terror, leaving their equipment behind in a frantic effort to escape this assault, so unexpected in the midst of their triumphal advance.[19] While the two recently arrived Republican bombers remained to carry on the destruction of the column, the original two craft flew back to Barajas to obtain a new load of explosives. Then they returned to attack the column again. This was repeated five times during the day. According to the reporter from *El Socialista*, at one point during the operation three rebel Junker planes appeared, and the Republican fliers prepared for a fight. However the Fascist airmen, evidently afraid to give battle, would not approach any closer than about 1,500 meters, and there was no actual combat between the two units.

During an afternoon lull in the bombing, the Nationalists on the Medellin road managed to rally some of their soldiers and took refuge, together with some of the trucks that had been salvaged from the debacle, in the hamlet of Santa Amalia. To try and conceal their vehicles as much as possible, the rebel officers ordered that they be parked in the shade, close to the civilian houses around the edge of the village square. However the Republican fliers quickly spotted them, noted Angulo in his account, aimed carefully, and placed a number of bombs directly in the square, causing much destruction of the enemy materiel nearby. By evening, after nearly eight hours under an intermittent rain of a reported 1,200 10- and 50-kilo bombs, the elements of the Castejon column were so dispersed that they no longer offered a target for air attack.

Malraux evidently took the French reporter Louis Delaprée along on one of the Republican sorties that day, for the latter subsequently vividly described his feelings about the "massacre" of the Castejon column from the air. During the Medellin attack, he wrote,

> man did not confront man directly. The rebel struck down on the Merida road or on the Guadiana bridge had scarcely had time to catch sight of the great black wings of the enemy, to hear the staccato rhythm of the machine-guns, before he was already nothing more than a corpse. As for the flyers, deafened by the thunder [of the bombs], they did not glimpse any men on that highway but only a procession of insects. The order had been given to disperse them; they did more, they annihilated them.
>
> I shall never forget this vignette. In the middle of the road a truck is halted; the driver, his head on the steering-wheel, seems to be sleeping, but the cargo of this trucker crushed by fatigue is not at all what one meets up with every day; twenty dead men, fallen one on top of another like ninepins, twenty dead men struck down by the same machine-gun burst: that is what is being carried by this driver, dead himself.[20]

One of the Moors from the column, later taken prisoner himself, also graphically described the attack on the square in Santa Amalia: "The panic was frightful. During the whole day [the Republican planes] let loose their bombs on us. We didn't know where to hide. During the afternoon we were able to do so in the hamlet of Santa Amalia. We were not even half of the number we had been in the morning. And even in the village the bombardment continued, with such accuracy that I remember that a single bomb which fell in the square caused 12 deaths and very many wounded."[21] Finally the People's Militia from nearby Don Benito arrived and took what was described as many prisoners and a large quantity of war materiel.[22] The captured trucks contained numerous personal effects as well as various religious objects looted from churches and monasteries by the Moors. Orders and maps discovered in an officer's trunk in one of the lighter vehicles made it clear that the enemy's primary plan was to advance along the main road toward Trujillo as rapidly as the Republican resistance would permit.[23]

When the Republican fliers returned to Barajas at the end of that day, they were not eager to speak about the Medellin raid because of the attack that circumstances had forced them to make on the hamlet of Santa Amalia; they were deeply distressed at the injury that they had doubtless caused to innocent people. *Politica*, a leading Republican paper of Madrid, in commenting on an interview with one of the pilots after the sortie, took the occasion to emphasize the difference between the basic spirit of the Loyalists and that of the rebels who were attacking them: "Our men returned to Barajas. They did not seek to destroy the little village of Estremadura [Santa Amalia]. In it there were innocent people, women and children, who were blameless in what was happening. The bombing of inhabited areas is always a terrible thing. Unlike artillery which can determine precisely the point where the shell is going to fall, one can easily understand that aerial bombs do not have mathematical accuracy, and that the explosion always varies by a few meters. In such conditions—and since it is a question of Spanish towns with, in general, narrow streets, a deviation of a few meters may have fatal consequences and cause victims among those who do not at all deserve to have their lives ruined in so terrible a manner." According to *Politica*, this concern for the inhabitants of Santa Amalia on the part of the fliers pointed up clearly "the character of the elements which are confronting each other at this moment in Spain. On one side, among the Loyalists, moderation and consideration for innocent people, and on the Fascist side barbarism and unlimited cruelty."[24]

The first news of the daylong Medellin battle of Monday, August 17, was revealed to the citizens of Madrid somewhat unexpectedly. At about 5:00 P.M., Senor Ramos, the Republican minister of finance, emerged from a conference at the War Ministry. To waiting reporters, eager for news, he said that "at Medellin, the Loyalist forces which are operating in Estremadura have routed a rebel column which was moving toward Don Benito."[25] Pressed for further details, he replied that this was "the first and only information" which the government had thus far received. It was not until about 10:00 P.M. that the War Ministry issued a communiqué that gave a few more details of what *Politica* called "the resounding victory of the Loyalist forces" over a major enemy contingent. According to that bulletin, "on the Estremadura front our forces have repulsed a strong enemy attack against Medellin and Santa Amalia. The rebels have left behind 300 individuals and more than 30 trucks. The column was made up of more than 300 vehicles. The Republican airforce intervened with great effectiveness."[26] Subsequent Republican bulletins emphasized that one of Castejon's primary objectives had been to "establish contacts between Andalucia and Castile," but in reporting the same incident, a pro-Franco Portuguese paper noted that the column had been moving against the "concentration of Communist aviation" at Don Benito.[27]

For the next several days, the Spanish Republican press—and a number of pro-Madrid newspapers abroad—featured news about the victory at Medellin and about the major role played in it by "the glorious airforce of the Republic." Successive articles furnished more and more details about the whole encounter. A number of these commentaries about this "greatest success achieved by government forces since the beginning of the month" emphasized its military importance.[28] Typical of these was the statement by Indalecio Prieto, given to *El Liberal* of Bilbao and subsequently reprinted by several French papers:

> The rebels had two objectives in view: to attack Madrid from the West, and to reinforce the rebel troops advancing on Oviedo in order to save Colonel Aranda. Oviedo is the key to the military situation in the North. Once that city has surrendered to the government forces, the situation of the rebels will be desperate, not only in the Oviedo region but also in León . . . and that surrender will allow the miners from Asturias to reach the Castilian plateau. If the miners have not entered Oviedo before now, it is because they are seeking to avoid calamities. That situation could not continue any longer, but the rout of the rebels at Medellin permits the miners henceforth to devote themselves entirely to the attack against Oviedo.[29]

Other accounts in the Republican press and in pro-Republican foreign newspapers emphasized more strongly the psychological significance of the "magnificent action of the airforce." As the *Heraldo de Madrid* pointed out, "the influence which it had on the morale of the enemy may be seen from the terror it produced from the first moment. No resistance was offered. The only concern was to flee. However the flight took place in so disorganized a manner that it facilitated the efficacious intervention of our heroic aviators. It should be noted that that column contained the best that the enemy had in Andalusia. It included many men accustomed to having the airforce always on their side. It is the first time that they encountered—to their misfortune—an airforce determined to inflict an incontrovertible disaster on them. Thus the results could not be more satisfactory. Thanks to a decisive and unforeseen rout, their morale was totally destroyed."[30] This view was seconded by one of the participating fliers, interviewed shortly afterwards. He noted that Medellin "was the most outstanding and marvellous operation which we have carried out. It was of enormous value above all because it left the morale of the enemy destroyed. One must take into account the manner in which it was accomplished. It was just short of a complete collapse."[31]

Thus for a brief moment at the time, Medellin seemed to be a highly significant event in the military and psychological struggle to stop the rebel advance on Madrid. However subsequent historians have placed it in proper perspective as a minor skirmish—and a very fleeting Republican success—in General Yagüe's campaign. In point of fact, Colonel Castejon's column was halted for no longer than 24 hours, and as early as August 18 Radio Seville had already issued a bulletin (studiously ignored by papers

Malraux at the time of *L'Espoir,* 1937

in Madrid and Barcelona) to the effect that "Colonel Castejon's column has occupied Santa Amalia, where government forces resisted energetically but were finally beaten ... Continuing its advance, following strong resistance, the Castejon column occupied Don Benito."[32] The following day, August 19, rebel headquarters announced that the whole area around Don Benito had been secured and that "Colonel Castejon's column is now said to be marching on Madrid. The government can offer opposition only with troops formed by volunteers chosen at random, without discipline or organization, and which will not be able to resist the pressure of the forces of General Franco."[33] Radio Seville was not far wrong, for within a few days Castejon's forces had indeed reached Trujillo and subsequently linked up with other units of the African army that had come north and east via the Caceres road. After a brief rest, this whole force under Yagüe moved forward along the Tagus Valley to Navalmoral de la Mata, which fell on August 23, and shortly afterward was besieging Talavera de la Reina, the last major city before Toledo.[34]

This then was the basic historical reality with which Malraux had to work in writing the two Medellin chapters, which conclude the "Careless Rapture" section of his novel. Just what did he do with this material, and why? There is not space here to go into the various details that he incorporated into his account to flesh it out and to give it the impression of reality or immediacy—details that he knew because of having participated in the Medellin raid and in others like it during the months when he commanded the Escadrille España. In any case, these are essentially minor elements. However, there are three major areas in which Malraux made important alterations or additions to historical reality that are very revealing of his overall purpose and literary method.

The first of these relates to the details of the raid itself. In Malraux's fictionalized account, the air attack is made against Medellin—a town that the Nationalist enemy had not been able to reach—rather than Santa Amalia, where the Franquistes actually took refuge. He probably used Medellin because newspaper reports at the time had featured this name. Moreover, it was a larger, more important place than the hamlet of Santa Amalia, and this helped make the whole battle seem more significant. (It is interesting to note in passing that in order to simplify his account and make it more forceful, Malraux omitted any reference to the Republican airfield at Don Benito, which, historically speaking, had been the primary target of the Castejon probe, nor did he bring out the fact that the Medellin troops were actually only a detachment from the main column on the Trujillo highway.)

In addition, in his novel Malraux radically alters the circumstances of the actual air attack. It is not a pair of bombers, arriving at five different times during the day, which disperses the Castejon column; rather it is a single late afternoon sortie of six planes that causes the damage. This change was doubtless due in part to Malraux's desire to concentrate the event and thus make it more striking. Moreover by using three French military planes (manned by foreigners) and three Douglases of the Spanish commercial airline (manned by civilians), he was also representing in a dramatic way the union of all those idealists throughout Europe who were joined in the struggle against the rising tide of authoritarian fascism in Spain. In the Medellin raid, this symbol becomes concrete, so to speak, in the persons of the French pilot Darras (closely modeled after Malraux's friend Guidez) and the Spanish flier Sembrano (patterned after the Spanish civilian airline commander, Novarro).

As Darras, a former World War I ace and a longtime militant unionist and anti-Fascist, seeks out the enemy column near Medellin, he thinks: "Now his quarry was what he had been fighting for so many active years—in his mayoralty, in workers' organizations laboriously built up, defeated, resurrected—the enemy he fought today was fascism. After Russia, Italy, Germany and China, now it was Spain's turn. The hope which Darras was fostering in the world had hardly been given a chance. Yet here in Spain was fascism once more—almost under his wings" (MH, 98). It was to give this "hope" a new chance for life that he had committed himself to the Republican cause. Sembrano, the leader of the three Spanish crews, is a dedicated pacifist. He had accepted an active military role only because virtually no Republican airforce officers had remained loyal to Madrid when the revolt broke out. In spite of its shortcomings, the Popular Front Republic seemed to him to be the only hope of the suffering masses of his countrymen, and he had joined those who were struggling against enormous odds to keep it from being swept away by the forces of reaction. As Sembrano looks down on the arid plain near Medellin, he, too, reflects: "He realized, far better than [a foreigner], the plight of the Estremadura militia—that they were helpless, and only the air-force could save them ... Now as ever pacifist at heart, Sembrano was, however, a far more competent bomber than any [other] Spanish pilot; only, to appease his conscience, whenever he flew solo he came down very low to drop his bombs. Somehow the sense of danger, the risks he was going out of his way to run, solved, for him, the ethical problem" (MH, 101). The meditations of these two characters during the raid make it clear that they symbolize the fundamental elements of the anti-Fascist cause as it was represented by the two major "idealist" groups associated with Malraux's squadron.

A further change that Malraux makes in the actual events of the Medellin incident involves the attack by enemy planes. An eyewitness report at the time indicates that only three Franco craft had appeared and that they had remained at a distance from the Republican bombers. In Malraux's fictionalized account, *six* enemy planes actually attack his squadron. This change was doubtless made in part to increase the drama and enlarge the scope of the encounter. However, even more important, the machine-gun attack by the German craft and the subsequent escape, through superior speed, of the Republican planes underline both the importance that technology would play in the winning of the war and the fact that German technology (at least as far as aircraft was concerned) had been vastly overrated. This is further emphasized when Magnin goes to Madrid that evening to complete his report to the Air Ministry. As he drives through the suburbs of the capital, he reflects on the importance of the military information that he had just learned from his squadron's encounter with the German planes over Medellin: "Until this war the Junkers had constituted the bulk of Germany's air force. They were commercial machines converted into war planes, and such had been the general belief in German efficiency that they had been regarded as a formidable weapon of offence. But their armament, though good, was inadequate, and ordinary American commercial planes such as the Douglases could outdistance them easily . . . For two years Europe had quailed before the constant menace of a war which Hitler was not equipped to wage" he concludes (*MH*, 108-109).

However, as Professor Bernard Wilhelm was one of the first to point out,[35] the most important change that Malraux made in historical reality was his altering of the date of the Medellin sortie: from August 17 to August 14. Why? The author himself gives us a clue in one of the very first paragraphs of his account. There he notes that on its way to Medellin in the late afternoon of August 14, the Magnin-Sembrano planes pass over Badajoz, where the pilots wave or drop colored scarves into the empty town arena before flying onward. In its real sortie, the squadron certainly would have had no occasion to go near Badajoz, which was some 85 kilometers to the west, *beyond* the target at Medellin-Santa Amalia. Moreover, it would not have wasted time and precious fuel in a futile gesture of defiance against a stronghold that had already been taken by the Nationalists several days earlier.

Yet the fall of Badajoz was a major event in the history of the war, particularly during the first year, and it was evidently for the purpose of introducing it into his text that Malraux pushed the Medellin raid back three days, to August 14, thus making it contemporary with the taking of the Portuguese border city. In the novel, the importance of this Franco victory is made specific during the conversation that Magnin, Garcia, and Vargas have at Air Operations headquarters immediately following the Medellin operation. After praising the squadron for its success, Garcia relates the unfortunate news about the capture of Badajoz. According to him, the loss of the city was a disaster, for it meant that the shipments of arms, planes, and other munitions that Franco had been receiving from Italy via ports in North Africa and southern Spain would now be increased to a flood because of the additional German materiel that would come via Portugal. The opening of the Badajoz road to the Nationalists, noted Vargas, would make it certain that "within a fortnight we'll have a hundred up-to-date machines against us" (*MH*, 111). (According to *Man's*

The reporter and/or writer

Hope [p. 110] and to contemporary newspaper reports, only a week earlier 14 German planes and 150 technicians had arrived in Lisbon and were only awaiting an appropriate opportunity to enter Spain.)

This potential technological improvement of the rebel forces was enormously significant. Shortly after Magnin's arrival at Air Operations, Garcia resumes the report on the taking of Badajoz, which he had been reading aloud to Vargas. The details in that account make it clear that it was superior *equipment*—particularly artillery, tanks and machine guns—that had enabled the Nationalists to take the city so rapidly, in spite of the fierce resistance of the Republican militia. Vargas then points up this aspect of the meaning of the Medellin victory and of the Badajoz defeat, when he comments: "Just think what happened today, Magnin. You held up that column with six machines—in what you likened to a frontier skirmish. The column turned its machine guns on the militia and Badajoz has fallen. And, mark you, they were anything but cowards, our militia. Yes, this war's going to be a war of mechanized equipment" (*MH*, 113).

Malraux's conviction that the Spanish conflict was a war in which technology would play a crucial role was an idea whose importance he hoped to convey in his novel. When the work was published late in 1937, things were not going very well for the Republicans. Most of the nations in the international community who wanted to help the Madrid government were prevented from doing so by their pledge to honor the nonintervention pact initiated by France in late August 1936—a pact that was ignored by the Fascist states. In short, as portrayed in *Man's Hope*, the Republican success at Medellin and the Nationalist victory at Badajoz were due to a superiority in the *weaponry* that the two sides were receiving from abroad, a fact of modern warfare that could not be ignored. By combining the two incidents into a single powerful episode, Malraux underlined the crucial role that technology would play in the Spanish conflict, and it was certainly one of the primary reasons he altered the date of his squadron's Medellin sortie.

Another reason for Malraux's changing of the Medellin date to make it coincide with the fall of Badajoz is suggested in the last dispatch from the Republican defenders, cited by Garcia at the end of the report that he reads to Magnin: "*The fascist prisoners have been released, safe and sound. All 'milicianos'* [militiamen] *and doubtful characters are being courtmartialed and shot. Twelve hundred have been dealt with so far . . . Firing squads have been busy all afternoon. We can still hear the volleys*" (*MH*, 112). Garcia comments that this kind of massacre was a deliberate Fascist tactic: "To protect his rear, Franco will have to practise large-scale terrorization; he's begun it at Badajoz," he says (*MH*, 117). The extent of this cruel barbarism—unheard of in previous conflicts and made known to the outside world by various foreign correspondents who visited the site—made a deep impression on international public opinion at the time. The seasoned newspaperman Jay Allen's stunned account of the atrocity, probably the most widely known, leaves no doubt but that for contem-

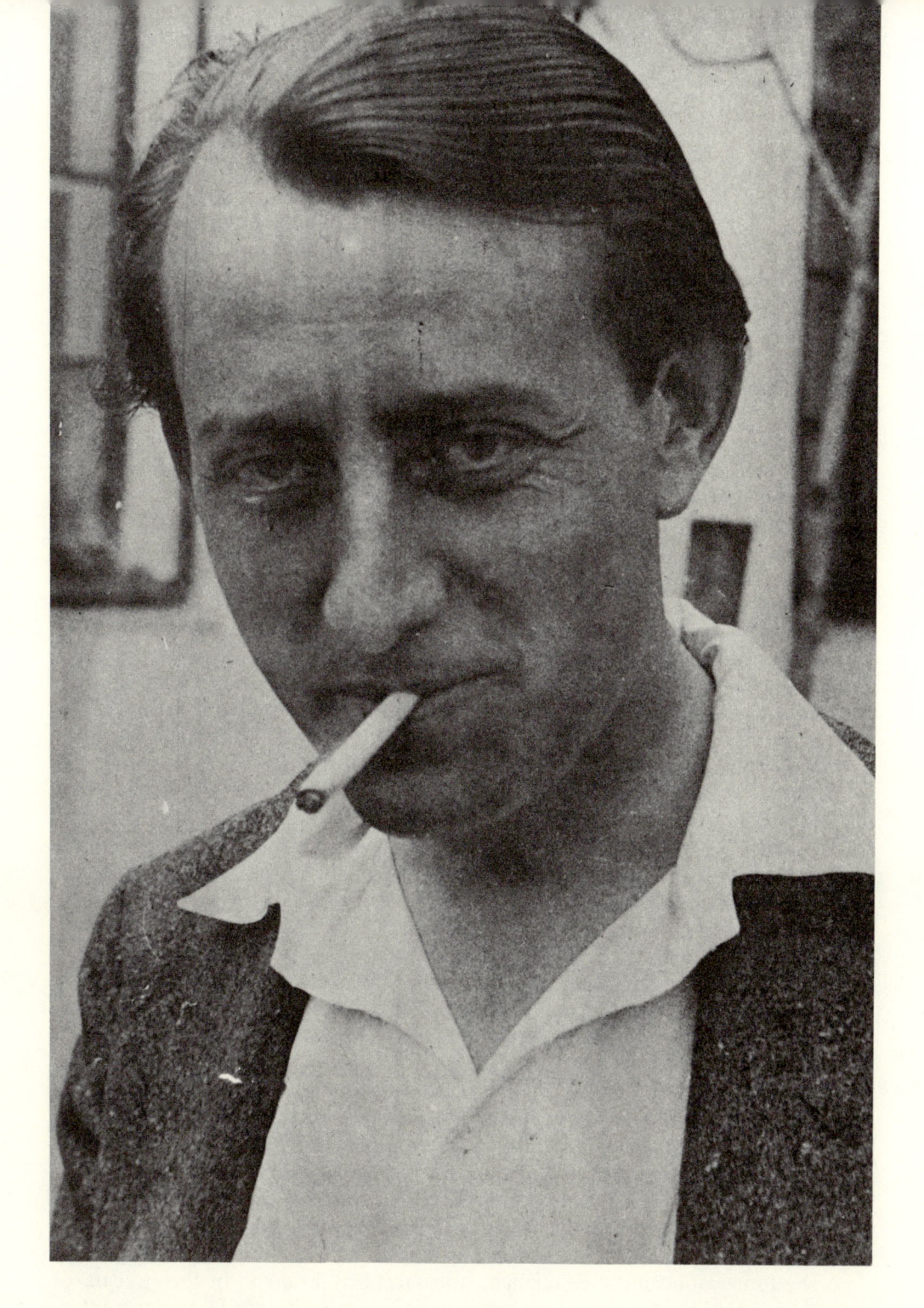

Malraux at the time of *La Condition humaine*, 1933

poraries it was a crime that transcended any previously known limits.[36] In including the incident in his novel, Malraux was well aware that for much of the world Badajoz represented all that was negative and inhumane in the Fascist cause: it symbolized the fundamental "scorn for man" that was a foundation of such authoritarianism, and it helped to explain why so many intellectuals in Europe and America had sided with the Republicans.

However, the final, primary reason for Malraux's altering of history so that Badajoz and Medellin—two victories by the opposing sides, due to their respective technological superiority—would become contemporary was to provide an appropriate introduction to the long discussion that Vargas, Garcia, and Magnin have concerning the *nature* of the whole conflict (*MH*, 113-118). After noting that Magnin had won his battle and that the Republican militia at Badajoz had lost theirs because "this war's going to be a war of mechanized equipment," Vargas warns that the Republicans were taking a great risk: for, he says, "we're running it as if noble emotions were all that mattered" (*MH*, 113). In other words, they were still relying on an emotional popular outburst, a "lyric illusion," to carry the day and to win the ultimate victory, as if the Spanish conflict were comparable to the French Revolution.

Garcia then emphasizes this point by observing that in everyone's mind there remained some dangerous myths concerning the nature of revolutions. The first of these was that the "People" had brought about the fall of the ancien régime in 1789. That may have been true, he says, "but the fact that a hundred pikes can knock out some inefficient muskets doesn't prove that a hundred shot-guns can beat the modern war plane. Then the Russian Revolution—it's made confusion more confounded! Politically speaking, it's the first revolution of the twentieth century; but don't forget that, militarily speaking, it was the last of the nineteenth. The Czarists had neither tanks nor planes; the revolutionaries used barricades. What was the idea behind these barricades? To resist the imperial cavalry, for the people never have horses. Today Spain is littered with barricades—to resist Franco's war planes!" (*MH*, 114). For Garcia, there was no question: the popular movement in which they were involved— and which had brought about a few victories, as in the Sierra and at Medellin, to counterbalance innumerable defeats symbolized by the fall of Badajoz—was not a real *revolution*, because it was not sustained and directed by an organized cadre of any kind. In short, it was not disciplined.

Garcia then defines discipline as "an organization of the factors which give an army in the field its maximum efficiency" (*MH*, 115), and he goes on to emphasize that the social transformations that they all so eagerly desire could not come about without the winning of a war against the forces opposing such change, epitomized by Franco. In such a situation, nuances of political or social belief were infinitely less important than the very practical consideration of being efficient enough to win the struggle. The lyric élan that had united the people against the rebels in the initial days of the uprising was a beautiful thing, which Garcia characterizes as an "Apocalypse of fraternity." This emotion is moving, he says to Magnin: "I can well understand it. It is one of the most moving things on earth, and one of the rarest. But all of that's got to be transformed—or perish" (*MH*, 116).

The organized cadres and the technical aid received from Germany and Italy had permitted Franco to transform his *coup d'état*—which had failed, thanks to the People made strong by their hope of an Apocalypse—into a new struggle, a modern technological war that was not at all of the same nature as the initial insurrection. It was not possible to fight this new kind of long-term war with the same haphazard means that had initially been successful against the *pronunciamiento*. Moreover, by its very nature an Apocalypse could not sustain itself; it had no future (and the new type of war required a future) because it had no form. "Our humble task," concludes Garcia, "is to *organize* the Apocalypse" (*MH*, 118). It is on this note that the "Careless Rapture" or "Illusion lyrique" section of the novel ends. The next division, which takes place about a fortnight later, shows the beginnings of the structuring for which Garcia has called and which will transform the "Illusion lyrique" into something lasting. Appropriately, it is entitled "Prelude to Apocalypse."

This brief examination has made it clear that, as in the case of the Descent from the Mountain, Malraux took a number of elements from historical reality, in this case, a reality that was also highly autobiographical, and used them to convey certain ideas about revolution in general and about the Spanish civil war in particular. As with the scene of the crash in the mountains, he did not hesitate to alter, combine, or otherwise modify real facts in order to make a more forceful presentation of a larger Truth with which he was grappling. Thus to say, as some conservative critics did at the time, that *Man's Hope* was little more than an ideologically slanted "documentary" is comparable to maintaining that *Starry Night* is only a picture of Van Gogh's garden in moonlight. In *Man's Hope*, as in his other novels, Malraux remained true to his long-held belief that the novelist "must create a coherent and special world, just like any other artist." He also reaffirmed that it was from a historical and personal experience that he himself usually preferred to take "those elements of reality which I need in order to create my universe."[37]

Notes

1. Major portions of Malraux's remarks—made at a June 1929 meeting of the Union pour la Vérité—have been reprinted under the title "Révolte et révolution," *Magazine littéraire*, No. 11 (October 1967), pp. 28-31.

2. Walter G. Langlois, "The Novelist Malraux and History," *L'Esprit créateur*, XV, No. 3 (Fall 1975), pp. 345-366.

3. *Man's Hope*. Translated from the French by Stuart Gilbert and Alastair Macdonald (New York: Random House, 1939). See pp. 3-118. In our discussion, quotations from this translation (which has a distinctly British flavor) will be indicated in the text by *MH* and the page numbers.

4. Cf. Jean Herbette, "Communication (par téléphone), No. 826, Saint Sébastien, 18 juillet [1936], in *Ministère des Affaires étrangères. Documents diplomatiques français 1932-1939*, tome II: *1er avril-18 juillet 1936* (Paris: Imprimerie nationale, 1964), p. 737.

5. Hugh Thomas, *The Spanish Civil War* (London: Eyre and Spottiswoode, 1961), pp. 244-246, gives details of this campaign.

6. Thomas (p. 246) indicates that the city fell on August 10, whereas in *Man's Hope* (p. 97) the date is given as August 8. Certain contemporary newspaper accounts suggest that the date may have been as late as August 12. See, notably, "Les Armées des généraux Mola et Franco auraient fair leur jonction à Mérida," *Echo de Paris*, August 13, 1936, p. 1.

7. See "Don Benito, centro da aviação communista" (Don Benito, Center of Communist Aviation), *O Século* [Lisbon], August 17, 1936, p. 5.

8. Jean d'Esme, "Les Noirceurs de la guerre; Merida, Badajoz, paisibles sous le soleil, ruisselantes encore du sang des massacres" (The Atrocities of the War: Merida, Badajoz, Peaceful under the Sun, Still Dripping with the Blood of the Massacres), *L'Intransigeant*, August 26, 1936, p. 3. The story is dated Merida, August 21, and it contains information about the bombing of Merida by planes from Don Benito as well as Castejon's account of his attack against Badajoz. Apparently, because of a misunderstanding on the part of the interviewer, the assault is mistakenly indicated as having taken place on August 15 rather than August 14. All other details conform to reports from other sources. In the present discussion, all translations from French, Spanish, and Portuguese sources are mine. I should like to thank my colleague and friend, Professor Richard Landeira, for his help with the materials in the latter two languages. His assistance was invaluable, and I am deeply grateful to him.

9. Thomas, pp. 246-247.

10. French and Portuguese newspapermen were the first to make reports about the Badajoz massacre to the outside world, but to Americans the best-known account is that of Jay Allen, a reporter for the *Chicago Tribune*. His text has been widely reprinted, most notably in *The Civil War in Spain: 1936-1939*, ed. Robert Payne (London: Seeker and Warburg, 1962), pp. 96-101, under the title "The Massacres."

11. Prieto's remarks were quoted in a number of French newspapers. See, notably, "La Victoire loyaliste de Medellin," *Le Peuple*, August 20, 1936, p. 3.

12. "La Situation militaire," *Écho de Paris*, August 16, 1936, p. 3, and "La Prise de Badajoz consolide la liaison opérée entre les colonnes de Franco et de Mola" (The Capture of Badajoz Consolidates the Link-up Between the Columns of Franco and Mola), *Écho de Paris*, August 16, 1936, pp. 1, 3.

13. "La Guerre civile en Espagne," *Le Temps*, August 18, 1936, cites a Seville dispatch dated 17 August, which notes that "Hier, la colonne du commandant Castejon est sorti de Badajoz pour se rendre à Merida..." (Yesterday, the column of Major Castejon left Badajoz to proceed to Merida...).

14. "La Ocupación de Don Benito," *Faro de Virgo* [Colon], August 19, 1936, p. 4.

15. "En el frente de Extremadura: La severa derrota sufrida por los facciosos cerca de Medellín" (On the Extremadura Front: The Severe Defeat Suffered by the Rebels Near Medellin), *El Día Gráfico*, August 20, 1936, p. 10. Details of the Medellin skirmish were published in all of the major Republican papers of Madrid and Barcelona, but these reports generally differed very little, and we shall usually cite only one source for our information.

16. "Detalles de una gran victoria," *El Día Gráfico*, August 21, 1936, p. 13.

17. The lengthy and detailed account of Federico Angulo was widely reprinted in the Spanish Republican press at the time. We shall quote from the text published in *El Socialista*, for which Angulo had worked before the outbreak of the rebellion. See Guitérrez de Miguel: "Como fue detenida en Medellín la columna motorizada rebelde que trataba de acercarse a Castilla. La magnífica enteresa de la fuerzas que defendían

el pueblo dio tiempo a que la avación deslocara la columna, destruyendo su material móvil. La brava conducta de nuestro camarada Federico Angulo" (How the Motorized Rebel Column Which Was Trying to Proceed to Castille Was Detained at Medellin. The Magnificent Conduct of the Forces Which Were Defending the Town Gave Time for the Air Force to Break Up the Column, Destroying its Mobile Equipment. The Courageous Conduct of our Comrade Federico Angulo), *El Socialista*, August 19, 1936, p. 1.

18. See "Como fue detenida en Medellín . . .," *El Socialista*, August 19, 1936, p. 1.

19. "La acción de los aviadores . . .," *Política*, August 22, 1936, p. 3.

20. Louis Delaprée: *Mort en Espagne* (Paris: Editions Pierre Tisné, 1937), p. 73. The dispatch, telephoned from Madrid, is dated August 23. It was printed as "La Rafale des mitrailleuses" (The Burst from the Machine Guns), in *Paris-Soir*, August 24, 1936, p. 3.

21. José Carbó: "A los moros que engañaron, los Fascistas les dan medio kilo de pan diario para cuatro" (To the Moors Whom They Mislead, the Fascists Give Half a Kilogram of Bread a Day for Four), *Política*, September 3, 1936, p. 3.

22. "La Guerre civile en Espagne: Dans la province de Badajoz," *Le Temps*, August 19, 1936, p. 3.

23. "En Estremadura: Comment s'est produit l'anéantissement de la colonne rebelle" (In Extremadura: How the Annihilation of the Rebel Column Was Brought About), *Le Populaire*, August 19, 1936, p. 3.

24. "La acción de los aviadores . . .," *Política*, August 22, 1936, p. 3.

25. "Una columna rebelde puesta en fuga en Medellín," *Mundo Obrero*, August 17, 1936, p. 5.

26. The bulletin was cited in a number of accounts, notably in "En el frente de Extremadura se had infligido un severo castigo al enemigo" (On the Extremadura Front A Severe Defeat Has Been Inflicted on the Enemy), *El Sol*, August 18, 1936, p. 1; in "En Extremadura sufría ayer el enemigo el más tremendo descalabro registrado durante la criminal sublevación . . . La gloriosa aviación de la República descargó centenares de bombas sobre une columna facciosa formada por más de trescientos vehículos" (In Extremadura Yesterday the Enemy Suffered the Greatest Loss Recorded During the Criminal Uprising . . . The Glorious Aviation of the Republic Released Hundreds of Bombs on a Rebel Column Made Up of More than Three Hundred Vehicles), *Política*, August 18, 1936, p. 4; and in "Noticias oficiales de la insurrección", *Heraldo de Madrid*, August 18, 1936, p. 4.

27. "Noticias oficiales: En Medellín ha sido vencida una columna que se dirigía a Don Benito" (Official Bulletins: At Medellin A Column Which Was Proceeding to Don Benito Has Been Overcome), *El Socialista*, August 18, 1936, p. 3 notes that the "fuerte columna enemiga . . . se dirigía a Don Benito con el fin de establecer enlaces entre Andalucía y Castilla" (the strong enemy column . . . was moving to Don Benito for the purpose of establishing links between Andalucia and Castile). For the pro-Franco report of the incident, see "Don Benito, Centro da **aviação** comunista," *O Século* [Lisbon], August 17, 1936, p. 5.

28. As an example, see "La Victoire loyaliste de Medellin," *Le Peuple*, August 20, 1936, p. 5.

29. "Prieto commente la victoire de Medellin," *L'Humanité*, August 20, 1936, p. 3.

30. "El gran triunfo de los leales en Medellín," *Heraldo de Madrid*, August 18, 1936, p. 4, and—in the same paper, same date (p. 1): "En Medellín, las tropas leales ponen en fuga a una columna facciosa que se dirigía a Don Benito" (At Medellin, The Loyalist Forces Put to Flight an Enemy Column Which Was Moving Toward Don Benito).

31. "En Estremadura sufrió ayer . . .," (In Extremadura Yesterday . . .), *Política*, August 18, 1936, p. 4, and "Se rechaza un fuerte ataque enemigo sobre Medellin" ("A Strong Enemy Attack on Medellin is Repulsed"), *Claridad*, August 18, 1936, p. 6.

32. "La Guerre civile en Espagne: Dans la province de Badajoz," *Le Temps*, August 19, 1936, p. 3. The original Franco communiqué was dated Seville, August 18. See "O avanço do coronel Castejón" ("The Advance of Colonel Castejon"), *A Voz* [Lisbon], August 19, 1936, p. 1, which quotes from that bulletin and notes that Cas-

tejon was able to take Santa Amalia and Don Benito only after "a ferocious resistance."

33. "La Guerre civile en Espagne: La situation militaire," *Écho de Paris*, August 24, 1936, p. 3, and "La Guerre civile en Espagne: Dans la province de Badajoz," *Le Temps*, August 19, 1936, p. 3.

34. For details of this stage of the campaign, see Thomas, p. 248.

35. Bernard Wilhelm: *Hemingway et Malraux devant la guerre d'Espagne* (Berne: Faculté des lettres, 1966), p. 86.

36. See Thomas, p. 247, notes 1 and 2, and Jay Allen's account (cited above, note 10).

37. Gaëtan Picon: *Malraux par lui-même* (Paris: Éditions du Seuil, 1953), p. 58.

Author's Preface

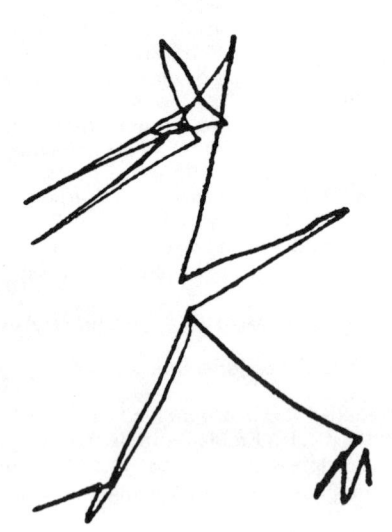

One of Malraux's sketches done on an "Author's Preface" of a book

15

Life Made into Fiction

PHILIPPE CARRARD

Malraux's work has often been considered a first-hand account of an actual experience. To many commentators, *L'Espoir* in particular has seemed a mere reportage. Geoffrey Hartman, for example, considers the novel "practically a battle-field reportage";[1] for W.M. Frohock, "relatively few of the action scenes sound like novelistic invention": *Man's Hope* "must be taken to lie at the borderland between journalism and fiction";[2] and for Claude-Edmonde Magny, "beginning with the reportage constituted by *L'Espoir*, the connection between Malraux's work and reality becomes more and more abstract."[3] Actually, relatively few events related in the book could have been materially witnessed by Malraux; and indication of source, whether implicit or explicit, is never given for the reporting of events not witnessed by the author. Events observed by Malraux have almost always been rearranged for literary and dramatic effects; see Langlois' article, p. 167. Finally, several basic devices used by Malraux are generically novelistic devices. Thus, without resorting to the verification procedures of the historian, using textual analysis only, it can be shown that *L'Espoir* is encoded according to the conventions of fiction; in other words, that the tacit contract which Malraux makes with his reader (beginning with the subtitle "novel" is already a true "attestation of fictitiousness"[4]) is a fictional rather than a journalistic contract.

I would like to examine some aspects of this encoding of *L'Espoir* as fictional narrative. My working hypotheses are that every type of narrative (tale, short story, autobiography, and so on) assumes some implicit rules; that the immediate perception of the text by the reader (according to style of type, printing process, information given by the title, and so on) conditions him to accept a certain type of discourse. In short, texts are produced and received along what Jauss calls "horizons of expectations,"[5] horizons which they may satisfy, transgress, or renovate. In the case of *L'Espoir*, I shall presuppose that there is a code of fiction and a code of journalism, even though in actual practice hybrid combinations may be found in, for example, such texts as *In Cold Blood* or the writings of the "New Journalism." It should be clear that everything can happen at the level of actualization, and when I say that the reporter "may" or "is supposed to," I am considering only the code level.

The analysis will focus on a passage that is particularly interesting, because it is among the very few to report an episode where Malraux's participation is well established by other people's testimony: the bombing of the nationalist motorized column near Medellin by the Malraux led Espana Squadron ("L'Illusion lyrique," section II, chapter II, pp. 514-525 in *Romans*, Pléiade, 1966). Unlike Walter G. Langlois, I will not compare this passage with historical reality, nor will I follow the successive stages of the text. The making of fiction will be examined in *L'Espoir*, and in *L'Espoir* alone. Occasionally, to buttress the argument, I will have recourse to brief comparisons between Malraux's text and the articles of a journalist, the Spanish correspondent of *Paris Soir*, Louis Delaprée.[6] These confrontations, which suppose that genres are defined by their oppositions, should help establish the specificity of fiction on three points at least: staging, narrative focus, and the use of descriptions.

Staging

From the point of view of narrative analysis, Malraux's participation in the mission shows clearly which options were offered to the novelist. As Malraux had first-hand knowledge of what happened, he might have borrowed the perspective of only one character and thus reproduced the incomplete perception (that of a bombardier?) that he himself had of the event. Or he might have reconstituted the entire operation, given a panoramic view of the mission by using a narrator endowed with extensive competence. Malraux, however, chooses to objectify the experience and to make it relative, to go beyond the fragmentary aspect of a testimony and what he calls himself "the absurdity of the omniscient novelist"[7] ("l'absurdité du romancier omniscient"). The narrative is organized by cutting the chapter into scenes, the scene being defined as the typographic unit limited by a blank space longer than the usual separation between paragraphs. A play of perspectives is made to correspond to this cutup. The story unfolds according to the point of view of four participants: Darras, Scali, Sembrano, and Magnin. They have different jobs in three of the six planes engaged in the bombing (Darras and Magnin are on the same plane). The following is a list of scenes and indicates which characters are endowed with the point of view in each of them.

1. Approaches and bombing. Indeterminate perspective, then that of Darras (copilot) (pp. 514-517).
2. Bombing. Perspective: Scali (bombardier) (p. 516-518).
3. Bombing. Perspective: Darras (p. 518).
4. Bombing. Perspective: Scali (p. 518).
5. Bombing, then arrival of Junkers. Perspective: Sembrano (pp. 518-520).
6. Bombing, then arrival of Junkers. Perspective: Scali (p. 520).
7. Combat against Junkers followed by flight. Perspective: Sembrano, then Magnin (function not indicated) (pp. 520-521).
8. Discussion between Magnin and "Sûreté" (military security) delegate. Perspective: Magnin (pp. 521-523).
9. Magnin's visit to the wounded House. Perspective: Magnin (pp. 523-524).
10. Magnin's meditation about the bombing. Perspective: Magnin (p. 525).[8]

First of all, particularly one must ask about the function of the cutup, the typographic interval separating the scenes. What is the relation between these units? If we examine scenes 1 to 7, those that deal with the bombing itself, we see that the blank hardly ever indicates a hole in the temporal sequence (there will be such a hole between scenes 7 and 8 and also, but less so, between scenes 8 and 9): Malraux does not have recourse to ellipsis. He does not "cut" at a particularly dramatic moment as he does in other circumstances, for example, the execution of the Fascist civil guards ("L'Illusion lyrique," section II, chapter V) or Hernandez's death at the end of "Exercice de l'Apocalypse" ("Exercise of the Apocalypse"). These relations may be called those of concatenation in that the moments isolated by the narrative yield one unto the other in succession without any pauses. Actually, if there is a pause, it is so brief that it is not perceived as such. In other words, the typographical interval constitutes a kind of spacing: it sets aside two events that follow immediately and indeed literally stages them.

Although the blank does not introduce a temporal break, it is a very definite mark of displacement in space. As the list of scenes indicates, all changes of scene correspond to the passage of one airplane into another. First Darras's perspective, then Sembrano's alternates with that of Scali.

Yet each of these characters is in a different aircraft. This arrangement is of a specifically literary nature. For if the narrative is conducted according to the point of view of certain protagonists, it is not the protagonists themselves who tell their own story, but a narrator who, though never saying, "I," is nevertheless present in a virtual way.[9] In this passage, the narrator is a witness whose principal characteristic is omnipresence; he can go from one place to another very rapidly and can even change plane in flight. Could this narrator be a real witness? Could he be a war correspondent who might have accompanied the soldiers? It is obvious that even on this simple point of organization, the Malraux text differs from a reportage. Because even if a reporter can use what he has learned from different sources, he cannot feign omnipresence. He cannot use it as a narrative convention without running into serious problems of credibility. His text would be constituted only by paraleipses, by excessive information inappropriate for the vantage point chosen.[10] Delaprée thus appears very careful to give credence to his story of events taking place at the same time. After having described a funeral of a revolutionary of the right, he makes a transition by saying that "at *the very hour* when his corpse was being buried, the *news came* of a sacrifice carried out by a hero of the left" (underlining is mine). This is followed by the account of an Asturian miner who had blown himself up along with the Fascist general staff with whom he was negotiating. The narrator's changes of position, independently of what is actually being said, are enough to exclude the Medellin episode from the journalistic domain and to make of it a fictional text. Decoded as such, this text appears highly plausible. The pact established with the reader is not of a referential nature: it does not attempt to give him or her information that needs to be checked. Its aim is not resemblance to reality but rather the effect of reality (what Barthes calls "coup de réel"), verisimilitude. And the device of an omnipresent narrator, a device that can hardly be allowed in a reportage, does not disturb the reader to the extent that he has accepted the pact—that his competence, the implicit knowledge he has of the operations of literary discourse, has allowed him to recognize the text as fictional narrative.

Narrative Focus

An examination of the uses of perspective in the scene itself, rather than in the connections between the scenes, will lead us to a very similar conclusion. By *perspective* or *focus* we mean the way in which narrative information is regulated in the story. Malraux has recourse to what Pouillon calls the story "with" and Genette "internal focus":[12] that is that he limits the narrator's statements to what a given character or "reflector" can be assumed to know or to perceive.

Spatially, the text observes this restriction very carefully and indicates an interest in exploring the possibilities of focus. The story, in

Malraux in 1944

effect, describes the combat as it is seen from the plane itself. This device is not to be found in specialists of aerial literature, for example, Saint Exupéry before 1942 and *Pilote de guerre.* The story is organized according to the vision of the four characters mentioned above. Malraux sets forth the conditions: distance from the action, obstacles that block the view, and so on. Thus, the text remains faithful to Darras's and Scali's perspectives: the aerial bombing carried out by Darras's plane is not seen according to his own perspective because "the second pilot cannot see below himself" (p. 517) but according to Scali's perspective. When Scali himself wants to follow the trajectory of his own projectiles, he has to leave the trapdoor that blocks his view and must use a "side window" (p. 518). Other dramatic effects reinforce these limitations motivated by a specific angle of vision. Here Malraux adopts the viewpoint of the pilot Sembrano and does what Anglo-Saxon criticism calls a "double take."[13] Two shots of the same event are given through the same reflector, and the two interpretations can vary considerably. When the planes are bombing the trucks parked in Medellin's plaza, Sembrano sees (shot 1) a Douglas coming to meet him; its pilot "has probably lost the [file]" (p. 519). A few seconds later, he sees (shot 2) the same Douglas and "two others" (p. 520). This means that danger is ahead because only three Douglas planes (including that of Sembrano) are engaged in combat. Everything is ready for the dramatic climax (coup de théâtre) or, to speak like Ricardou, the writing climax (*coup d'écriture*). Surprise (the Douglases are actually Junkers) is linked to an "error" of perception just as the fragmentary aspect of the story was linked to a restriction of the visual field or as the image ("Magnin watched the Junkers grow as if they had been blown up," p. 521) will later be motivated by an optical illusion. Like the staging techniques, these focusing devices are of a literary nature. A reporter would have to be extraordinarily close to a character to find himself face-to-face with the same obstacles and be victim to the same errors or to the same illusions. As a powerful auxiliary of a certain modern verisimilitude, the principle of internal focus can be used in a reportage only under the following two conditions: (1) the point of view must be that of the reporter; (2) it must be that of a character who had been watched closely or perhaps even been followed by the reporter. (In the latter case the reporter must be able to justify and explain the outcome of such constant surveillance.) Delaprée almost constantly uses the first alternative.

Many items are introduced so as to justify his presence: "I saw," "witnessed," "observed," "met," "followed," and so on. He even specifies that he observes the Oviedo dynamiters through a "field glass" (p. 136), that he follows the rocket processions through a periscope placed in governmental trenches; that because he cannot reach front combat lines, he is present during the fighting from a "central telephone station" in Madrid (p. 174, p. 193); or still, that he observes the combats from the Clinico Hospital "lying near a muddy gutter" (p. 179). But whether the narrator-witness of *L'Espoir* uses the first alternative (and does not go through the intermediary of a reflector) or the second alternative (focusing on one of the protagonists), he does not much care about motivation: he explains neither how he could have witnessed the event himself nor how he accompanied his character to the heart of the action. At that level also, then, it is not possible to read the Medellin episode and maintain all the while that we are dealing with a reportage. The reading contract would be broken almost right away, and with such a rupture the referential value accounting for the journalistic text would disappear. We have here another proof that Malraux's text must be read according to terms of another contract, the contract of a fictional text.

Malraux's use of internal focusing is not limited to these spatial restrictions. The narrator recounts events as seen through the eyes of his characters, but he can also place himself inside a given individual and report what that character says to himself. The quotation can be made directly and introduced by a verb such as *think* or *say to oneself*. For example, while Sembrano flies over the battered truck and then the city of Medellin, he "thinks": "It will take Franco more than five minutes to fix all this up" and "Perhaps the trucks are in the city (. . .) and they should all be shot up; or perhaps the trucks are outside and to avoid a massacre of the militiamen they still have to be destroyed" (p. 519). But the quotation can be given in free indirect discourse without an introductory verb. The last paragraph of the fourth scene where the reporting of events is mixed with the reporting of words is interesting in this respect. The following quotation underlines the statements belonging to this latter type of discourse. The adverb *surely* and the exclamatory construction indicate that the character is talking to himself; the use of the imperfect shows that there is mediation from the narrator:

> *Two, three* . . . Impossible to see far beyond the trap. Through a lateral hole: on top, some guys were running hands up high— *they were probably climbing up on a mound.* Five, six . . . Machine gun platoons were shooting the planes. *Seven, eight* . . . It stopped running, underneath twenty red spots slamming at once. [p. 518]

Internal discourse, both direct and indirect, is even more abundant in the three scenes we haven't yet studied. According to a movement very typical of Malraux, the report of events is followed by the analysis of their meaning. Meaning is supplied as a counterpoint: efficacious action does not do away with the annoyance of administrative formalities, with the possibility of a fifth column, or with the reality of pain. Certain conclusions about German aviation and about implications for Europe are drawn from Magnin's internal discourse, mainly free indirect discourse.

> Magnin thought about France. Until this war, Junkers had formed the bulk of the German bomber force. They were modi-

fied civilian aircraft planes, and the reputation of German technology was such that the Europeans saw in them a fleet of warplanes. Their armament, although excellent, was not sufficient, and they were unable to chase the Douglases, these American commercial planes. Of course, they were a match for the stagecoaches purchased by Magnin on all European markets. But they wouldn't have held out against newer French or Soviet designs. Everything was now to change: the world's great bloody maneuvers had begun. For two years Europe had shrunk from the menace of a war that Hilter did not have the technical ability to begin (p. 525).

It is clear that a reporter could not have drawn such conclusions, using this type of discourse. A journalist may quote words actually spoken, but is not allowed within the consciousness of a character. If he resorted to this type of omniscience he would not be more credible than if he pretended to be omnipresent: his text would become a kind of hybrid, similar to these fictionalized biographies where private thoughts and conversations are reported without any reference to a source.

The rules of the novel game are different. A "homodiegetic" narrator,[14] present as a character in the story he tells, may explain how he obtained information and how he can read somebody else's consciousness. Such motivations are often found in Proust. Marcel often legitimizes his own access to a character's thoughts by quoting a conversation with him or with someone who knew him well. In a similar fashion, a "heterodiegetic" narrator, absent from the story he tells, will justify a fact, using the pronoun *I*. In the epistolary novel, for instance, he delegates his prerogatives to an "extradiegetic" editor, an editor who relates "in a prologue, an epilogue and/or notes at the bottom of a page his so-called acquaintance with the missives."[15] But the heterodiegetic narrator who does not use the first person cannot take advantage of this possibility. Whether he "opens up" one or more consciousnesses, or whether he places himself within the character or analyzes him from without, the problem remains the same. As soon as he does not use "I," he can no longer legitimize his knowledge of someone else's inner life. Such is the narrative situation in *L'Espoir*: the justification of thoughts remains arbitrary. This arbitrariness, however, is accepted by the reader: the rules of verisimilitude vary according to genres, and fiction has other requirements than reportage. Thus, the reader who has accepted the text as an imaginary story is not at all disturbed.

Description

The literariness of the text is also obvious in the use of descriptions because they go much beyond the accepted range of setting in journalistic writing. In particular, they are often related to a major aspect of the novel: the metamorphosis of the political and military conflict into a metaphysical conflict, where man fights what Malraux calls "destiny": "everything that imposes upon (man) the consciousness of his condi-

Malraux at Verrières, 1971

tion,"[16] "the cosmos and its elements of indifference and mortality, universe and time, earth and death."[17] The descriptions may textually actualize this other dimension of the combat in many ways.

In the first place, landscape can be presented as outside the conflict. For the aviators who are about to bomb the motorized column, the earth appears "covered with peace"; "peace" referring not only to "deep calm," but also to "state of what is not at war." The opposition is then between the spectacle's serenity and the combat to come and also between appearance and reality. The aviators are about to fly over Badajoz without noticing anything abnormal. Yet at that moment Badajoz was the stage of bitter fighting:

> It was cool in the planes, but along the ground, heat could be seen just as we can see hot air tremble above chimneys. Here and there, large peasant straw hats appeared in the wheat. From the Toledo to the Estremadura, beyond the earth, from one horizon to the next, covered with peace, the harvest-colored earth dozed an afternoon's sleep. Ridges and hills formed flat silhouettes in the dust that came toward the sun; beyond, Badajoz, Merida—taken by the Fascists on the eighth—Medellin, still invisible, paltry points in the shivering plain's immensity. [p. 515]

In other passages, this peace will be explicitly defined as indifference. Cosmic detachment and human activities will be contrasted while their relation is questioned. For instance, "indifferent sea of clouds" and the peacelike "beginning of world" in which Magnin flies en route toward another aerial mission (the bombing of the clandestine field) are compared to "man's relentlessness" (p. 185). Metaphysical questioning also manifests itself in images, more particularly to those which refer to art or history. Although there is but one occurrence of this type of image in the chapter under analysis, it is a significant one. Before being designated by its name, the city of Badajoz is described in a metonymic and metaphoric way as: "roofs without trees, old tiles gray from the sun, Berber skeleton on African soil" (p. 515). The metaphor is both geographical and historical: it refers to the similitudes of typography between the two countries, to the geologic epoch when the Mediterranean did not separate the two regions and also to the Islamic invasions and their deep influence on Spanish culture. In the same category, one should note the type of monument Malraux's aerial observers identify: "Badajoz, its Alcazar, its empty arenas" (p. 515); "the antique Merida theater, its ruins" (p. 516). These are monuments that inscribe the past in their typography. Such parallels in space and time will become systematic in Malraux's later works to the degree that they are perceived, in the *Antimémoires* for instance, as mere tics of writing. Here, however, their function is specific. Establishing a relation between Spanish and African geography means confronting human time with what Sartre calls "universal time, the time of nebulae and planets, of tertiary folds and animal species."[18] Furthermore, the evocation of Moslem conquests suggests metaphorically that, beyond their immediate causes, men's combats have the same object: to shape destiny and affirm the self against the world's inertia.

Should a journalist be a metaphysician? In practice, he cannot, of course, be denied this right. However, whereas he may draw a lesson from the events, it does not seem that he should engage in philosophical speculations lest he go beyond his scope, or rather beyond his genre. Delaprée often draws conclusions of a military nature. He also moralizes, for instance about child soldiers or about massacres that he judges useless: "Jacobeans of Spain: do not allow children to play with death any more" (p. 102); "Oh, elderly Europe, always busy with your little games and great intrigues, let God not allow all this blood to strangle you" (p. 161). But he refrains from all philosophical or metaphysical development, whether implicit or explicit. The matter, it should be noted, is not only a matter of content. Insistent historical rapprochements, or images referring too specifically to art or culture, would constitute "grammatical" errors in a reportage; in other words, they would be perceived as mistakes against the code, as would the use of an omnipresent or omniscient narrator.

A last point remains to be settled. We do not deal with *L'Espoir* in the same way we would be dealing with other historical novels. If we read *War and Peace*, or *The Charterhouse of Parma*, we know that these books were published respectively fifty years after the Russian Campaign and twenty-four years after Waterloo; we also know that neither Tolstoy nor Stendhal took part in the events they report. When we read *L'Espoir*, on the other hand, we know that Malraux was in Spain. Thus, it is to some extent legitimate to ask ourselves questions such as: does Malraux have first-hand knowledge of what he is talking about? Is he telling the truth? Is all the relevant information included? It even seems possible to go one step further. When reading *L'Espoir* would we be as moved or have so much pleasure, if we did not know that Malraux was a participant in the bombing of the motorized column before being a scriptor of the event? Do certain essential aspects of the book, the epic enlargement of the war or the celebration of man for instance, gain in value because Malraux was there and wrote with hardly any distance from the events. Finally, does the book not *benefit* from the circumstances of its writing and publication? Whatever the answer, one thing remains certain: in a book of this type, our awareness of the context is a dimension of our interpretation.

Translated by Jeanine P. Plottel

Notes

1. *Malraux* (New York: Hilary House, 1960), p. 31.
2. *Malraux and the Tragic Imagination* (Stanford: Stanford University Press, 1952), p. 106.
3. "Malraux le fascinateur," *Esprit*, 149 (Oct. 1948), p. 522.
4. Lejeune, *Le Pacte autobiographique* (Paris: Seuil, 1975), p. 22. About the notion of reading "pact" or "contract," see the same work, particularly pp. 26 and 36-37.
5. "Littérature médiévale et théorie des genres," *Poétique*, 1 (1970), p. 79.
6. These articles, which Malraux knew and occasionally uses in *L'Espoir*, have been collected in *Mort à Madrid* (Paris: Pierre Tisné, 1937). This is the book we quote in the course of this study.
7. "Esquisse d'une psychologie du cinéma" in *Scènes choisies* (Paris: Gallimard, 1946), p. 331. Contemporary description would say "narrator" rather than "novelist."
8. The end of scene 9 coincides in the Pléiade edition with the bottom of p. 524. There is no typographical blank at the beginning of p. 525, but such a blank was clearly marked off in the Gallimard edition of 1937. It seems to us required by the separation between paragraphs indicating advances in time and displacement in space.
9. About this point, see Genette, *Figures III* (Paris: Seuil, 1972), pp. 251, 4.
10. The term *paraleipsis* is borrowed from Genette, op. cit., p. 213.
11. About the notion of literary competency, see Culler *Structuralist Poetics* (Ithaca, N.Y.: Cornell University Press, 1975), particularly pp. 113-114.
12. Pouillon, *Temps et roman* ("Time and the Novel") (Paris: Gallimard, 1946), p. 74; Genette, op. cit., pp. 206-207.
13. About this point, see for example Hartman, op. cit., p. 62, and Tarica, "Ironic Figures in Malraux's Novels," in *Image and Theme: Studies in Modern French Fiction*, ed. W. M. Frohock (Cambridge, Mass.: Harvard University Press, 1969), p. 41.
14. We borrow the terms *homodiegetic* and *heterodiegetic* from Genette, op. cit., p. 252.
15. Dallenbach, *Le Récit spéculaire: Essai sur la mise en abyme* (Paris: Seuil, 1977), p. 119.
16. *Les Voix du silence* (Paris: Gallimard, 1951), p. 628.
17. "De la représentation en Orient et en Occident," *Verve* 3 (Summer 1938), p. 69.
18. "La Temporalité chez Faulkner," in *Situations I* (Paris: Gallimard, 1947), p. 73.

16

Visual Imagination in *L'Espoir*

BRIAN THOMPSON

The novelist, Malraux believes, is obliged to draw his material from the real world: it is the *transfiguration* of this raw material in the creative imagination that distinguishes the real novelist.[1] "Like the painter, the writer is not the transcriber of the world; he is its rival."[2] For Malraux, the notion that the work of art reproduces a model is as mistaken in literature as in the plastic arts.[3] The artist imposes his "vision" on the world: he may be an El Greco who, according to Malraux, drew the black drapes of his studio in order to crucify Toledo in the depths of his own artistic genius[4] or a Balzac whose work is now recognized as an "oeuvre de visionnaire," the work of a visionary.[5] *L'Irréel*, *L'Intemporel*, and *La Tête d'obsidienne* show that the work of art is remote from the model that may have served as its raw material. Art makes the invisible visible and makes tangible the values of the artist and his or her civilization. Its elements are interrelated and harmonized as those in real life never are.

Does this theory correspond to Malraux's own practice? Even in *L'Espoir*, for example, where the role of imagination is, we are told, reduced to a minimum? I shall examine a series of interrelated scenes in *L'Espoir* that share several elements characteristic of Malraux's personal vision: striking interplay of light and darkness, importance of visual experience in communication and understanding, obsession with blindness. The "raw materials"—both the outer world and inner obsession—are transfigured and come to express economically one of the fundamental themes of *L'Espoir:* man's solidarity and fraternity in the face of destiny in an indifferent universe.

The first of these scenes is from the subsection marked "The Night of November 6th" near the beginning of Part II ("The Manzanares"),[6] where Magnin's "multiplace" bomber clashes with a Fascist antiaircraft beacon. The rapid interplay of light and darkness effects a buildup of tension. Antiaircraft shells explode on all sides; the shafts of light from the beacons below "slash" the darkness of night in front of and behind the plane; bombs exploding below cause eerie lights. Contrary to traditional usage and normal expectations, the light itself is dangerous and must be avoided at all costs; darkness is sought out as a safe haven. A reversal of traditional attributes is explicitly made between "menacing light" and "protective night." But as the passage progresses, only the immediate situation invites this apparent reversal of values. On a deeper and more constant level of human experience the traditional values and associations are powerfully reestablished. How is this reversal brought about?

The Significance of Light and Darkness in Malraux

Malraux suggests this reevaluation in his close and unexpected association of menacing light with fraternity and of protective night with becoming lost or going astray. Under Malraux's pen the expression *perdu dans . . .* (lost in . . .) may, on the surface, seem to refer simply to visual phenomena but very often takes on metaphysical implications. Throughout the passage the associations connect night less with protection than with vast solitude, obscurity, and cold. The narrator's question—*Combattent-ils l'ennemi ou le froid?* (Are they fighting the enemy or the cold?)— implies that the real enemy is not the antiaircraft beacon: a cold, dark, indifferent universe supplies an even larger arena of combat against man's solitude.

The plane is over the "nocturnal" Balearics, invisible in the darkness. Each crew member's face is frozen; each man is alone in the immensity of the night sky and sea, "solitaire jusqu'au fond de l'obscurité de la mer" (solitary to the far reaches of the darkness of the sea). At the end of the passage, the plane is once more "lost" in the immensity of the night which stretches as far as the eye can see. The expression *la mer sans phares* (the beaconless sea) now connotes less a welcome lack of deadly antiaircraft beacons than an absence of lighthouses—also *phares*— to guide our way in the dark. The value of the very word *phare* has changed, and the passage as a whole seems to invert the meaning of the adjective *protectrice* (protective).

The light from the antiaircraft beacon undergoes a similar transformation. On the level of immediate experience, it is indeed a danger, to be avoided and then escaped at all costs. It is "menacing," "dazzling," "overwhelming." Yet at the same time it lights up the interior of the plane, which has been in almost total darkness. Magnin's momentary misinterpretation of visual phenomena in such a critical situation—one of Malraux's favorite techniques—involves the reader very immediately in the action of the scene. For an instant, readers curse with Magnin, but then must, like Magnin, correct their mistake by noticing the shadows cast from without. They then see through Magnin's eyes when, for the first time since takeoff, they are able to see their fellow crew members. They, too, see Attignies's face and *la bonne tête de Pol* (Pol's good humored mug)—the very formulation predisposes readers to consider what they see favorably. Malraux intervenes to clarify his point: although the menacing light may be dangerous, it fills the plane with fraternity. The men, drawn forth from darkness and solitude, can suddenly see themselves engaged in a common struggle, subject to a common destiny.[7] Malraux's use of italics emphasizes the importance of the instantaneous visual recognition and awareness: *ces hommes se voient* (these men see one another). This visual epiphany is a moment of intense awareness beyond mere rational, verbal communication. When faced with the immensity and indifference of the universe, with the "human condition," man's hope is fraternity: this fraternity is found beyond and through common danger. The beacon is not only a mortal danger. Light regains its traditional role of revelation when it reveals to the crew their common destiny and their solidarity. Such newfound awareness gives them the strength to endure, and as they go off into the darkness, they carry images of *les visages fraternels un instant apparus* (fraternal faces seen for a moment). The word *but* in the final sentence makes clear the opposition between such fraternity and night's real nature: *l'obscurité glacée de la mer sans phares* (the icy darkness of the beaconless sea).

Malraux stresses the privileged role of vision as a recognition and awareness even more by two striking images of its opposite, blindness. The city below is compared to a blind man, helplessly screaming. Above, the plane is invisible; so the city can literally not see the source of its own imminent destruction. Once the beacon has lost the plane, its search is compared to a blind man's groping with a sword. Its very movement is rendered by the choppy rhythm of the sentence and further underlined by alliteration: "le phare coupe, coupe, comme un aveugle qui tâtonnerait avec un sabre" (the beacon slashes, slashes, like a blind man feeling his way with a sword). It is especially in *L'Espoir* that blindness becomes explicitly associated with destiny, as it is at least implicitly in all Malraux's novels and even in his books on art.[8] In this passage it is juxtaposed to the fraternal vision of one's comrades. Vision, the mere fact of *seeing* one another, here triumphs over blind destiny.

Many other passages confirm this close interplay of light and darkness, vision and blindness, with hard-won fraternity in the face of danger. For example, during the siege of the Alcazar (*E* 543-545; *MH* 130-133), Hernandez, Garcia, le Négus, Mercery, and several other militiamen are trapped in the darkness of a cellar by an approaching flamethrower. We follow the approach of the flamethrower, through the eyes of the men trapped inside, along the corridor toward the door. We see the step-by-step advance of the sputtering flame together with them. The bearer remains unseen; war seems to have been transformed into a combat against an elemental force. The trapped men are cowering in terror against the walls, and Hernandez feels they are reaching the breaking point. Their frantic shadows on the wall convey their growing anxiety:

> The spray of crackling gasoline was approaching step by step, and the the frenzy of the militiamen was multiplied by its convulsive bluish flames which were projecting clusters of crazed shadows onto the walls, unleashing a horde of phantoms strung out around the madness of the living men. [*E* 543; *MH* 131]

The shadows jump dramatically from wall to ceiling as le Négus manages to kill the bearer just as he reaches the threshold. The tremendous tension built up by the highly kinetic visual imagery is relaxed as the room returns to semidarkness.

The similarity of the scenario with that of the episode in the "multiplace" bomber is striking: men hidden in darkness are sought out by a deadly ray of light (or flame); tension is increased by the rapid interplay of light and shadow; the menacing light is finally overcome or escaped; and the men return to darkness with relief. Even the theme of blindness is again present, here literally rather than figuratively. One of the Republican defenders is burned by the approaching flame:

> "I can't see anymore!" he yelled, at ground level, "I can't see anymore! Get me out!"

Here, too, light is menacing, blinding, deadly; darkness is protective. But once again, the passage ends with a reversal, and light is reestablished in its traditional role of revelation. Le Négus lights a cigarette, and each of the others follows suit, appearing for a moment in the flickering light— it is their "return to life." As in the "multiplace," the very flame that threatens the men with death then serves to reveal their fraternity and solidarity as they *see* one another in the darkness surrounding them all:

> Le Négus lit a cigarette; and all those who were following them did the same at the same time: the return to life. Each man appeared for a second in the brief glow of the match or lighter; then everything returned to semi-darkness. [*E* 544; *MH* 132]

Malraux at the shooting of *Sierra de Teruel (L'Espoir),* 1939

After a moment of near dissolution, their solidarity is further underlined by the verbal formulation: "tous ... de même ... à la fois. .. chaque homme ... " (all ... the same ... at the same time ... each man).

The fraternal lighting of cigarettes plays a similar role of illumination and revelation during the defense against oncoming Fascist tanks (*E* 631-632; *MH* 234-235). Gonzalez and his group of dynamiters follow the decomposition of the night and the gradual approach of dawn; light, for them, will signal combat and perhaps death. As they wait, a distant explosion illuminates their faces: they watch each other, ominously, as they would look at dead men. Again, light holds negative connotations of danger and death; darkness means relative security from attack. The tanks finally arrive as dawn breaks, and the Republicans light their cigarettes one by one. They will then light their bombs from these same cigarettes.

> Gonzalez, then Pepe, then each of the others lights his cigarette. Everywhere, dark shadows of men begin to glide towards the oncoming tanks.

The same link of fraternity and solidarity takes place as glowing cigarettes move forward together. Light—in the immediate context—is again connected to danger: seen by the tanks, it could mean discovery and death. Some of the Republicans fail to conceal their cigarettes properly: " *'Idiots!' devrait penser Gonzalez* " (Idiots! Gonzalez ought to think) (*E* 632). Logically, Gonzalez ought to curse his careless comrades (the conditional, *devrait*, is important here; it is missed in the *published* English translation). But he is caught up in a movement of fraternity above such logic.

> He moves forward with them, uplifted by the same tide, by a pure and fraternal exaltation.

And Malraux intervenes with a characteristic superlative to underline the importance of the experience.

> Never will he know more fully what it is to be a man.

A visual experience is again used within the context of a highly stylized interplay of light and darkness to convey human solidarity and fraternity in the face of death. Traditional symbolic values first seem reversed, but a deeper level of human experience reestablishes light as an element symbolic of human fraternity and life itself.

Are these scenes faithful accounts of actual experiences or carefully contrived literary set pieces? Apparently neither: they are products of the novelist's imagination.

Although Malraux *was* actively involved in certain phases of the

Spanish civil war, he was not omnipresent; as far as we know, he saw no action against flamethrowers and tanks. Indeed, Malraux pointed out to me that it is an error to suppose that the artist necessarily transposes his experience into a mimesis. The painter who has noticed a wonderful blue flower will use the same color to paint a table. I think we can find traces of just such a transposition immediately following the flamethrower episode. Le Négus reflects that the bearer hesitated a moment instead of turning the flame on Le Négus and burning him alive. He concludes that it is impossible to kill someone who is *looking* at you. A similar experience of a man he simply calls "the Frenchman" confirms his statement. It seems the Frenchman was Malraux. Some thirty years later, the *Antimémoires* recount an experience underlying this passage and show how "raw material" is transfigured. Upon seeing a bearded enemy pilot for the first time, Malraux was momentarily unable to fire: the beard changed an anonymous "enemy" into an individual and combat into murder. The human face may establish solidarity even among enemies, at a very elemental and visceral level.[9] Experience, though important, may thus be quite removed from its eventual artistic expression.

I asked Malraux whether the symbolic interplays of light and darkness, vision and blindness, had been consciously contrived. His answer, I must admit, surprised me both by its vehemence ("Never, never, never!") and by its emphasis on the role of the subconscious in artistic creation. For Malraux, the truly powerful image never results from a deliberate effort but always from an encounter between something the novelist has chosen—the scene at hand—and something which emerges from his memory, a memory at once visual, affective, and emotive. "This encounter takes place at a subconscious level—I don't like the word, but no matter—which is extremely profound and which accounts for what we would call, in music, its lyricism."

This encounter, adds Malraux, is often between images that, at a subconscious level, are somehow opposites—positive and negative poles in electricity. This is precisely what we have observed in *L'Espoir*: vision and blindness, light and darkness, life and death; light that blinds and reveals, darkness as a safe haven or endless abyss. Malraux—or any other artist—transcends the limits of his own time, his own place, and even his own psychology through the workings of the creative imagination. Nourished not only by personal experience but by all the "previously elaborated forms" of the world of art, the imagination "plugs into" something beyond itself, into man's quest for transcendence and for the absolute.

"All that I have written," Malraux told me, "consists of posing the contradiction between appearance, in the metaphysical sense—that is, what one could call 'life'—and the realm of the absolute, whatever it might be."[10] It is through the creative imagination, his own and the one expressed by the arts of all mankind, that Malraux sought and perhaps caught a glimpse of what he called the secret, the enigma, the fundamental mystery of life. We may apply to Malraux what he wrote of Rembrandt:

"He discovered, in an invented light and shadow, communion with the fundamental mystery."

Notes

1. In Gaëtan Picon's *Malraux par lui-même* (Seuil, 1953), p.40, Malraux notes: "... le romancier, pour créer son univers, emploie une matière qu'il est contraint de puiser dans l'univers de tous. Encore cette matière est-elle *moyen* de création, ou rien. Le grand romancier est Balzac, non Henri Monier. C'est la puissance transfiguratrice du réel, la qualité atteinte par cette transfiguration, qui font son talent; il est évidemment un poète" (the novelist, in order to create his univers, uses a material that he is obliged to draw from the universe of all. Yet this material is a *means* of creation, or nothing. The great novelist is Balzac, not Henri Monnier. It is the power of transfiguring the real, it is the quality of this transfiguration, which make for his talent; he is obviously a poet.)

2. *L'Homme précaire et la littérature* (Gallimard, 1977), p. 152: "... comme le peintre, l'écrivain n'est pas le transcripteur du monde, il en est le rival" (... like the painter, the writer is not the transcriber of the world, he is its rival).

3. Ibid., p. 123: "... en littérature comme dans les arts plastiques, l'illusion repose sur le préjugé que l'oeuvre réproduit le modèle" (... in literature as in the plastic arts, the illusion is based on the prejudice that the work reproduces the model). As Malraux stated most emphatically to me in October 1974: "there are no models for me, nor for Rembrandt or Goya either. The idea that you have in any art a transcription is always a wrong idea. Something else is at work and the mediator is generally another work of art." Much of our conversation has recently appeared in *Malraux et l'art*, the fourth volume of the Série Malraux published by Lettres Modernes, under the title *L'art et roman: l'imagination visuelle du romancier (Entretien avec André Malraux)*.

4. *Les Voix du silence* (Gallimard, 1951), pp. 433-435.

5. In the conversation referred to in note 3. One example not unrelated to our discussion below: Balzac's vision of the world as hyperbolic antitheses leads him even to change Esther's hair from blond to blue-black part way through *Splendeurs et misères des courtisanes*, apparently so as to offer a more complete contrast to the blond "Anglaise" as well as, later, to her own wedding dress and white camelias. (Edition Garnier, 1964, pp. 159, 227, 341).

6. *L'Espoir* in the Pléiade edition of the *Romans* (Gallimard, 1947), pp. 663-664 (henceforth cited as *E*). *Man's Hope*, translated by Stuart Gilbert and Alastair Macdonald, is available in the Random House Modern Library series (New York, 1941), henceforth cited as *MH*. This passage is on pages 273-275. For the purposes of this study, I have retranslated all passages cited in English as literally as possible.

7. Gilbert and Macdonald mistranslate this passage, missing this close association between danger and revelation: "It was their comradeship in arms which had brought then into that cabin filled with menacing light ..." (*MH* 274). Malraux's text reads as follows: "La fraternité des armes remplit la carlingue avec cette lumière menaçante ..." (*E* 663).

8. See, for example, my brief article of "The Image of Blindness in Malraux's Meditations on Art," in *Mélanges Malraux Miscellany*, III, 2 (Autumn 1971), pp. 16-25, or my dissertation, "Vision and Blindness in the Novels of André Malraux" (Harvard University, 1970).

9. *Antimémoires* (Gallimard, 1967), p. 99, and in *Anti-memoirs*, translated by Terence Kilmartin (London: Hamish Hamilton, 1968), p. 65. Generally, war remains blind and impersonal, "le tir d'un aveugle contre un inconnu" (a blind man firing at someone unknown) (*E* 689; *MH* 305). For Malraux, the Fifth Column bombings, in which Fascists clearly *looked* at the women and children before throwing their bombs, mark "the first step toward bestiality" (*E* 689; *MH* 306).

10. Malraux suggests that this may be why the blind man is such a fascinating figure, for he is defined by his rupture from, his ignorance of, the world of appearances.

11. *La Tête d'obsidienne (Picasso's Mask)* (Gallimard, 1974), p. 83 (my translation).

17

Malraux's *Storm in Shanghai*

LE ROY C. BREUNIG

The fact that Malraux was born with the century prompts one to look back on his life in terms of decades, his twenties coinciding with *the* twenties, his sixties with the sixties, and so on. I have chosen to glance at only one of these blocks, the thirties, not only because it witnessed the publication of the novel that is usually considered his masterpiece—and I shall limit myself to that work—but also because as impressionable students, soon to become soldiers, my generation lived through the ideological battles that our immediate elders, those of Malraux's age, were waging and that were in a way crystallized in *Man's Fate*.

The New Republic repeated recently what has already become a cliché in France: that all of Camus and much of Sartre came out of the mold of Malraux's novels.[1] For most readers today it is axiomatic that *La Condition humaine* is a great existentialist novel.

But that is not at all the way the thirties saw it. When the book first appeared in England in 1934, it was entitled *Storm in Shanghai*, the publishers apparently intending to sell it as a thriller, a political thriller. In the United States the Haakon Chevalier translation was called more appropriately *Man's Fate*, but almost without exception the critics ignored the implications of this title and treated it more in the spirit of the English version.

It was Edmund Wilson who discovered Malraux on this side of the Atlantic. Writing in *The New Republic* in 1933, just after the novel had originally appeared in Paris, he almost alone seems to have got the point of the French title inspired by Montaigne. But then he goes on to conclude: "There is ... something else in the book besides the mere theme of escape [sic] from the human situation.... His [Malraux's] interpretation of recent events seems now essentially Marxist—though he never, as I have said, slips into the facile formulas; and though the criticism his characters make of the line of the Comintern is more or less that of Trotsky, he maintains in relation to Trotsky, too, an attitude of independence. Marxism, Gisors observes, is not a doctrine but a will; and it is simply that, in Malraux's world, the only men he respects are animated by the Marxist will ..."[2] For Wilson there was no doubt about it; Malraux was a Marxist.

When in June 1934 the translation appeared in New York, most of the reviews were, like Wilson's, variations of the Marxist criterion. In a front page article in *The Saturday Review of Literature*, Pearl Buck, whose *Good Earth* had appeared three years before, does not let us forget that, unlike the rather frivolous French adventurer whose work she is presenting, *she* really knows China. Malraux, she writes, was "caught up by the fascination, rather than by a profound belief in the cause of the Chinese people.... One is confirmed ... after reading the book that the real revolution which China is yet to have cannot come out of such figures as these, or at least out of such incomplete followers of the great Marx, however satisfactory many Marxians will certainly find this book. Rather the true revolution will come, not thus frantic and superficial but deep and basic out of the real Chinese people."[3]

Writing in the *Nation*, Lionel Abel sees in *Man's Fate* a successful proletarian novel. According to the Marxists, he says, D. H. Lawrence, Proust, Mann, and Joyce all attest to the decay of the bourgeois world. "The bourgeois values are no longer creative, they say, and the corollary is that art and individuality are being recreated by the proletariat." *Man's Fate* supports this Marxist view. "The Shanghai insurrectionists ... united against a common enemy as brothers in arms, hold on to their personal styles of dignity even though unable to communicate them except to themselves."[4]

One senses some wishful thinking in this article. Abel seems to be persuading himself that one can be simultaneously a revolutionary and an individual. And we are reminded of the urgency of this question in the thirties when the phrase "come the revolution" had the ring of reality.

Abel's remarks about the decadent bourgeoisie are echoed in—of all places—the *New York Times Sunday Book Review* in order to reach a very different conclusion. R. L. Duffus claims somewhat smirkingly that al-

André Malraux and Jean Grosjean at Verrières, 1971

though it will be the bourgeoisie that reads it—for only the bourgeoisie can afford the $2.50 that the novel costs—it will undoubtedly be received as good proletarian literature. It *must* be, because Leon Trotsky endorses it. Duffus then condemns the naive optimism of the translator, Haakon Chevalier, who in his preface alludes to the heroes of the novel and their bond of brotherhood "in pursuit of a goal to which the future of humanity is intimately linked." "Nonsense," says Duffus. This is a novel of decadent pessimism. It is not a proletarian novel at all, but the story of a thoroughly bourgeois reaction. The unhealthy qualities in the book are the product of a bourgeois disintegration. "They are the result of just such a divigation *[sic]* as in Flaubert produced *Salammbo*. They may not interfere with the book's popularity—they may even add to the sales. But they do reveal an uncertainty of purpose, a philosophical as well as a literary weakness that makes M. Malraux with all his gifts no more than a good second-rate."[5]

And what said the *Partisan Review*, the prestigious "journal of the anti-Stalinist left-wing, cultural avant garde," which struck with awe the young Trotskyists of the CCNY Alcove 1 in the mid-thirties, according to a recent account by Irving Kristol?[6] The *Partisan Review* ignored Malraux until 1938, when F. W. Dupee described his shifting relations with the revolutionary movement, accusing him in effect of opportunism and hypocrisy. Professor Dupee quotes a remark from *Man's Fate* uttered by Kyo to the Comintern representative: "In Marxism there is the sense of a fatality and also the exultation of a will. Every time fatality comes before will I am suspicious." And Professor Dupee goes on to accuse Malraux of oscillating between Trotsky and Stalin and of ascribing each shift to the recurrence of the "will." For example, "once the Comintern, confronted by Hitler in power, reverted to the old policy and proclaimed the people's front, it seems to have recaptured its title to the Marxist will; and Malraux once more reversed his sympathies. Trotsky now became 'a moment in the past' and those who continued to uphold revolutionary principles became so many utopian moralists."[7]

Almost without exception, then, the reaction in America to *Man's Fate* was political. The reason is not far to seek: in that decade which went from the Crash to the Blitz we *were* political. Writing in *The New Republic* in 1938 on *Man's Hope*, the novel inspired by the Spanish civil war, Ralph Bates placed Malraux among the "progressive forces of the world."[8] We of the thirties were progressive because we still believed in progress, in the perfectability of man. We were concerned, intellectually as well as pragmatically, with the ways and means, political, economic, social, of enhancing the well-being of mankind. As the thirties unfolded, fascism and our opposition to it merely served to strengthen our kinship with what we thought to be Malraux's revolutionary optimism. I recall my enthusiasm as a graduate student sitting one evening in the periodical room of the Cornell Library reading Haakon Chevalier's "Return of the Hero" in the *Kenyon Review:* "Malraux has brought the hero back into the novel. If as seems likely, faith in man's capacity to control his social destiny increases and the bonds of human fellowship are strengthened it may well be that Malraux's novels herald the beginning of a new heroic literature."[9]

"The bonds of human fellowship," writes Chevalier. One can almost hear the strains of "Avanti Popolo" and the "Groupons-nous et demain" of the Internationale.

That was 1940. Only a few years later in one of the first post-war essays on Malraux, Claude-Edmonde Magny was to write: "Malraux . . . has reiterated only one point under the most diverse forms: the absolute impossibility for any individual to communicate with any other, even with those who belong to the same group."[10] It was, of course, the watershed of World War II that separated Magny from Chevalier. This war, which caused so many literary names to topple, those whom we had studied so assiduously in our Marcel Braunschvig anthology, *La Littérature française contemporaine*, in the mid-thirties: Barbusse, Dorgelès, Rolland, Romains (not to mention the conservatives Bordeaux, Bourget, Estaunié, even Daudet and Loti)—this war brought Malraux into his own at a time when Pascal and Kierkegaard were tending to crowd out the names of Stalin and Trotsky in literary criticism.

Malraux himself helped in the postwar evaluation of his novel. An anthology that was to replace Braunschvig for the students of the fifties, Gaëtan Picon's *Panorama de la nouvelle littérature française*, included (in French, of course) the following quotation from Malraux's *La Psychologie de l'art:* "A few years ago I told the story of a man who does not recognize his voice that has just been recorded because he hears it for the first time through his ear and no longer through his throat; and because our throat alone transmits our inner voice I called the book *La Condition humaine*."[11] It is hard to imagine a more graphic illustration of Sartre's notion of the "Other."

A new adjective, *tragic*, creeps into the commentaries on *Man's Fate* after the war. We find it used by two of the American pioneers of the new focus on Malraux: W. M. Frohock, at the time an assistant professor at Columbia, whose *André Malraux and the Tragic Imagination* was to appear in 1952, and Bert Leefmans, a graduate student of Professor Frohock, whose "Malraux and Tragedy: the structure of *La Condition humaine*" came out in the *Romanic Review* in 1953.

Actually, the word *tragic* was not completely new, and it seems appropriate to end this little glance at the thirties with a tribute to the one American critic I could find who, when *Man's Fate* first appeared in 1934, came closest to seeing it for what it was to become. The French writer Ernest Hello once said of the true critic that he "must be as accurate as posterity; he must speak in the present the words of the future."[12] John Chamberlain of the daily *New York Times* was just such a critic when he wrote: "Malraux may lack the marvelous invention of incident that one finds in Dostoevsky, he may lack the cosmic brooding of Joseph Conrad, but he has nevertheless something in common with these writers; he too sees man, the perpetual idealist, beating his head against the stars and falling into the mire. The perception of this as 'man's fate' is what endows his writing with the tragic sense of life."[13]

Notes

1. Stanley Hoffmann, "The Poignant Silence," *The New Republic*, December 18, 1976, p. 11.
2. Quoted in *Malraux: A Collection of Critical Essays*, ed. R. W. B. Lewis (Englewood Cliffs, N.J.: Prentice-Hall, 1964), p. 29.
3. "Revolutionists in a Novel of China," *Saturday Review of Literature*, June 30, 1934.
4. "Malraux and the Individual," *The Nation*, October 17, 1934, pp. 443-444.
5. "A Frenchman's Prize Novel of Chinese Revolt," *New York Times Sunday Book Review*, V, p. 1, June 24, 1934.
6. "Memoirs of a Trotskyist," *New York Times Magazine*, January 23, 1977, p. 43.
7. "André Malraux," *Partisan Review* (March 1938), pp. 49-50.
8. "Malraux's Best Novel," *The New Republic*, November 16, 1938, pp. 49-50.
9. (Winter 1940), p.46.
10. Quoted in Lewis, op. cit., p. 116.
11. Picon, *Panorama . . ., nouvelle édition revue et augmentée* (1951), p. 303.
12. Quoted by Apollinaire in *Apollinaire on Art* (New York: Viking, 1972), p. 419.
13. "Books of the Times," *New York Times*, June 25, 1934, p. 19.

"Essuie-Plume"—an ink sketch by Malraux

18

Malraux's *El Nacional* Interview

ROBERT S. THORNBERRY

Biographers and literary historians rely upon the press, among other sources, to provide information on a particular author or period. In the case of France, where the *moraliste* tradition is to this day still very strong, the writer often represents the conscience of his fellow countrymen by attempting to elucidate, in the form of interviews and newspaper articles, matters of immediate moral, social, or political concern. Frequently, the sum of these pieces constitutes a by no means insignificant part of an author's total literary output, for example, Bernanos's *Français, si vous saviez (1945-1948)* and Camus's *Actuelles* (1950, 1953, 1958) or Mauriac's wider-ranging *Bloc-Notes* (1958-1971, 7 vols.). Though sometimes quickly consigned to oblivion by the passing of time, they do testify to his preoccupation with the pertinent issues of his day. As such they are indeed an indispensable tool for those critics in search of details and insights that will ultimately—or so it is to be hoped—deepen one's appreciation or enhance one's understanding of a writer or period.

With Malraux, whose earliest incursions into journalism occurred in a remote corner of Frane's colonial empire, we have a significant case in point. The editorials that he wrote for *Indochine* and *Indochine Enchaînée* in 1925 and 1926 are interesting not only because they provide examples of a propensity for polemics that is seldom associated with him but, more importantly, because they record the early phases of the young author's awakening social and political consciousness. From that time until his death half a century later, Malraux contributed hundreds of articles and interviews to newspapers, magazines, and reviews in numerous countries throughout the world. This material, much of which is inaccessible, often reveals aspects of the man and his work that are either little known or undervalued.

Few periods in Malraux's many-sided career have been as fertile in this respect as the three years of his commitment to Spanish democracy: first, as commander of the International Air Force, which fought alongside the Spanish Air Force between August 1936 and February 1937; secondly, as spokesman for the Republican government during a lecture tour that took him to eight cities in North America in the late winter and early spring of 1937; thirdly, as a creative artist who transmuted these experiences into two major works: the novel *L'Espoir* (1937) and the film *Sierra de Teruel* (1938), later baptized *Espoir*. From 1936-1938 and particularly throughout his fund-raising visit to the United States and Canada, Malraux was willing to use the press as a weapon in the anti-Fascist struggle. As a result we find, in the *Literary Digest* and in *Collier's*, early versions of incidents that were to appear in a modified form in *L'Espoir* and also various interviews where Malraux recounted his own personal experiences and related them to the wider political and ideological conflicts of the time.

Though the major conflict of the 1930s was undoubtedly that which pitted democracy against totalitarianism, it would be a mistake to reduce the complex network of political struggles and intrigues, especially those of the left, to a single monolithic event. Popular Front strategy in both France and Spain dictated that the parties of the left and center should set aside their individual differences and unite in a common front against fascism. This uneasy alliance was relatively short-lived, and various factors soon emerged to emphasize its basically tenuous nature. In particular, Trotsky's incessant and well-documented indictment of Stalin's motivations in using the Popular Front served as a constant reminder of the many compromises involved. In addition, the insidious Moscow trials, whereby Stalin sought to incriminate Trotsky and his followers of conspiracy to undermine the Soviet state, were jarring evidence of something sinister within the Communist system. The fragile unity of the Popular Front was further strained when, in November 1936, André Gide, whose so-called "conversion" to communism had once been hailed as a major victory of the left, published *Retour de l'URSS*. This slim volume, primarily a series of impressions of a visit to the Soviet Union, represented a resounding volte-face on Gide's part. Not only were many of his observations critical, if not downright hostile, but he even went so far as to write: "Je doute qu'en aucun autre pays aujourd'hui, fût-ce dans l'Allemagne de Hitler, l'esprit soit moins libre, plus courbé, plus craintif (terrorisé), plus vassalisé."[1] (I doubt that in any other country today, even in Hitler's Germany, the mind is less free, more oppressed, more fearful (terrorized), more subservient.) This comparison threw segments of the left into utter disarray. As is evinced by the *El Nacional* interview of March 1937, Malraux, like so many others, nursed the hope that Gide would, in his announced sequel to *Retour de l'URSS*, qualify his denunciations of the Soviet Union and thereby render them useless to the enemies of the left.

The timing of Gide's book had been anything but propitious. With the gradual "defection" of the democracies under the guise of "nonintervention," the USSR became in late 1936 the only European power to supply arms and ammunition to the beleaguered Republic regularly. Furthermore, through the Comintern, it had inspired, and was in the process of organiziing, the International Brigades, which rapidly passed into legend. Consequently, many Republican sympathizers were prepared to ignore the internal situation as long as the Soviet Union continued to provide support for the people of Spain. Malraux, despite many serious reservations, which he examined at great length and with considerable subtlety in *L'Espoir*, was one of those who fell into this category. His reluctance to discuss these reservations during his stay in North America stems from his position as official spokesman for the Spanish government and from a decision not to involve himself in any dispute that would weaken his efforts to advance the Republican cause. In so doing, he refrained from full debate with the Trotskyists and anarchists who attended his speeches mainly to ask awkward questions about the Moscow trials and the fate of radical groups and parties in Spain. By the same token, he hardly ever broached these subjects in interviews given to American and Canadian reporters.

Almost all of these interviews, which appeared in *The New York Times*, *The New York World Telegram*, *The Sunday Worker*, *The Toronto Star*, *Le Devoir*, and *La Presse*, are available to Malraux scholars and readers.

Such is not the case, however, regarding an interview conducted in New York on March 1 by Ernesto Madero of *El Nacional*, one of Mexico City's largest daily newspapers. Published in that same newspaper exactly one week later (in Spanish, needless to say), it has never, until now, been translated into English. Though containing statements that had already appeared or that were later to appear almost verbatim in either the American or Canadian press, the *El Nacional* interview is mainly characterized by Malraux's relative lack of restraint in voicing his opinion on personalities —Blum and Trotsky—and events—the Moscow trials—that he was not otherwise willing to discuss quite so candidly.

Not that Malraux had been particularly eager to do so, especially as far as Russia was concerned. Nevertheless, when Madero insisted in pursuing the matter, Malraux's initial resistance disappeared and his answers were both direct and succinct. In a clear definition of his own political choice, he stresses the need to subordinate long-term objectives to the short-term goal of achieving victory in Spain, a priority that then led him to formulate one of the harshest criticisms he ever leveled at Trotsky. Attacking a whole category of individuals—and not only Trotsky whom he included among "unscrupulously futile critics"—he denounced their responsibility in "prevent[ing] the organisation of the people." Furthermore, he used the argument regularly advanced by *L'Humanité* and other orthodox communist publications that their behavior "favour[s] the aggression of international fascism."[2]

The interview was published in the March 8 issue of *El Nacional*. As Trotsky was living at that time in Coyoacán, just outside Mexico City, and Malraux must surely have known this, how could he not have heard of those passages that concerned him directly? That same day, he accused Malraux, in a vehemently worded indictment, of "issu[ing] an appeal to forget everything except the Spanish revolution" and of leaving Spain "for the purpose of conducting a campaign in the United States in defense of the judicial work of Stalin and Vyshinsky."[3] As a corrective to the *El Nacional* interview, Trotsky's accusations have a degree of credibility; without this frame of reference they would continue to appear as they must have done for forty years: utterly gratuitous.

This then is where the chief interest of the Mexican interview lies. Aside from brief references to Blum and Gide or possible evidence of mythomania, Malraux's dialogue with Madero offers a partial explanation as to why his once frank but cordial relationship with Trotsky degenerated so suddenly. From March 1937 until Trotsky's death in 1940, the polemic continued though, with the exception of a single article[4] by Malraux—not to mention *L'Espoir*—it was always on Trotsky's initiative. My translation of the "missing" interview, which follows, should contribute to a better understanding of a crucial stage in Malraux's political metamorphosis.

Notes

1. André Gide, *Retour de l'URSS* (Paris: Gallimard, 1950), p. 61.
2. See the English translation.
3. A shortened version of Trotsky's communiqué appeared in "Trotsky versus Malraux," *The Nation*, Vol. 144, No. 13, March 27, 1937, p. 351.
4. The article in question is Malraux's reply, which is dated March 13, to Trotsky's communiqué of March 8. It is also published in *The Nation*, March 27, 1937, p. 351.

MEXICO SHOWS THE WAY TO DEMOCRACY[1]

André Malraux, the Famous French Writer Speaks of This Country's Progress

What Has Been Achieved

Knows to What Extent Peasants and Workers Have Evolved under the Present Régime

"Neutrality"

Strongly Condemns the Policies Followed by Other Countries with Respect to Spain

by Ernesto Madero, exclusive interview for *El Nacional*

New York, March 1st—*The Daily Worker*, "champion of the people's rights and democratic freedoms" in the United States, announced André Malraux's arrival in New York.[2] I immediately tried to locate him and managed to contact him in the offices of *The Nation*, whose editorial board was preparing a private dinner in his honor.[3] After several hours of waiting, my interview with this extraordinary man was arranged; for 3:30, in the Mayflower Hotel.[4]

I showed up punctually at the appointed place.

—"Mr. Malraux left several hours ago and apparently will not be back," was the first distressing news.

I was about to leave when, on the table where my informant was working, I saw a note with my name on it. It said: "Mr. Malraux is expecting you at his publisher's offices on 57th Street." Without wasting a second, I went off to look for him, across Central Park, impressive and beautiful, covered in snow that fell endlessly and remorselessly.

Upon entering Random House I found another message, that I wait in a small room. I passed the time flicking through magnificent editions and looking at the portraits of many writers covering the walls. Among those present in this reception room were the faces of Thomas Mann, John Strachey, the famous dramatists Eugene O'Neill and Clifford Odets; Leane Zugsmith, Waldo Frank, Callagham [sic].

I was reading a few lines when a young woman, who looked like a private secretary, informed me that Mr. Malraux was asking for the reporter from Mexico. And, pencil at the ready—with an indefinable feeling of excitement—I had the honor of shaking the hand that wrote *Les Conquérants*. The first words were exchanged; a woman writer accompanying him volunteered to act as our interpreter; but Malraux amiably declined,[5] indicating his preference to be alone with me. When we were left by ourselves, we went and sat by the window overlooking the street. Twenty floors below, people were running for shelter from the heavy snowfall.

Leader of the Malraux Squadron

We sorted out the language problem and quickly arrived at an agreement. Malraux would answer in French and I would put my questions in English.

—"I was in Spain from five days[6] after the outbreak of the rebellion until three weeks ago.[7] Every day[8] in contact with the People's Army." Malraux, an excellent aviator,[9] organized the effective Malraux Squadron,[10] which has been fighting daily in defense of the Spanish Republic.

—"For reasons of a military nature, I cannot tell you"—he goes on in reply to my questions—"how many planes and pilots there are at our[11] disposal at the moment; but on innumerable[12] occasions, I flew as squadron leader, at the head of more than a dozen and a half aircraft in each line of our bomber formation.[13]

"Personally, in my six months' service as pilot, I brought down 44 enemy planes."[14]

As he speaks, Malraux continually stares at me with a searching look. His eyes, completely blue, convey the impression of not missing a single detail around him. He frequently smoothes his hair, which is entirely blond, fine, abundant and almost long. I watched him closely, even insignificant details. His speech was quick, sonorous and clear; his hands nervous and interesting; his French suit impeccable, but his shoes were heavy, like those of a miner.

The Development of Mexico

I mention a couple of things about Mexico.

—"I am perfectly aware how your country is developing," he states. "I am familiar with the Mexican government's policy, its tendencies and aspirations. In fact, I have followed its general evolution: problems solved, strikes, and complications.

"I do not speak"—he goes on—"in the usual fashion when one is interviewed by a representative of a foreign newspaper, and which forces people not only to make statements that are already known but also to give praise that is for the most part false. I speak with the complete sincerity of one who can say to all and sundry that Mexico was the first country to show the world how democracy must be defended."[15]

As Malraux stooped slightly to adjust the heating, the fine lines of his forehead became apparent to me. I felt proud, not just because I had the unforgettable experience of talking with him in confidence, but at hearing the author of *La Condition humaine*—is it redundant to say the author of genius?—speak in such terms of my country.

We prolong the conversation about Mexico. I realize that he is perfectly aware how President Cárdenas[16] redistributed the land among its legitimate owners, the peasants; he comments on the extent of worker organization with mathematical precision; and, raising his voice, he emphasizes Mexico's intelligent and tireless efforts toward economic emancipation from imperialism.

The Question of Spain

Malraux, like all men who share an idealistic view of the world,[17] focuses on the creative strength of Mexican intellectuals, by revealing his own personal conviction:

—"I truly believe that the recent congress of the LEAR[18] was one of the firmest statements you have made. It is certain that efforts to convene the Continental Congress shortly will have a definitive outcome. And I would say that this chapter in the creative activity of Mexican intellectuals is fundamental, because it is of greater importance than a congress of intellectuals in the USSR. In the Soviet Union it would represent one more, normal step in the life of the country; in Mexico, it has the full value of a vigorous awakening of an entire continent, which, in itself, is a forceful event.

"I shall not be able to attend that meeting, because I have to return to Spain. I know ahead of time how fruitful the successful realization of the conference you have in preparation will be."

The conversation returns to Spain. I inquire, insistently, about "neutrality," the League of Nations, the Nonintervention Committee, and so on.

"Léon Blum, following the unmistakable path of Social Democracy, has naturally fallen into the most cowardly of betrayals;[19] and I say this with the argument I hold as a revolutionary who is unable to depart from a dialectical view of life or from the honest application of historical materialism."[20]

André Malraux measures my words carefully and then speaks after a short pause.

The Role of France

—"In view of what has already been said about neutrality—France, England, the United States—I have nothing more to add. However, I must state most categorically that, had France helped the Spanish government immediately after Franco initiated the military coup, in less than three months the power of the Popular Front government would have been consolidated throughout the peninsula.[21] But we didn't have rifles or planes or cartridges.

"In July of last year, Franco's troops did not amount to 14,000 men,[22] including soldiers and Moors, whereas the Madrid government could have raised more than a half million militiamen in a matter of days. Even now, if Germany and Italy were to send a half a million soldiers, they would lose the battle, because the government in Valencia[23] has the necessary war materials."[24]

On several occasions I endeavor to make him talk about Trotsky.

—"We would have to define who is Trotsky, the Trotskyists and Trotskyism..."

—"Trotsky?" I interrupted, "but everyone knows who he is."

—" . . . and to do so for each country," he continued without hearing me. "Which would be a useless waste of time."[25]

—"But Trotsky has been declaring that the USSR has not really helped Spain. And he holds the government of the Soviet Union criminally responsible as the direct cause of the Spanish workers' failure to gain power.[26] Trotskyism . . ."

His Impression of the USSR

Malraux objects:

—"You are too insistent, as I see from the tenacity of your questions, on my talking about Trotsky, Trotskyism in Russia, the Moscow Trials,[27] and the Soviet Constitution. In this regard I wish to tell you that the fate of mankind is at present at stake in Spain and that we should all set matters of opinion and argument[28] to one side, so as to devote ourselves wholeheartedly to defending and assisting the Spanish people. It is almost criminal to waste hours, entire months, speculating upon matters that should be left until later: not because they are devoid of interest, but because we must urgently surrender our lives in support of Spain, at a time when the blood of her children is being shed in a titanic struggle against the most barbaric and inhuman forces.

"We would not deserve to go on living, were we to abandon the struggle: the armed struggle in Spain, as well as that directly engaged against those who are trying to prevent peoples from uniting. It is necessary to put a stop to those unscrupulously futile critics[29] who prevent the organization of the people and thereby favor the aggression of international fascism.

"With respect to the USSR, I shall mention very briefly that I was there[30] only before the Constitution, bitterly opposed by reactionary elements, was approved. The Constitution entails the historical substitution of the Dictatorship of the Proletariat by a constitutional regime hitherto unknown. History, like the very life of a nation, cannot be measured in millimeters; consequently, it is not possible for the Soviet Union to emerge from one period or stage and enter upon another overnight. It is, however, obviously true that the present Constitution is a firm expression of the triumph of socialism and the only true Democracy."

Malraux's way of speaking is overwhelming; his gestures and mannerisms are always precise. While going over the international situation, I mention France and hear him respond in the following words:

The Return of Gide

—"Well now, everyone is aware of what would happen in France should the Fascists—and of course that day will never come—take over Spain. In France, at this very moment, a powerful coalition consisting of the Communist and Socialist Parties and, in general, of all those whose political beliefs transcend party lines,[31] is being formed to fight for national defense. This new, superior alliance will comprise many millions of people and will undoubtedly be a bulwark of liberty."

"And *Retour de l'URSS* by André Gide?"[32]

Malraux looks at me perplexingly, with an inscrutable smile. (Basically a very eloquent one, in my opinion.) He answers evasively:

—"I know that Gide is rapidly preparing another book. I do not know what tone it will have. I will hope he publishes it.[33] At any rate, I do not have to say that of all writers, I shall always maintain the position befitting the intellectual who has never veered from his purpose. I do not wish to talk about André Gide."[34]

Guessing that he was probably working on something, on account of the papers he had had to leave in order to receive me, I venture:

—"Are you writing anything?"

—"Yes. Something on Spain. It will have the intimacy and philosophical orientation of *La Condition humaine*."[35]

Time to relax. We exchange looks, smiling, halfway across the room. Once I have obtained his autograph and picture, he cordially places his hand upon my shoulder: "I hope we shall soon meet in Spain. What a business!" he exclaims.

We shake hands. I leave with a magnificent copy of *Man's Fate*, containing a kindly dedication that is more expressive and longer than I had anticipated.

Impression of the Thinker

I can still hear the echo of André Malraux's voice, talking about the tragedy of Spain; our Spain, which international fascism has destroyed; the Spain that belongs to mankind and that barbarism tries to carry off. Unique Spain—fertile cradle of genius, of Cervantes and García Lorca—[36] which will rise on the ruins of this hecatomb to attain even greater and more exemplary heights . . .

As I went through Central Park, my feet sank into the snow. André Malraux, a man barely thirty-five years old, one of the greatest philosophers of our time, a thinker whose genius and greatness will endure forever, remained silently at the window.

A biting cold numbs my muscles until I arrive at the house of Liza Kraitz, a generous and self-effacing friend in whose helpful company these modest columns were written. In four hours' time, I shall be crossing the Atlantic on my way to Spain.[37]

Notes to the Translation

1. *El Nacional: Diario Popular* (Mexico City), Año VIII, Tomo XV, Núm. 2824 (2ª Epoca), 8 de marzo de 1937, pp. 1, 3, 4.

2. On February 25, 1937, the official organ of the Communist Party of America, *The Daily Worker* (Vol. XIV, No. 48, p. 1), announced that André Malraux had arrived the previous evening in New York, where he was greeted by Louis Fischer, correspondent for *The Nation*, and Marcel Acier of the American Writers' Union. In an earlier article published on February 19, *The Daily Worker* (No. 43, p. 1) had quoted a brief UP release to the effect that the entry ban on Malraux, who was to begin his visit in January, had been lifted by the State Department. Of the numerous newspapers reporting his tour of the US, *The Daily Worker* provided the most extensive coverage.

3. On February 26, a few days prior to meeting Ernesto Madero, Malraux had already addressed a small group of intellectuals at a private dinner given in his honor by the editorial board of *The Nation*. A revised version of his speech appeared in that same review on March 20 (Vol. 144, pp. 315-316) under the title "Forging Man's Fate in Spain." *The Nation*'s Spanish correspondent, Louis Fischer, another guest of honor, recalled the occasion several years later in *Men and Politics:* "[Malraux] delivered a beautifully poetic speech. I had preceded him with a factual address outlining the history and background of the Spanish conflict" (New York: Duell, Sloan & Pearce, 1941), p. 413.

4. On March 3, 1937, Malraux gave a press conference at the Mayflower Hotel. For details see *The New York Times*, March 4, 1937, p. 25.

5. If Malraux had not dispensed with the services of an interpreter, it is possible that some of the difficulties alluded to in the following notes would not have arisen.

6. Most accounts of Malraux and Spain (Hoffmann, Frohock, Marion, and so on) agree that he landed in Madrid two days after the military uprising of July 18, 1936. Furthermore, in a letter dated July 17, 1970, Malraux informed me that he had arrived there "le surlendemain" of the Fascist rebellion. In fact, as Walter Langlois has shown, the first of Malraux's two visits to Madrid in July 1936 was a short one— only 24 hours— and it is the second one that is of greater significance ("Aux sources de *L'Espoir*," *André Malraux 2*, "Visages du romancier," Nos. 355-359, 1973(5), pp. 93-133).

7. The last major offensive in which Malraux's volunteer air force participated took place in the southern sector immediately after the fall of Malaga on February 8, 1937. It involved protecting Republicans, fleeing along the coast road from Malaga to Almeria, from repeated strafings by Italian fighter planes. For a full account of this and other incidents involving the International Air Force, see Robert S. Thornberry, *André Malraux et l'Espagne* (Genève: Droz, 1977), Ch. I.

8. This is not to be taken literally for Malraux's many activities on behalf of the Spanish Republic, particularly his efforts to purchase arms and ammunition involved travel in other countries.

9. Had the *El Nacional* interview not remained in oblivion for some forty years, one could see here the genesis of the myth of Malraux-pilot. Though Malraux was commander of the International Air Force, he was, of course, not a pilot. The missions were organized by a professional pilot, Abel Guides, and coordinated with the Republican Air Force by Captain Martín-Luna. See *André Malraux et l'Espagne*, pp. 38-39.

10. Originally called the Escadre or Escadrille España, it was renamed the Escadrille André Malraux (or Escadre Antifasciste Malraux) in early November 1936, both to mark the departure of the mercenaries and in honor of Malraux's leadership. See Julien Segnaire's article, "L'Escadrille 'André Malraux,' *Magazine Littéraire*, No. 11, October 1967, p. 16.

11. It is likely that "our" refers here—and despite the context—to the Republican Forces at large, and not to the International Air Force, which had been, to all intents and purposes, disbanded in mid-February 1937, just prior to Malraux's departure for North America. Nevertheless, one can read in *The Literary Digest* that "casualities and desertions [have] caused the unit to fluctuate in numbers from 250 to as low as five. At the present time, the squadron averages sixty members" ("André Malraux Seeks Aid for Loyal Air Corps," April 3, 1937, pp. 15-16).

12. "Innumerable"—numerous would be the *mot juste*—is either an exaggeration on Malraux's part or a misunderstanding on the part of Madero. Sixty-five is the most commonly accepted figure for the number of missions flown by Malraux, although there is no documentary evidence to substantiate this. The statement, "I flew as squadron leader" is ambiguous, for it suggests Malraux was pilot in command. In the Montreal newspaper *La Presse* he is quoted as saying; "En tant que commandant de l'escadrille, je ne combats point dans les airs" (As commander of the squadron, I am not involved in air combat) (5 avril 1937, p. 5).

13. According to interviews that I conducted in 1970 with Julien Segnaire, political commissar of the Escadrille André Malraux, and with other survivors, the International Air Force never had more than six planes at any given time. The figure eighteen may be explained as a reference to missions carried out in conjunction with other

squadrons, but in that case there would be even less likelihood of Malraux flying as "squadron leader."

14. Undoubtedly, this is the most bewildering sentence in the whole interview. Can it be attributed to confusion on the part of Madero (who never queried how the author of *Les Conquérants* could have accomplished such a feat) brought about in part, or at least aggravated, by the language barrier? Or is it an example of Malraux's "mythomania"? It is most curious that not even Trotsky should have noted the singularity of Malraux's "claim," which, could it be substantiated, would make of him the most fearful ace on either side. See Jesús Salas, *La guerra de España desde el aire* (Barcelona: Ediciones Ariel, 1969, pp. 459-462) for a breakdown of air victories on the Nationalist side. The leading pilot, Joaquín García Morato, who flew throughout the entire war, is credited with forty victories.

15. A reference to the Mexican government's open support of Republican Spain. In September 1939 the president announced that 20,000 rifles and 20 million rounds of ammunition had been sent to the Spanish government.

16. Lázaro Cárdenas (1895-1970) was president of Mexico from 1934 to 1940, a period characterized by the implementation of socialist policies that, in addition to those mentioned by Malraux, included the expropriation of foreign petroleum interests.

17. The Spanish text reads here: "Malraux, como todo hombre de trascendente concepción universal . . ."

18. This could refer either to a Liga de Escritores y Artistas Revolucionarios, whose aims would presumably resemble those of the Association des Ecrivains et Artistes Revolutionnaires, a Communist-inspired coalition of intellectuals whose main concern was to help stem the rising tide of fascism in Europe. Alternatively, in view of Malraux's reference to a "Continental Congress" symbolizing the "vigorous awakening of an entire continent," it could mean "Liga de escritores americanos revolucionarios."

19. As Malraux was *actively* opposed to fascism, his antipathy to the defeatism of the Nonintervention Treaty is understandable. What is noteworthy here is his harsh criticism of Socialist Premier Léon Blum.

20. An equivocal statement when one recalls that Malraux, despite his acceptance of certain Communist policies, never subscribed to the "dialectical view of life" or the "honest application of historical materialism." In fact, many of his articles and speeches of the 1930s are distinctly anti-Marxist. See in particular "L'art est une conquête," *Commune*, Nos. 13-14, septembre-octobre 1934, pp. 68-71.

21. Given that the military uprising failed in several major industrial centers or areas—Madrid, Barcelona, Valencia, and important sections of the Basque provinces— this is a reasonable hypothesis. Had the Popular Front government of France provided military assistance during the early weeks of the war, there is a distinct possibility that Franco would have lost within a matter of months. It was primarily the responsibilities of the major democracies, Great Britain and France, and to a lesser extent, because of distance, the United States, to come to the aid of another democracy. The subsequent involvement of the Soviet Union south of the Pyrenees was a direct result of the democracies' vacillation over the Spanish question.

22. This figure is very definitely wrong. Hugh Thomas writes: "The total of men under arms in 1936 was, on paper, just over 100,000 in the Peninsula and 30,000 in Morocco, together with 33,000 civil guards, 14,000 carabineers and 18,000 assault guards." Furthermore, he specifies that the army of Africa, some 30,000 men, was wholly with Franco. *The Spanish Civil War* (Harmondsworth: Penguin Books, 1977). See in particular "Rising and Revolution," Ch. 19, pp. 330-331.

23. In early November 1936, the government of Largo Caballero decided to leave Madrid for Valencia on the grounds that administration could not be carried on in a war zone (Thomas, *The Spanish Civil War*, p. 475).

24. When Giral decided on July 19 to arm the people, the government might have had approximately half a million militiamen. But, as Malraux has pointed out in "L'Illusion lyrique" (Part 1 of *L'Espoir*), numerical superiority combined with revolutionary fervor are not in themselves sufficient to combat highly trained and disciplined professional troops.

25. At one and the same time an example of evasiveness and political astuteness. Malraux was evidently reluctant to answer questions on the Russian revolutionary, but

he was also shrewd in insinuating that some of the groups calling themselves Trotskyists were in many instances quite far removed from the ideas and theories that Trotsky himself had carefully worked out in his political writings.

26. At that time the central thesis of the Stalinists was that the social and political revolution be made subordinate to the necessity of winning the war. While giving the impression of supporting a bourgeois democracy against the encroachments of fascism, the USSR took advantage of the chaos to eliminate those dissident groups on the left, specifically the anarchists and Trotskyists, that threatened Stalinist domination. Trotsky, on the other hand, insisted that the war against fascism and the revolution were part and parcel of the same process and that they must be waged simultaneously.

27. Though Madero had not referred to the Moscow Trials, it was obvious that his questions were leading in this direction.

28. The Spanish here reads: "cosas de juicio y discusión."

29. The Spanish here has: "los disolventes sin escrūpulo."

30. A reference to Malraux's visit to the Soviet Union in the summer of 1934 as a speaker at the First Congress of Soviet Writers.

31. The Spanish here reads: "fuerzas de trascendencia." literally, "forces of transcendence." A probable reference to the Popular Front's continuing efforts to unify all parties and individuals of the center and left against fascism.

32. See my introduction.

33. The "other book" would be *Retouches à mon "Retour de l'URSS,"* published in June 1937, in which Gide did anything but recant: "L'URSS n'est pas ce que nous espérions qu'elle serait, ce qu'elle avait promis d'être, ce qu'elle s'efforce encore de paraître; elle a trahi tous nos espoirs. Si nous n'acceptons pas que ceux-ci retombent, il faut les reporter ailleurs" (The USSR is not what we hoped it would be, or what it had promised to be, or even what it is still trying to appear to be; it has betrayed all our hopes. If we refuse to let these hopes be dashed, we must place them elsewhere.) (Paris: Gallimard, 1950, p. 174).

34. Several days after talking to the *El Nacional* reporter, Malraux expressed similar reservations when Edwin Seaver of *The Daily Worker* asked the same questions: "It was too soon for anyone to venture any final statement about Gide's book. Too soon, because Gide is now working on a new book, which is to be devoted to a "reconsideration of what he wrote when he returned from the USSR. Let us wait and read what Gide has to say further before we attempt any rash judgments" (March 9, 1937, p. 9). And years later, during a conversation with Roger Stéphane, Malraux said he objected not to what Gide had said, but rather to the timing of the book's publication and to Gide's inability to see how it would be used against the Popular Front: "Gide a eu tort de ne pas y inclure des critiques ou des approbations qui l'eussent rendu inutilisable par les capitalistes, qui auraient empêché M. de Wendel d'en acheter cent mille exemplaires." (Gide was wrong not to include criticism or praise that would have made it incapable of being exploited by the capitalists, that would have prevented M. de Wendel from purchasing one hundred thousand copies.) (Roger Stéphane, *Fin d'une jeunesse*. Paris: La Table Ronde, 1954, p. 60).

35. When F. W. Dupee asked exactly the same question, Malraux replied: "Yes, about Spain. It will have the intimacy and philosophical quality of *Man's Fate.*" Interview conducted in New York and reprinted in *The Daily Clarion* (Toronto), April 1, 1937, p. 4.

36. This lyrical invocation of Spanish civilization is not without political undercurrent: Cervantes was an example of the writer-warrior, and Lorca was one of the first victims of Spanish fascism.

37. I would like to thank Dr. Richard Young for clarifying parts of this interview and for generously helping me with many finer points of the translations.

PART 6

TEXTS AND DOCUMENTS

19

"Professions délirantes" from Malraux's *L'Homme précaire et la littérature*

JEAN HYTIER
TRANSLATED BY JEANINE PARISIER PLOTTEL

Writers of Valéry's generation voiced strong reservations about Flaubert's works. Some of them were exceedingly harsh. Only one exception can be cited—a professional critic, a truly remarkable one, the richest in ideas since Sainte-Beuve: Thibaudet. Suarès, for example, who was himself bitterly frustrated but quite able to recognize his victim's accomplishments, nevertheless devoted an entire essay to disparaging him, with the title: "Pour en finir avec Flaubert." There is no end to Flaubert; and that is indeed the best evidence of his greatness.

In the course of these last thirty years, an extraordinary renewal of interest has manifested itself with heretofore unequaled force; such recognition has been ceaselessly asserted not only by scholars and historians but also by creative interpreters. There has been, and still is, Flaubert criticism of admirable wealth and insight. Among its representatives (and I beg forgiveness for any omissions): Jean Seznec, Georges Poulet, Marie-Jeanne Durry, Jean-Pierre Richard, Erich Auerbach, John C. Lapp, Raymond Giraud, Alison Fairlie, Jean Bruneau, Jean Rousset, Harry Levin, Nathalie Sarraute, Jean-Paul Sartre, Victor Brombert, Claudine Gothat-Mersh, and Enid Starkie.

The pages of Malraux devoted to Flaubert in his last book, *L'Homme précaire et la littérature*, published shortly before his death, especially the chapter "Professions délirantes" (an expression borrowed from Valéry, who so designated literature; but we may be allowed to believe the allusion was also to any activity involving flights of imagination: teaching, law, and medicine fall within its scope)—these pages are so eloquent and exalted that they constitute a conclusion to the magnificent effort of continuous reinterpretation and rediscovery we have witnessed. Yes, of course: a current and provisional conclusion, consistent with Malraux's own most intimate thinking, but nevertheless and at the same time a *durable* one. Because, indeed, we know that Malraux used Flaubert in the same way he used other hallowed names: as an illustration of his fundamental thesis about metamorphosis.

It is quite certain—but nobody before him made the point as forcibly—that we project our acquired culture unto notable surviving works of the past and unto the present creations that seduce us. For example, the various debates about pure poetry allowed a different appraisal of Racine's verses. It was Malraux's global and cavalier view upon the ever-changing panorama of art and letters that conferred originality to his perspective, and that accounts for its human, aesthetic, and metaphysical resonance. While bewitching his reader by his affirmative and enigmatic style, he often noted observations that revealed the heart of a text. Casts of lead and flashes of lightning characterized his manner. But by choosing to dominate overall views and to exemplify the perpetual enrichment of our artistic treasure, he granted the illusion of escaping our destiny for a moment and of acceding to the divine. Then, without entangling himself in details, Malraux considered the masterpieces of literature, transformed by the grace of our "inner library," with the same eye that had contemplated *monuments*.

"Professions délirantes"

from

André Malraux's

"L'Homme précaire et la littérature"

translated by

Jeanine Parisier Plottel

as

"Flaubert: The Writer's Library"

Flaubert lived with his library the way Victor Hugo lived with Juliette Drouet. Sometimes his library was material he read or reread for his own work-in-progress; sometimes it was an Olympus. The point was not consulting books but engaging in a dialogue with a superhumanity. Great dead men didn't really fool him. His superlatives fitted works rather than men. He didn't confuse Frédéric Lemaître with Ruy Blas, whom he admired. However, French classicism willingly confronted the library with the level of civilization expressed by Racine; Flaubert unwillingly confronted life with Homer and Cervantes

When writing *Salammbô*, he did not judge his characters, who are never real characters. He expected a sequence of poetic moments from his book, just as he expected visions from the first *Tentation de Saint Antoine*. History overflowed with extraordinary minutes.

But when dreaming about Cleopatra's galleys, he didn't compare them to Croisset's barges; when dreaming about Cervantes, Flaubert couldn't help comparing him to Charles Bovary. Did he always do this? He always had Olympus pass judgment on Yonville. Because he was not so much a novelist as an avenger (of what?), this generous man, drunk with admiration, found that contempt was the only basis for his contemporaneous characters. Guilty of creating Homais, he reestablished justice by creating Bournisien.

At the time of *Madame Bovary*, he noted with sadness that "all one's characters should be liked equally well"; years later, he wrote with bitterness about the characters he planned for the future: "And because I am fair, I will fling them all in the same mud." A justice whose fair-mindedness did not weigh lightly in the conflict between naturalism and romanticism. The former postulated an average humanity and had faith in such a humanity, but Flaubert's own belief lasted only while he wrote modern novels. Was it easy to create fifty characters without a single "positive" character, and to do this almost without any awareness? He was so intoxicated by his dialogue with the written work that the work begun with a dictionary of heresies preying upon Saint Anthony ended with the library preying upon Saint Bouvard: he would copy it! The powerful virus other writers find in satire was found by Flaubert in disparagement and belittling, . . . at a mysterious level, however. The first French novelist to experience the absurdity of man's fate, he found his experience determined by the world of writing at the root of his mockery rather than by death itself. Such, I believe, was the thing he called art. The Promised Land—salvation.

Not only was the sarcasm in *Madame Bovary* and in *L'Education sentimentale* ignored by each and every critic, but for naturalists the latter novel became the bible of objectivity. Now we may plead the case for *Madame Bovary*'s objectivity. Even Homais lacked a scientific ellipsis of the type: "Bouvard did not even believe in matter." But if we were to compare *L'Education sentimentale* with its first unpublished version, finished ten years before *Madame Bovary*, we would understand what he expected from the style of his modern novels, expectations that can be found only there.

The profound difference, in spite of style's continuity, between *Madame Bovary* and *Salammbô*, was due not only to the substitution of archaeology for observation. The sustained style—none of his disciples would discover an equivalent one—when applied to Yonville's trivia, gave it the same sarcastic dimension that the bellow of cattle gave Rodolphe's and Emma's amorous dialogue. Style inverts the mechanism; derision results from the gods, not from the calves. The speeches of the cattle show were haltingly stammered in front of Shakespeare, in front of the entire Flaubert internal library. Perhaps here we grasp what allowed him to exhaust himself with Charles Bovary as much as with the crucified lions, and we also grasp what conferred to the heartbreaking universe of his greatest works the background legitimizing his passion for Cervantes. The empirical domain of his values was steady for the same reason that it was vague. His occasionally secretive works had as their author a being who seemed unambiguous. On the margins of universal absurdity, a domain of salvation spread itself out, the only true domain in the religious sense of the word. Gustave was sick, too bad. He could save his niece only by ruining himself, and so

Malraux at Verrières

Malraux with Hemingway (left) and Robert Haas of Random House, 1934

he ruined himself. Cut *Madame Bovary?* Young Maxime De Camp could go f— himself! He didn't like Stendhal and said so. Did any other writer ever write a book about a saint, a book in which Christ was shown only to get it done and over with? The only meaning to be found in the world was in *Saint Antoine*'s succession of scenes and in the days of Frédéric Moreau. Clouds adrift.... Only oratory *existed*, a house of books. Everything would be simple if he were to write *Salammbô* all his life, if he were to become Théophile Gautier's successor. But Gautier wrote neither *Bouvard* nor the *Correspondance.* Neither did Leconte de Lisle. How could this priest of art-for-lack-of-anything-better be changed into an operatic engraver, into a loudmouthed Cellini? Might his genius escape from the enigmatic world of books?

He was its prisoner.

One day, the word *bourgeois,* to which artists gave the meaning "enemy of art," would also simultaneously take on the meaning "enemy of the people," and then, "enemy of the proletariat." The principle was derived whereby damned geniuses gave their greatness unto poverty, and poverty placed its ghastly seriousness in front of Monsieur Prudhomme. But before *bourgeois* took on the implications that are now so familiar to us, before the Commune, Flaubert's character had already evolved from caricature to myth. In Henri Monnier's works, Monsieur Prudhomme wasn't even a man of property. But Monnier's meticulous scenes showed better than anything else the extent to which Flaubert's conception of the Bourgeois was symmetrical to his notion of the wretchedness of the artist and aggrandized by the same Manichaeism. The fullness and breadth Flaubert gave him was unattained by Chatterton in Vigny and was always yearned for by Romanticism; such a Bourgeois was more mythical than Jean Valjean. Even than Don Quixote, because it was an imaginary creation, not a type: a fabulous gargoyle, just as Perceval was an unreal knight, just as unreal as the *Mona Lisa.* Flaubert's characters reflected the fantastic with impassive jubilation; but because he knew such incarnation was impossible, he carefully refused to actualize it. The Bourgeois went beyond "les deux bonhommes" in the same way that Don Juan went beyond Werther. When Don Juan became the Molière Don Juan, the mythic dimension no longer protected him. The same was true for the Bourgeois when he became the Bourgeois of the *Correspondance:* he then revealed the common denominator of the ill-assorted guises or appearances. It turned out to be—who would have believed it?—a hatred of values preserved by the house of books.

By dint of opposition, the Bourgeois emphasized aspects that were barely perceptible: sometimes the quality of emulation and always the value of make-believe. The stress was on the subordination of ethics to aesthetics—providing it be underlined that Flaubert refused to be an aesthete or a well-lettered man in the Goncourt-Chinese sense; he possessed neither paintings nor precious objects. Fancy's helmet, which placed him opposite the Bourgeois's forepart, also indirectly placed him opposite the Bichons, who suspected something was up; the library was saved, not victorious—at best, the trap where universal absurdity would *perhaps* be caught. The next game was at stake rather than posterity or genius, and along with it fraternity and its mediators against fancy in a frock coat where Foolishness was conjugated with nothingness. Like groupings in antiquity, where some Neptune at the limit of his strength subdued two Atlantises for centuries to come, Daumier's Flaubert would chase these two jeering silhouettes beset by a shadowy nation. The constant, profound, and involuntary defiance of reality by the inner library of the master of French realism stood unrivaled. Only once was the true stake unveiled, and we understand why he could find solace only in reading and in friendship from companions-in-chains. Readers have always felt Flaubert's duality; it was first attributed to the decor. In fact, the opposition of Emma Bovary to Salammbô, a figurine whose importance was totally lacking, hardly expressed this duality. It was embodied rather by the contrast between Charles Bovary and the curt Dr. Larivière, marionettes for their disconsolate creator. All of Yonville summoned an incurable appeal to the dignity of man—a word Flaubert never used. Do we need it in order to understand the lugubrious complaint sweeping through the *Correspondance* and covering the last part: "My heart is filled with corpses like an old cemetery"?

It is natural for biographies to be attached to the picturesque. Flaubert's type of picturesque, as we imagine it from his letters and his friends, was Rabelaisian. Recollections of *le Garçon*, vivid style of the bachelor and eternal student. But aren't we giving too much importance to hoaxes and to the Goncourts' nasty gossip? Should we thus belittle a man about whom Gide said: "His *Correspondance* was my Bible," a correspondence containing the story of the death of his friend Le Poittevin, a story that Gourmont, hardly given to sentimentality, felt should be read kneeling. At the depth of sadness, face-to-face with death, he contrived to nickname himself Saint Polycarp. I am afraid that he called himself Saint Polycarp all his life: his sallies and paradoxes were related to Gautier. Gautier, however, found his best work in himself. But if we freed Flaubert from his chechia, from his heinormous *[sic]* stories, from his puppets—untarnished by the passing of a century—and from the monstrous myth that reigned over them like a Mephistophelian friend of Pécuchet, we would find a grief for the pettiness of the living, a piety for the unexplained nobleness of man, that are quite foreign to *le Garçon*. If we had to choose the noblest form of a French writer of that period, can we be absolutely certain that the Flaubert of silence would be unworthy of our choice? Silence and secrecy surfaced unawares when he wrote about the furtive servant honored at the end of the agricultural fair of *Madame Bovary:* "Thus, this half-century of servitude posed for the bourgeois in full bloom."

None of his works hid such nostalgia more harshly than *Bouvard/et Pécuchet.* The book was cherished by the members of the Flaubert Club and excited not only admiration for a master but also collusions, a taste for Saint Polycarp, and recollections of *le Garçon;* from the time of Thibaudet and Gourmont, communion has been celebrated through the most gripping hoax of our literature, and we have exalted a super-Flaubert, an essential Flaubert.

It is one of our few enigmatic books. Flaubert worked hard at a meticulous trompe l'oeil, not in order to paint coccinellas on a daisy, but in order to imitate a litho, a monochrome caricature. And it was the caricature rather than the illusion that gave rise to caution. Caricature of what?

"Their stupidity fascinates me," he wrote. The fascination is beyond doubt. But the stupidity? That of the two "bonhommes"? What for? Why did he infallibly destroy the realist illusion he sought? As would be expected, critics concentrated on complacency. From the very beginning of his task, Flaubert was conscious of its improbabilities and felt constrained to the point where what had been conceived as a drawing (or so he claimed from time to time) was executed as a caricature. No matter. The two heroes are obviously booby-trap heroes, masks of themselves. Bouvard is disguised as Bouvard.

Les Deux copistes, an insignificant novella read thirty-five years earlier, was sought out as the origin of Bouvard. One might as well seek the source of *Ubu* in the chronicles of the Polish kings. By specifying what can't be specified, realism complicated the issue. *Bouvard* came from further back, from the Jacquemart, from the eternal couple: Don Quixote and Sancho, Footit and Chocolat—archetypal like the little tramp and the colossal policeman. The book superposed the narrative thread of a chronicle of events upon alleged satire about two fellows, neither being the book's actual theme or subject. Stupidity remains? Complaining made Flaubert happy, and he reluctantly became aware of having committed himself to an adventure; beyond stupidity, the elusiveness of his book fascinated him just as the elusiveness of *Un coup de dés* . . . later fascinated Mallarmé. His jokes allow us to forget what a lucid writer he was . . . out of the ordinary. He cultivated the absolute originality of his gropings. This chapter-outline maniac discovered the wild beast he had always seen only in a cage. He dreamed about a book "without any subject whatsoever, a book that would hold together only through the power of style itself." It was not this book he wrote, but its cousin. After Bouilhet died, he continued his somnambulant monologue alone. The less he understood what he was doing (and yet, he controlled it), the more he knew himself capable of doing it and the more he became his own accomplice and subordinated sarcasm to the aberrant masterpiece whose key was unknown to him.

Would the Jacquemart, the virulence of works apparently written for marionettes—who, to our great surprise, act them out so badly: Ubu Don

Malraux and Gide, 1934

Malraux, Gorki, and Koltzov in the USSR, 1934

Quixote, Bouvard—separate his last novel from its predecessors? Flaubert wrote the *Trois Contes* as a distraction. Even *Un coeur simple*? Why did the "Bouvardists," who were after all careful "Flaubertians," remain deaf to the summons served them by Flaubert's paralyzed genius by means of Bouvard's and Félicité's hopeless dialogue? He didn't contrast Félicité with Bouvard. In the face of humanity redeemed by books, human stupidity is invulnerable. Not necessarily a specific type of stupidity: man's condition in the century. But the impotence of *Un coeur simple*, of *Saint Julien*, exclamations of ineffectual and desperate revenge, portends that we should acknowledge that Flaubert's creation was equivalent to *La Comédie humaine:* his two tales also attempted to exorcise the *mythic* Bourgeois through whom, beyond any and all Bouvards, the absurdity of the world incarnated.

Bouvard was perhaps predestined to this incompletion of ruins, which suits it so well, and perhaps we were never meant to be sure what it was the two friends were supposed to have copied out in the last chapter. But suppose Flaubert had died a few years later than he did. Once the "bonhommes" had been dismissed, he had resolved to pounce upon a fourth tale: *Léonidas aux Thermopyles,* as he had pounced upon *Saint Julien*. He had, therefore, chosen Sparta; neither Renan's Attica nor the Greece of Atreus that had again become mysterious. The city without any arts, of course. Whistling of Persian arrows, clear uproar of spears against shields, a tricolor morning world against an overdressed *Hérodias,* motionless flight of eagles to the Phedriades. The accent that attuned Flaubert to the Doric might have made it a dazzling work (the success of *Trois Contes* had equaled the *Education sentimentale*'s failure). "It will be squat!" With what joy he would have translated again: *"You who pass by, go tell Lacedaemon—That those who fell here died according to its law. . . ."*

But beyond the Spartan sacrifices, the invincible unreality of the two scribes would again have met M. Homais and his colleagues, and these sacrifices would have been as empty and vain as Julien's faith and Félicité's devotion.

An extreme case. Its secret dialogue reveals the creation of fiction and the creation of the library, but, usually, the former works more simply and more rigorously.

Was Bouvard a rabid accusation, by survivors, of absurd living beings? Why did the dialogue between Sparta and the grotesque come to be ensconced by two fools; and the problem of Evil, by the Karamazovs? The true Saint Antoine found refuge in *La Thébaïde,* not in detective novels, no matter how full of genius these might be. Why did the mind of a Crusade preacher come to be incarnated in the fancy of fiction in the case of a Dostoyevsky and a Tolstoy? The sacred text alone could provide a foundation for Dostoyevsky's thought. He used his fantasies to make up characters and not to make himself a starets or to shout his convictions along highways. In the same library where he found the Apocalypse and the works of the Orthodox Fathers, he also found Gogol. The Gogol of *Dead Souls* and of *Revizor*.

The fantasy world of the theater does not command his attention. He found another kind of fantasy in *Dead Souls;* in Balzac, whom he translated; in Dickens, whom he loved; in Flaubert, perhaps. A fantasy that was shaped little by little as the theatrical one had been; this amateur belonged to the species of late bloomers. But the captivating slowness of the novel was much more essential for Flaubert's genius than for Dostoyevsky's spasmodic genius.

"His confrontations were theatrical confrontations, scenes," Gorky used to say: "He had but one rival, Shakespeare. You see, I asked myself: what would his creation have become had it been impossible, forbidden, what do I know? to write novels? The Karamazov are a kind of Greek-Russian tragedy."

Did Meyerhold stage him? We may dream about it. For its enthusiasts, the theater has always been a magic place. If a spell had been cast upon Dostoyevsky, would he have been led, as was Meyerhold (and sometimes Molière), to gestures and spectacles? Or to the Greek-Byzantine tragedy glimpsed by Gorky?

If we imagine Dostoyevsky writing the grand dialogue of the Karamazov for the stage, Shakespeare comes indeed to mind. Meyerhold would have staged his play in a sensuous communion with lightning, costumes, and actors; we know, and the *Notebooks* help us, that Dostoyevsky wrote his book in such a state of communion. With written fantasy.

Valéry is right in classifying literature among delirious and frenzied professions. Writing seems clear. Everyone knows he or she has been unaffected by the intoxication of the stage, the costume, the sets, the rehearsals, the manuscript that gradually becomes the play; nor has it been a matter of directing a film, mechanical witchcraft. But everybody writes letters; everybody dreams; everybody is unaware that written imagination is much more like witchcraft of fiction than like letters or daydreaming. A phantasm is inside the writer: he knows the repertory and the kinship of his creatures. The major characters of Balzac and Dostoyevsky belong to Balzac's and Dostoyevsky's fantasy where they take shape—and they are not interchangeable. Dostoyevsky does not tell himself about the Karamazov brothers the same way a young girl tells herself about her future fiancés. He works at elaborating a novel; but the implied requirements of meeting with fictional beings everyday go beyond work. The task that the novelist seems to control the most, corrections, is connected to his most extravagant undertaking: establishing a continuous relationship with his fictions (possible definition of madness). Almost every analysis of novels involves aesthetic categories: writing, composition, narrative, superiority or inferiority of the arabesques of *La Princesse de Clèves* over the *Illusions Perdues* block. Before determining whether a Balzac novel is well written or badly written, we must become fully aware that it is written. I mean: neither recited not acted nor filmed. Balzac's proofs are more instructive than any possible account; they disclose what preceded them, the game of creativeness from the first line of the manuscript. Writing and typography tell Balzac (his imagination had left this unspoken) that between such and such a paragraph an event took place and that analysis was required: paste-on over the proofs—that he can omit a given passage—and he knows the strength of ellipses: suppression. Additions go so far as to introduce new characters. When a reader says that the author corrects, he means improvement and purification. The initial procedure is quite different and is based on the fact that his written daydream is no longer the daydream to which he surrenders himself. He has left the stream. The flow he watches still belongs to the current; corrections of style will come later. But a shuttle goes from his riveted imagination to his disposable imagination, that is, the imagination that allows us to grasp written fantasy, the novelist's raw material. In the same way, from the first rehearsal to the last performance, the stage belongs to the playwright. Imagination belongs to the realm of dreams; fantasy, to the realm of shapes.

The fantasy of the novel lives by its own laws and its own coherence, a coherence that is as demanding as the requirements formulated by the world of music for its librettos and ballets. We do not compare Bizet's *Carmen* to Mérimée's hypothetical model. What kind of existence would an operatic character have outside the operatic world?

Literary creation is born into the world of creations and not into that of Creation. How could it be possible for the secret of the novel still to elude us today? Rather than an ideal or a faithful photograph of the nineteenth century, it may be defined as the fantasy of writing.

Of *our* writing: art in a low voice, in manuscript and in print, a world of monomania where the crazed Balzac intoxicates himself with Rubempré, the crazed Dostoyevsky with his Karamazov, who will in turn intoxicate the crazed solitary reader. Mrs. Bloom's stream of consciousness cannot be recalled; neither can *Ulysses*.

We have noted that the creation of fiction is born in the interval that severs the novel from its tale, but we have failed to see how the dialogue of the author with his or her imagination unfolds itself through writing: alterations, additions, freedom unlimited by some interpreter or other or by oral narrative, by memory, bound only by the shuttle between author and characters, the margin whereby they proliferate, inseparable from the novelist's insight that neither interlocutor nor a spectator is being addressed but a reader. How would the ancients have grasped the novel? Upon the very scenes where the voice of antiquity had made Oedipus howl, the silence of antiquity did not go beyond Daphnis and Chloe.

It was not because the ancients lacked machines or newspapers that they did not invent the novel. And they certainly had imagination: what they missed was our library.

Chronology

1901-1918 — Georges-André Malraux was born in Paris on November 3, 1901. His parents, Fernand Malraux and Berthe Lamy, separated in 1905. André was raised by his mother, maternal grandmother, and an aunt in Bondy, a small suburban town.

1919 — Buyer for René-Louis Doyon's bookshop, "La Connaissance," which specialized in rare books.

1920 — Malraux's first article, "Les origines de la poésie cubiste," was published in the first number of *La Connaissance*. Worked for Simon Kra (Editions du Sagittaire) and then for Daniel-Henry Kahnweiler.

1921 — *Lunes en papier*, dedicated to Max Jacob, with woodcuts by Fernand Léger. Marriage with Clara Goldschmidt, whom he was to divorce after World War II.

1922 — Began to publish regularly in the *Nouvelle Revue Française*.

1923-1924 — First Indo-Chinese adventure. Archaeological expedition to Cambodia's "Royal Way." Malraux was arrested and tried for removing seven bas-reliefs from the Banteaï-Srey temple. He was sentenced to three years in prison. A petition was signed on his behalf by most of the well-known writers of the period, including Aragon, Arland, Breton, Gide, Jacob, Mauriac, Maurois, and Paulhan. Malraux finally received a one-year suspended sentence.

1925-1926 — Second Indo-Chinese adventure. Cofounder with Paul Monin of a newspaper, *L'Indochine*, in Saigon. The paper was forced to close because of it attacks on government policy; Malraux subsequently published another paper, *L'Indochine enchaînée*. Affiliated with the Young Annam Movement and with the Kuomintang and then returned to Paris. Published *La Tentation de l'Occident*.

1928-1929	*Les Conquérants; Royaume farfelu.* Director of Gallimard's Department of the Arts. Visited the USSR and Persia.
1930-1931	*La Voie royale.* Traveled to Persia, Pamir, Afghanistan, India, China, Japan, Canada, and USA.
1932	Joined the Association des Ecrivains et Artistes Révolutionnaires.
1933	*La Condition humaine*—Prix Goncourt. A daughter, Florence (Mme. Alain Resnais), was born.
1934	Archaeological flight to the city of the Queen of Sheba. Went to Germany with Gide for the liberation of Dimitrov. Soviet Writers' Congress in Moscow.
1935	*Le Temps du mépris.* International Congress of Writers for the Defense of Culture.
1936	Purchased airplanes for the Spanish Republic. *Coronel* Malraux organized and commanded an international air squadron, the Escadrille España, later named the Escadrille André Malraux. Among the many missions he himself flew, Medellin and Teruel were notable. Separation from Clara; liaison with Josette Clotis.
1937	*L'Espoir.* "La Psychologie de l'art," a forerunner of the book that was later to bear the same title, appeared in *Verve.* At the invitation of several universities and left-wing organizations, Malraux toured North America to raise funds for the Spanish Republic.
1938	Shooting of motion picture *Sierra de Teruel*, later called *Espoir.*
1939	World War II: Malraux enlisted in a French tank regiment.
1940	Taken prisoner in Sens but escaped to the Free Zone. Birth of a son, Pierre-Gauthier (mother, Josette Clotis).
1942	First contact with the Resistance.
1943	*Les Noyers de l'Altenburg* (published in Switzerland). Birth of Vincent, a second son.
1944	Malraux became *Berger* in the Resistance movement. He was particularly effective in unifying diverse elements of the Maquis in the Dordogne region, in obtaining arms from London, and in

halting the Das Reich division. Taken prisioner in Toulouse, he was later freed by the French forces. Death of Josette Clotis (she stumbled and fell under the wheels of a moving train). Execution of Claude Malraux, a half brother, member of the Resistance. *Colonel Berger* commanded the brigade Alsace-Lorraine, which distinguished itself in the liberation of the Vosges and Alsace, especially Strasbourg

1945　Death of Roland Malraux, another half brother, a member of the Resistance, a few days before the end of the war. Minister of information for the first De Gaulle government.

1947-1950　Director of propaganda for the R.P.F. (Rassemblement Peuple Français), the Gaullist party. Began to publish his essays about art, *La Psychologie de l'art*. Married Madeleine Malraux, the wife of his half brother, Roland.

1951　*Les Voix du silence*.

1952-1954　*Le Musée imaginaire de la sculpture mondiale*, 3 volumes.

1957　*La Métamorphose des dieux*, volume 1.

1958　Minister of information in the second De Gaulle government.

1959-1969　Minister for cultural affairs.

1961　Death of both of his sons, Pierre-Gauthier and Vincent, in an automobile accident.

1962-1963　Two trips to the USA. Guest of the Kennedys at the White House.

1965　Acute depression. Traveled to China and other Oriental countries. Resumed writing. The last ten years of his life were to be devoted to this pursuit.

1966　Reunion with Louise de Vilmorin, poet and novelist, author of *Madame De*.

1967　*Antimémoires*, an immediate best-seller.

1969　Death of Louise de Vilmorin. Malraux continued to live at her family estate at Verrières.

1970 *Le Triangle noir.* Death of De Gaulle.

1971 *Les Chênes qu'on abat . . .; Oraisons funèbres.*

1972 Malraux suffered a stroke and was hospitalized at the Salpétrière. Good recovery.

1973 Exhibition held at the Fondation Maeght in Saint-Paul de Vence, which showed works of his imaginary museum.

1974 *Lazare; La Tête d'obsidienne; L'Irréel.*

1975 *Hôtes de passage.*

1976 *La Corde et les souris; L'Intemporel.* Died of a pulmonary embolism, November 23. Private burial at Verrières-le-Buisson. National homage at the Louvre. Memorial mass at Saint-Louis des Invalides, with a homily preached by R. P. Bockel.

1977 *Le Surnaturel* and *L'Homme précaire et la littérature* (posthumous publications).

Bibliography

A SELECTED BIBLIOGRAPHY

(Unless it is otherwise indicated, all French books are published in Paris.)

1. Principal Works by André Malraux (arranged chronologically)

Lunes en papier. Éditions de la Galerie Simon, 1921.
La Tentation de l'Occident. Grasset, 1926. *The Temptation of the West.* Translated by Robert Hollander. New York: Vintage Books, 1961.
"D'une Jeunesse européenne," in *Écrits.* Grasset—Collection "Les Cahiers verts," 1927, no. 70, pp. 129-153.
Les Conquérants. Grasset, 1928. Rev. ed., Grasset, 1949. *The Conquerors.* Translated by Winifred S. Whale. London: Jonathan Cape, 1929. New York: Harcourt, Brace, 1929. Rev. ed. translated by Jacques Leclerc. Boston: Beacon Press, 1956. London: Mayflower, 1956.
La Voie royale. Grasset, 1930. *The Royal Way.* Translated by Stuart Gilbert. New York: H. Smith and R. Haas, 1935. London: Methuen, 1935.
La Condition humaine. Gallimard, 1933. *Storm in Shanghai.* Translated by Alastair Macdonald. London: Methuen, 1934; reprinted as *Man's Estate,* 1948. *Man's Fate.* Translated by Haakon M. Chevalier. New York: H. Smith and R. Haas, 1934.
Le Temps du mépris. Gallimard, 1935. *Days of Contempt.* Translated by Haakon M. Chevalier. London: Gollancz, 1936. *Days of Wrath.* Translated by Haakon M. Chevalier. New York: Random House, 1938.
L'Espoir. Gallimard, 1937. *Days of Hope.* Translated by Stuart Gilbert and Alastair Macdonald. London: Routledge, 1938. *Man's Hope.* Translated by Stuart Gilbert and Alastair Macdonald. New York: Random House, 1938.
Les Noyers de l'Altenburg. Lausanne, Switzerland: Editions du Hauts-Pays, 1943. Geneva: Skira, 1945. Gallimard, 1948. *The Walnut Trees of Altenburg.* Translated by A. W. Fielding. London: Lehmann, 1952. This is the first part of *La Lutte avec l'ange,* a novel whose manuscript was seized and destroyed by the Gestapo.
Esquisse d'une psychologie du cinéma. Gallimard, 1946.
La Psychologie de l'art, 3 vols. *Le Musée imaginaire,* vol. 1. Geneva: Skira, 1947. *La Création artistique,* vol. 2. Geneva: Skira, 1948. *La Monnaie de l'absolu,* vol. 3. Geneva: Skira, 1950. *The Psychology of Art,* 3 vols. Translated by Stuart Gilbert. New York: Bollingen-Pantheon

Books, 1949-1950. *Museum without Walls*, vol. 1; revised 1967, see *Les Voix du silence. The Creative Act*, vol. 2. *The Twilight of the Absolute*, vol. 3.

The Case for De Gaulle. A dialogue between André Malraux and James Burnham. Section by André Malraux translated by Spenser Byard. New York: Random House, 1948.

Saturne—Essai sur Goya. Gallimard, 1950. *Saturn: An Essay on Goya*. Translated by C. W. Chilton. New York and London: Phaidon, 1957.

Les Voix du silence. Gallimard, 1951. *The Voices of Silence*. Translated by Stuart Gilbert. New York: Doubleday, 1953. London: Secker and Warburg, 1954. (This is a revised edition of *La Psychologie de l'art* with the addition of a new section, *Les Métamorphoses d'Apollon*.) Volume 1, *Le Musée imaginaire*, was again translated as *Museum without Walls* by Stuart Gilbert and Francis Price. London: Secker and Warburg, 1967. New York: Doubleday, 1967.

Le Musée imaginaire de la sculpture mondiale, 3 vols. *La Statuaire*, vol.1. Gallimard, 1952. *Des bas-reliefs aux grottes sacrées*, vol. 2. Gallimard, 1954. *Le Monde chrétien*, vol. 3. Gallimard, 1954.

La Métamorphose des dieux. Gallimard, 1957. *The Metamorphosis of the Gods*. Translated by Stuart Gilbert. London: Secker and Warburg, 1960. New York: Doubleday, 1960. The French edition was revised and retitled *Le Surnaturel*, which became the first volume of the trilogy *La Métamorphose des dieux: Le Surnaturel*, vol. 1 (1977); *L'Irréel*, vol. 2 (1974); *L'Intemporel*, vol. 3 (1976).

Antimémoires. Gallimard, 1967. Rev. ed. 1972. *Anti-memoirs*. Translated (1967 ed.) by Terence Kilmartin. London: H. Hamilton, 1968. New York: Holt, Rinehart and Winston, 1968. This book was later considered as volume 1 of *Le Miroir des limbes*.

Le Triangle noir. Gallimard, 1970.

Les Chênes qu'on abat... Gallimard, 1971. *Felled Oaks*. Translated by Irene Clephane. New York: Holt, Rinehart and Winston, 1972. *Fallen Oaks*. London: H. Hamilton, 1972.

Oraisons funèbres. Gallimard, 1971.

La Tête d'obsidienne. Gallimard, 1974. *Picasso's Mask*. Translated and annotated by June Guicharnaud with Jacques Guicharnaud. New York: Holt, Rinehart and Winston, 1976. London: Macdonald and James, 1976.

Lazare. Gallimard, 1974. *Lazarus*. Translated by Terence Kilmartin. New York: Holt, Rinehart and Winston, 1977.

L'Irréel. Gallimard, 1974. (Volume 2 of the trilogy, *La Métamorphose des dieux*.)

Hôtes de passage. Gallimard, 1975.

L'Intemporel. Gallimard, 1976. (Volume 3 of the trilogy, *La Métamorphose des dieux*.)

Le Miroir des limbes. Pléiade-Gallimard, 1976. Comprises *Antimémoires*

(rev. ed.) and *La Corde et les souris.*
La Corde et les souris. Folio-Gallimard, 1976. (Volume 2 of *Les Miroir des limbes.*) Comprises: *Hôtes de passage, Les Chênes qu'on abat. . ., Le Tête d'obsidienne,* and *Lazare* (all in revised form).
L'Homme précaire et le littérature. Gallimard, 1977.
Le Surnaturel. Gallimard, 1977. (Volume 3 of the trilogy, *La Métamorphose des dieux.*)

2. Books about André Malraux

a. Bibliography

Langlois, Walter G. *André Malraux 2.* Minard, 1972. Malraux criticism in English; chronological bibliography of publications on Malraux in English, 1942-1970; preface by Peter C. Hoy.

b. Biographies

Chantal, Suzanne. *Le Coeur battant: Josette Clotis, André Malraux.* Grasset, 1976. Includes a letter from A. Malraux.
Friang, Brigitte. *Un autre Malraux.* Plon, 1977.
Galante, Pierre (with the collaboration of Yves Salgues). *Malraux—Quel roman que sa vie!* Plon, Paris-Match, Presses de la Cité, 1971. Translated by Haakon M. Chevalier. New York: Cowles Books, 1971.
Grover, Frédéric. *Six entretiens avec Malraux.* Gallimard, 1979.
Lacouture, Jean. *André Malraux. Une vie dans le siècle.* Seuil, 1973. Translated by Alan Sheridan. New York: Pantheon Books, 1975.
Madsen, Axel. *Malraux: A Biography.* New York: William Morrow, 1976.
Malraux, Alain. *Les Marronniers de Boulogne.* Plon, 1978.
Malraux, Clara. *Le Bruit de nos pas,* 6 vols. *Apprendre à vivre,* vol. 1. Grasset, 1963. *Nos vingt ans,* vol. 2. Grasset, 1966. *Les combats et les jeux,* vol. 3. Grasset, 1968. *Voici que vient l'été,* vol. 4. Grasset, 1973. *La Fin et le commencement,* vol. 5. Grasset, 1976. *Et pourtant j'étais libre,* vol. 6. Grasset, 1979.
Payne, Robert. *A Portrait of André Malraux.* Englewood Cliffs, N.J.: Prentice-Hall, 1970.
Suarès, Guy and Bergamin, José. *Malraux, celui qui vient: Entretiens.* Stock, 1974. *Malraux, Past, Present, Future.* Translated by Derek Coltman. Boston: Little, Brown, 1974.

c. Criticism

Blend, Charles D. *André Malraux: Tragic Humanist.* Columbus: Ohio

State University Press, 1963.
Blumenthal, Gerda. *André Malraux: The Conquest of Dread.* Baltimore, Md.: The Johns Hopkins Press, 1960.
Boak, Denis. *André Malraux.* Oxford, England: Clarendon Press, 1968.
Boisdeffre, Pierre de. *André Malraux.* Editions Universitaires, 1952.
Brincourt, André. *André Malraux ou le temps du silence.* La Table Ronde, 1966.
Carduner, Jean. *La Création romanesque chez Malraux.* Nizet, 1968.
Carrard, Philippe. *Malraux ou le récit hybride. Essai sur les techniques narratives dans 'L'Espoir.'* Minard, 1976.
Courcel, Martine de, ed. *Malraux: Life and Work.* With a major new essay, "Anti-Critique," by Malraux. London: Weidenfeld & Nicolson, 1976. New York: Harcourt Brace Jovanovich, 1976. French version: *Malraux: Être et dire.* Plon, 1976.
Delhomme, Jeanne. *Temps et destin.* Gallimard, 1955.
Dorenlot, Françoise. *Malraux ou l'unité de pensée.* Gallimard, 1970.
Duthuit, Georges. *Le Musée inimaginable.* Corti, 1956.
Ellis, Elisabeth. *André Malraux et le monde de la nature.* Minard, 1975.
Fitch, Brian. *Les deux univers romanesques d'André Malraux.* Minard, 1964.
Frohock, Wilbur Merrill. *André Malraux and the Tragic Imagination.* Stanford, Calif.: Stanford University Press, 1951.
———. *André Malraux.* London and New York: Columbia University Press, 1974.
Gaillard, Pol. *André Malraux.* Bordas, 1970.
———. *Les Critiques de notre temps et Malraux.* Garnier, 1970.
Gannon, Edward. *The Honor of Being a Man.* Chicago: Loyola University Press, 1957.
Gaulupeau, Serge. *André Malraux et la mort.* Minard, 1969.
Greenlee, James W. *Malraux's Heroes and History.* De Kalb: Northern Illinois University Press, 1975.
Greshoff, C. J. *An Introduction to the Novels of André Malraux.* Cape Town and Rotterdam: A. A. Balkema, 1975.
Harris, Geoffrey T. *André Malraux. L'éthique comme fonction de l'esthétique.* Minard, 1972. Preface by Brian Fitch.
Hartmann, Geoffrey H. *André Malraux.* New York: Hilary House, 1960.
Hébert, François. *Tryptique de la mort. Une lecture des romans de Malraux.* Montreal: Presses de l'Université de Montréal, 1978.
Hewitt, James R. *André Malraux.* New York: Frederick Ungar, 1978.
Hoffmann, Joseph. *L'Humanisme de Malraux.* Klincksieck, 1963.
Horvath, Violet. *André Malraux. The Human Adventure.* New York: New York University Press, 1969.
Jaloux, Henri. *Journal d'une fabrication. Oeuvre romanesque d'André Malraux.* Nouvelle Librairie de France, 1962.
Jenkins, Cecil. *André Malraux.* New York: Twayne Publishers, 1972.
Juilland, Ileana. *Dictionnaire des idées dans l'oeuvre d'André Malraux.*

The Hague and Paris: Mouton, 1968.
Kline, Thomas Jefferson. *André Malraux and the Metamorphosis of Death*. New York and London: Columbia University Press, 1973.
Langlois, Walter G. *André Malraux: The Indochina Adventure*. New York: Praeger, 1966. *André Malraux—L'Aventure indochinoise*. French translation by Jean-René Mayor. Mercure de France, 1967.
Lecerf, Emile. *André Malraux. Lettres inédites d'André Malraux à l'auteur*. Richard-Masse, 1971.
Lewis, R. W. B., ed. *Malraux—A Collection of Critical Essays*. Englewood Cliffs, N.J.: Prentice Hall, 1964.
Lorant, André. *Orientations étrangères chez André Malraux: Dostoievski et Trotsky*. Minard, 1971.
Marion, Denis, ed. *André Malraux*. Seghers, 1970.
Mauriac, Claude. *Malraux ou le mal du héros*. Grasset, 1946.
Meuris, Emmanuel. *Réflexions sur "Le Musée imaginaire" d'André Malraux*. Fraipont, Belgium: Meuris, Sur la Butte, 1948.
Morawski, Stefan. *L'Absolu et la forme. L'Esthétique d'André Malraux*. Translated from the Polish by Yolande Lamy-Grun. Klincksieck, 1972.
Moray, Aloys. *À la rencontre d'André Malraux*. Brussels: La Sixaine, 1947.
Moser, Yvonne. *L'Essai de la constitution d'un monde dans l'oeuvre d'André Malraux*. Aaron, Switzerland: Sauerländer, 1959.
Mossuz, Janine. *André Malraux et le gaullisme*. A. Colin, 1970.
Patry, André. *Visages d'André Malraux*. Montreal: Editions de l'Hexagone, 1956.
Picon, Gaëtan. *André Malraux*. Gallimard, 1945.
———. *André Malraux par lui-même*. Seuil, 1953.
Righter, William. *The Rhetorical Hero—An Essay on the Aesthetics of André Malraux*. London: Routledge and Kegan Paul, 1964. New York: Chilmark Press, 1964.
Sabourin, Pascal. *La Réflexion sur l'art d'André Malraux. Origines et évolution*. Klincksieck, 1972.
Savane, Marcel. *André Malraux*. Richard-Masse, 1946.
Smith, Roch. *Le Meurtrier et la vision tragique. Essai sur les romans d'André Malraux*. Didier, 1975.
Surchamp, Dom Angelico. *André Malraux (à propos de "La Métamorphose des dieux ")*. Geneva: Forces Vives, 1967.
Thornberry, Robert S. *André Malraux et l'Espagne*. Geneva: Droz, 1977.
Vandegans, André. *La Jeunesse littéraire d'André Malraux. Essai sur l'inspiration farfelue*. J. J. Pauvert, 1964.
Vandromme, Pol. *Malraux du farfelu au mirobolant*. Lausanne: Alfred Eibel, 1976.
Wilkinson, David. *Malraux—An Essay in Political Criticism*. Cambridge, Mass.: Harvard University Press, 1967.

d. Selection of Books Partially Dealing with André Malraux

Albérès, R. M. *La Révolte des écrivains d'aujourd'hui.* Corréa, 1949.
Astier, Emmanuel d'. *Portraits.* Gallimard, 1969.
Beauvoir, Simone de. *La Force des choses.* Gallimard, 1963.
Berl, Emmanuel. *Mort de la pensée bourgeoise.* Grasset, 1929.
Bespaloff, Rachel. *Cheminements et carrefours.* Librairie philosophique Vrin, 1938.
Blanchet, André. *La Littérature et le spirituel*, vol. 1. Didier, 1959.
Brasillach, Robert. *Portraits.* Plon, 1935.
Brée, Germaine. "The Archaeology of Discourse in Malraux's *Anti-memoirs*." In *Intertextuality*, New York Literary Forum, vol. 2. New York: New York Literary Forum, 1978.
Brée, Germaine, and Guiton, Margaret. *An Age of Fiction.* New Brunswick, N.J.: Rutgers University Press, 1957.
Brincourt, André and Jean. *Les Oeuvres et les lumières. À la recherche de l'esthétique à travers Bergson, Proust et Malraux.* La Table Ronde, 1955.
Brombert, Victor. *The Intellectual Hero. Studies in the French Novel 1880-1955.* Philadelphia: J. B. Lippincott Co., 1961. Reprinted from *Yale French Studies* (Winter 1957).
Caute, David. *Communism and the French Intellectuals.* New York: Macmillan, 1964.
Domenach, Jean-Marie. *Le Retour du tragique.* Seuil, 1967.
Doyon, Jean-Marie. *Mémoire d'homme.* La Connaissance, 1953.
Drieu la Rochelle, Pierre. "Malraux, the New Man." In *From the N. R. F.—An Image of the Twentieth Century from the Pages of the Nouvelle Revue Française.* Edited by Justin O'Brien. New York: Farrar, Straus and Cudahy, 1958.
Ehrenburg, Ilya. *Memoirs 1921-1941.* Translated by Tatania Shebunina and Yvonne Kapp. Cleveland, Ohio, and New York: The World Publishing Co., 1964.
Fischer, Louis. *Men and Politics—An Autobiography.* New York: Duell, Sloan and Pearce, 1941.
Flanner, Janet. *Men and Monuments.* New York: Harper and Row, 1957.
———. *Paris Journal 1944-1965.* New York: Atheneum, 1965.
Frank, Joseph. *The Widening Gyre.* New Brunswick, N. J.: Rutgers University Press, 1963.
Frohock, W. M. *Style and Temper. Studies in French Fiction 1925-1960.* Cambridge, Mass.: Harvard University Press, 1967.
Garaudy, Roger. *Literature from the Graveyard: J. P. Sartre, F. Mauriac, A. Malraux, A. Koestler.* Translated from the French by Joseph Bernstein. New York: International Publishers, 1948.
Gide, André. *Journal 1889-1939.* Bibliothèque de la Pléiade, 1959.
———. *Journal 1939-1949.* Bibliothèque de la Pléiade, 1959. English translation by Justin O'Brien. Harmondsworth (Middlesex), En-

gland: Penguin, 1967.
Goldberger, Avriel. *Visions of a New Hero. The Heroic Life According to André Malraux and Earlier Advocates of Human Grandeur*. Minard, 1965.
Goldman, Lucien. *Pour une sociologie du roman*. Gallimard, 1964.
Halda, Bernard. *Berenson et Malraux*. Minard, 1964.
Howe, Irving. *Politics and the Novel*. New York: Meridian Books, 1957.
Jarrell, Randall. *A Sad Heart at the Supermarket. Essays and Fables*. New York: Atheneum, 1962.
Knight, Everett W. *Literature Considered as Philosophy. The French Example*. New York: Macmillan, 1958.
Lacasse, Rodolphe. *Hemingway et Malraux. Destin de l'homme*. Montreal: Editions Cosmos, 1973. 2d ed. Nizet, 1974.
Magny, Claude-Edmonde. *Littérature et critique*. Payot, 1971. Reprinted from *Esprit* (October 1948).
Mauriac, François. *Journal. II*. Grasset, 1937.
Merleau-Ponty, Maurice. *Signes*. Gallimard, 1960.
Moeller, Charles. *Littérature du XXème siècle et Christianisme*, vol. 3. Tournai: Casterman, 1957.
Mounier, Emmanuel. *Carnets de route*, vol. 3. Seuil, 1953. Reprinted from *Esprit* (October 1948).
Peyre, Henri. *French Novelists of Today*. New York: Oxford University Press, 1967.
Picon, Gaëtan. *L'Usage de la lecture*. Mercure de France, (vol. 1) 1960, (vol. 2) 1962.
Reck, Rima Drell. *Literature and Responsibility. The French Novelist in the XXth Century*. Baton Rouge: Louisiana State University Press, 1969.
Regler, Gustav. *The Owl of Minerva*. Translated from the German by Norman Denny. New York: Farrar, Straus and Cudahy, 1960.
Riffaterre, Michael. *Essais de stylistique structurale*. Flammarion, 1971.
Roy, Claude. *Descriptions critiques*. Gallimard, (vol. 1) 1949, (vol. 5) 1960.
Sachs, Maurice. *Le Sabbat*. Corréa, 1946.
Saint Clair, M. (Mme. Théo van Rysselberghe). *Galerie privée*. Gallimard, 1947.
Savage, Catherine. *Malraux, Sartre and Aragon as Political Novelists*. University of Florida Monographs, no. 17. Gainesville: University of Florida, 1964.
Seylaz, Jean-Luc. "Malraux et le romanesque de l'intelligence." In *Lettres d'Occident—de l'Iliade à l'Espoir*. Neuchâtel: La Baconnière, 1958.
Simon, Pierre-Henri. *L'Homme en procès. Malraux, Sartre, Camus, Saint Exupéry*. Neuchâtel: La Baconnière, 1949. 2d ed. Payot, 1965.
———. *Témoins de l'homme. La Condition humaine dans la littérature*

contemporaine. A. Colin, 1955.
Stéphane, Roger. *Portrait de l'aventurier. T. E. Lawrence, Malraux, von Salomon.* Le Sagittaire, 1950. Reprinted from *Esprit* (October 1948).
Sulzberger, Cyrus L. *A Long Row of Candles: Memoirs and Diaries 1934-1954.* New York: Macmillan, 1969.
Tarica, Ralph. "Ironic Figures in Malraux's Novels." In *Image and Theme—Studies in Modern French Fiction.* Edited by W. M. Frohock. Cambridge, Mass.: Harvard University Press, 1969.
Tison-Braun, Micheline. "Les Héros et les hommes." In *La Crise de l'humanisme*, vol. 2 (Nizet, 1967).
Wilson, Edmund. *The Shores of Light.* New York: Farrar, Straus and Co., 1952.
——. *The Bit between My Teeth.* New York: Farrar, Straus and Co., 1966.
Wilhelm, Bernard. *Hemingway et Malraux devant la guerre d'Espagne.* Porrentruy, Switzerland: La Bonne Presse, 1966.

e. Issues Devoted to André Malraux

(1) Regularly Published

André Malraux, series. Edited by Walter G. Langlois. *Revue des Lettres Modernes.* Minard, (vol. 1) 1972, *Du "farfelu" aux "Antimémoires"*; (vol. 2) 1973, *Visages du romancier;* (vol. 3) 1975, *Influences et affinités;* (vol. 4) 1978, *Malraux et l'art;* (vol. 5, scheduled 1980), *Malraux et l'histoire.*
Mélanges Malraux Miscellany. Publication of the Malraux Society, Laramie, Wyoming. Edited by Walter G. Langlois. 1969—

(2) Special Issues

Esprit, no. 10 (October 1949). "Interrogation à Malraux."
Yale French Studies, no. 18 (Winter 1957). "Passion and Intellect."
Le Magazine littéraire, no. 11 (October 1967). "Les 3 guerres d'André Malraux."

On Malraux's Death

Nouvelles littéraires, no. 2560 (November 25-December 1, 1976).
Nouvelle Revue Française, no. 295 (July 1977).
Espoir, no. 19. Revue de l'Institut Charles de Gaulle. Plon, 1977.
Mélanges Malraux Miscellany, vol. 9, no. 2; vol. 10, no. 1 (Autumn 1977-Spring 1978).

About the Authors

PIERRE BOCKEL, dean of the Cathedral of Strasbourg and chaplain of the Brigade Alsace Lorraine, is the author of *L'Enfant du rire* (Grasset, 1973), for which André Malraux wrote the preface.

LEROY C. BREUNIG has taught at Cornell and Harvard and is now professor of French at Barnard, where he has been chairman of the French Department, dean of the faculty, and interim president. He is the author and editor of books and articles on Guillaume Apollinaire and on poetry and painting. A member of the editorial advisory board of *New York Literary Forum*, he writes while residing in Mykonos, Morningside Heights, and sometimes in Paris.

JEAN CARDUNER, a professor of French at the University of Michigan, is also director of the Middlebury French School and vice-president of the American Association of Teachers of French. His publications concerning Malraux include *La Création romanesque* (Nizet, 1968); "Les Antimémoires dans l'oeuvre de Malraux," *Kentucky Romance Quarterly*, vol. 16, no. 1 (1968); and "Le Miroir des limbes, L'Homme précaire et l'aléatoire" (to appear in *Twentieth Century Literature*). At present he is working on the relationship between literature, culture, and civilization in contemporary France.

PHILIPPE CARRARD teaches French at the University of Vermont. His works include *Malraux ou le récit hybride: Essai sur les techniques narratives dans "L'Espoir"* and other studies on Malraux. He has also written on contemporary French literature and on the literature of French-speaking Switzerland.

MARY ANN CAWS, executive officer of the Comparative Literature Program at the Graduate Center, City University of New York, is the editor of *Dada/Surrealism* and the director of *Le Siècle éclaté*, a French journal on the avant-garde; author of *Surrealism and the Literary Imagination, The Inner Theatre of Recent French Poetry, The Poetry of Dada and Surrealism, The Presence of René Char*, and many other works on contemporary poetics; and translator of volumes of Tristan Tzara and René Char. She is currently translating André Breton and Pierre Reverdy.

HANNA CHARNEY is professor of French and comparative literature at Hunter College and the Graduate Center, City University of New York. She has written on Paul Valéry; on problems of character and narrative structures in Thomas Mann, Butor, the *New Novel*, Flaubert, Valéry, Simone de Beauvoir, and Musil; on the relations between film and the novel in Flaubert, Rohmer, Pieyre de Mandiargues; and on detective fiction. She is co-editor of *Intertextuality*, volume 2, of *New York Literary Forum*.

TOM CONLEY, currently teaching problems of image/text relationships in Renaissance and modern literatures at the University of California at Berkeley, will return to the University of Minnesota this spring to resume work in the Departments of French and Comparative Literature. He has written on plastic dimensions of Montaigne, Lévi-Strauss, Godard, Marot, Renoir, Barthes, Blanchot, Hélisenne de Crenne, and others. A product of Columbia (M.A.) and Wisconsin (Ph.D.), he has studied in Paris under the auspices of fellowships granted by the American Council of Learned Societies and the National Endowment for the Humanities. A member of the editorial advisory board of *New York Literary Forum*, he is projecting a longer monograph on collisions of word and figure.

MARTINE DE COURCEL, a graduate of the Sorbonne with a degree in psychology, is the editor of *Malraux—Life and Work/Malraux—Être et dire*. In private life she is the wife of a former French ambassador to the Court of St. James's.

FRANÇOISE DORENLOT, a professor of French at City College of New York, City University of New York, is co-editor, with Robert Thornberry, of *Mélanges Malraux Miscellany*. The author of *Malraux ou l'unité de pensée* (Paris: Gallimard, 1970), she has written many articles about Malraux, the most recent of which appeared in Martine de Courcel's *Malraux—Life and Work*.

W. M. FROHOCK, professor emeritus of French at Harvard University, is at present a fellow of the Camargo Foundation in Cassis (Bouches du Rhône), France, where he wrote the essay included in this volume of *New York Literary Forum*. He is author of *André Malraux and the Tragic Imagination* and several briefer writings about Malraux, as well as books about French and American fiction.

JAMES ROBERT HEWITT, assistant professor of French at New York University, has made nineteenth-century and early twentieth-century literature his field of specialization. He has lectured and/or published on Rousseau, Musset, Proust, and Malraux. His two book-length studies are monographs on Marcel Proust and André Malraux. Professor Hewitt has also translated works by Arabel, Audiberti, Gascar, and Queneau. He is presently working on a critical biography of the romantic poet Alfred de Musset.

JEAN HYTIER, a Director of Letters in the first De Gaulle government and former French delegate to UNESCO, is a professor emeritus of Columbia University. A distinguished scholar, editor, and writer, he was awarded the Académie Française prize for his *La Poétique de Paul Valéry*. His notable achievements include editions of Pascal and Valéry, books on Iran and Gobineau, Gide, the techniques of modern French verse, and on the aesthetics and theory of literature.

BETTINA KNAPP, a professor in the Departments of Romance Languages and Comparative Literature at Hunter College and the Graduate Center, City University of New York, has written extensively on the theater. She is the author of *Antonin Artaud, Man of Vision; Jean Racine: Mythos and Renewal in Modern Theatre; Céline, Man of Hate; Maurice Maeterlinck* (an analytical study), and other books. Her book *Gérard de Nerval, the Mystic's Dilemma* is soon to be published.

WALTER LANGLOIS, professor of French at the University of Wyoming in Laramie, is primarily a literary historian. He has published several books and numerous articles relating to Malraux's life and work. His study of Malraux and the Spanish civil war is nearing completion. Professor Langlois is also head of the Malraux Society and editor of the *Mélanges Malraux Miscellany* and *Série André Malraux* (Paris: Minard).

EDOUARD MOROT-SIR, is at present professor and French general adviser at the University of North Carolina at Chapel Hill. Since 1975 he has been editor of the *North Carolina Studies in Romance Languages and Literature* and of *Romance Notes*. His publications include numerous articles in English or French on epistemology, literary criticism, history of French literature and philosophy, and French-American relations. Among his books are *La Pensée negative* (1947), *Philosophie et mystique* (1947), *La Pensée française d'aujourdhui* (1971), *La Métaphysique de Pascal* (1973), and *"Les Mots" de J.-P. Sartre* (1975).

HENRI PEYRE, professor emeritus of Yale University, is at present chairman of the French Program at the Graduate Center, City University of New York. He is the author of numerous articles and more than forty books, of which at least half were written in English and which were published by major houses.

JEANINE PARISIER PLOTTEL teaches French at Hunter College, writes about literature, and publishes *New York Literary Forum*. She is the author of a book about Paul Valéry, and her articles about Raymond Roussel, anamorphosis, and poetics have been published in numerous scholarly journals. Currently, she has a National Endowment for the Humanities fellowship to write about nonreferential texts.

BRIAN THOMPSON, associate professor of French and chairman of the French Department at the University of Massachusetts at Boston, has translated a number of books from French and German, including Gabriel Marcel's *Problematic Man* and Romano Guardini's *Pascal for Our Time*. He has also published articles on Malraux in *Mélanges Malraux Miscellany* and *Twentieth Century Literature.*

ROBERT S. THORNBERRY, associate professor of French at the University of Alberta, Edmonton, Canada, is co-editor of the *Mélanges Malraux Miscellany*. He is author of *André Malraux et l'Espagne* (Geneva:

Droz, 1977) and various articles on Malraux in *Mélanges Malraux Miscellany*, *La Revue du Pacifique*, and *Twentieth Century Literature*. His current projects include an account of Malraux's polemic with Trotsky.

MICHELINE TISON-BRAUN teaches at Hunter College and the Graduate Center, City University of New York. Her publications include *La Crise de l'humanisme*, volume 1 (1959) and volume 2 (1967), *Nathalie Sarraute ou la Recherche de l'authenticité* (1969); and *Tristan Tzara, inventeur de l'homme nouveau* (1977). A Guggenheim fellow, she is currently studying the problems of the personality in modern French literature.

Index

"Agnosticism and the Gnosis of the Imaginary" 85
Agnosticism in Malraux's writings and thought 86, 95
Alexander the Great 7, 31, 60, 68
"André Malraux and the Metamorphosis of Literature" 27
Antimémoires 23, 37, 38, 39, 41, 42, 49, 52, 55, 56, 57, 58, 59, 60, 61, 64, 65, 68, 69, 198, 246
"Archetypes: Dissolution as Creation" 149
"Artist as Exemplar of Humanity, The" 155
Balzac, Honoré 33, 34, 239, 240
Bernanos, Georges 10, 30, 77, 80, 215
Bockel, Pierre 75
Bosch, Hieronymus 34, 152
Brée, Germaine ix
Breunig, LeRoy C. 209
Camus, Albert 17, 30, 209, 215
Caravaggio, Polidoro Caldara da 6, 144, 146, 147
Carduner, Jean 37
Carrard, Philippe 189
Cat, Malrucian 62, 64
Caws, Mary Ann 143
Cézanne, Paul 9, 34, 136, 151, 158, 162
Char, René 29, 144, 145, 146
Chardin, Jean-Baptiste-Siméon 34, 156
Charney, Hanna 15
Chênes qu'on abat, Les (Felled Oaks) 23, 24, 65
China 30, 68, 210
Clotis, Josette 50, 52, 65, 76
Condition humaine, La (Man's Fate) 16, 17, 18, 20, 22, 23, 25, 28, 45, 58, 62, 69, 73, 76, 88, 91, 145, 209, 210, 212, 213, 220, 223
Conley, Tom 125
Conquérants, Les 23, 58, 69, 89, 167, 220
Corde et les souris, La 7, 23, 60, 64, 65, 247
Courcel, Martine de 32, 67
Création artistique, La 95, 99
Days of Wrath: see *Temps du mépris, Le*
Death in Malraux's writings and thought 58, 59, 60, 61, 62, 64, 65, 67, 69, 75, 76, 78, 80
De Gaulle, Charles 9, 23, 24, 37, 48, 49, 52, 56, 60, 61, 62, 65, 70, 76

Delacroix, Eugène 34, 151, 158
Descartes, René 27, 95
Destiny (or Fate) in Malraux's writings and thought 46, 47, 48, 50
"Dialectics of Character in Malraux" 15
Diderot, Denis 29, 33
Dorenlot, Françoise 21
Dostoyevsky, Feodor Mikhailovich 33, 39, 42, 46, 56, 64, 72, 78, 163, 238, 239, 240
Eliot, T. S. 5, 22
Espoir, L' (Man's Hope) 23, 31, 49, 66, 73, 92, 109, 157, 168, 169, 185, 189, 190, 194, 196, 199, 201, 202, 212, 216, 217, 218
Esquisse d'une psychologie du cinéma 31
Fate: see Destiny
Felled Oaks: see *Chênes qu'on abat, Les*
"Figures in the Carpet of Malraux's *Le Miroir des limbes*" 55
Flaubert, Gustav 31, 32, 33, 34, 212, 229, 230, 231, 232, 234, 235, 236, 238, 239
"Framing Malraux" 125
Franco, Francisco 169, 170, 171, 182, 184, 185, 221
Freud, Sigmund 39, 61, 70, 114, 127, 128, 130, 131, 132
Frohock, W. M. 3, 189, 213
Gide, André 28, 33, 38, 39, 159, 216, 217, 218, 223, 235
Gioconda, La: see *Mona Lisa*
Gothic sculpture 34, 44, 69
Goya, Francisco de 34, 126, 136, 151
"Haunted Model, The" 21
Hegel, Georg Wilhelm Friedrich 29, 95, 162
Heidegger, Martin 27, 160, 162, 163, 164
Hewitt, James Robert 55
Homme précaire et littérature, L' 10, 25, 32, 34, 46, 52, 68, 86, 110, 230
Hugo, Victor 34, 66, 80, 231
Hytier, Jean 229
Imag-paradigm in Malraux's writings 87, 90, 92, 99
Imaginary in Malraux's writings and thought 85, 86, 87, 88, 92, 94, 95, 97, 98, 99, 103, 104, 109, 120
Imagination in Malraux's writing 111
India 30, 68, 69, 70, 72

Intemporel, L' 6, 9, 72, 103, 104, 105, 132, 133, 135, 137, 139, 201, 246
Irréel, L' 3, 72, 73, 103, 104, 126, 130, 131, 139, 201, 246
Joyce, James 34, 39, 210
Jung, Carl Gustav 149
Knapp, Bettina 149
Lacan, Jacques 28, 111, 114, 118, 119, 120
Langlois, Walter 167, 190
La Tour, Georges de 6, 146
Lawrence, T. E. 39, 49, 57
Lazare 22, 57, 59, 61, 64, 77, 78, 144, 145, 146
Leggett, Lee 73
Leonardo da Vinci 34, 126, 127, 128, 129, 130, 131, 135, 136, 139, 160
"Life Made into Fiction" 189
Lunes en papier 64, 86, 87, 88
Madero, Ernesto 217, 219
Mallarmé, Stéphane 17, 149
Malraux, Alain 38, 41, 47, 49, 50, 52
Malraux, Clara 41, 50, 70
Malraux, Fernand 41, 42, 52, 75, 78
Malraux, Madeleine 50, 52
"Malraux and Death" 75
"Malraux and Medellin" 167
"Malraux's *El Nacional* Interview" 215
Malraux's sons 50, 52, 76
"Malraux's *Storm in Shanghai*" 209
Manet, Edouard 13, 34
Mann, Thomas 20, 210
Man's Fate: see *Condition humaine, La*
Man's Hope: see *Espoir, L'*
Marx, Karl 61, 162, 210
Master of Flémalle 135, 136, 139
Medellin incident 168, 169, 170, 172, 173, 174, 175, 176, 178, 179, 180, 182, 184, 190, 195
Métamorphoses des dieux, La 3, 10, 12, 13, 25, 44, 52, 72, 102, 103, 104, 108, 119, 126, 132, 139, 246
Métamorphoses d'Apollon, Les 95, 99
"Metamorphosis and Biography" 37
Metamosphosis in Malraux's writing and thought 3, 4, 5, 6, 8, 27, 32, 34, 42, 43, 44, 45, 46, 48, 57, 64, 65, 86, 102
Miroir des limbes, Le 10, 11, 23, 38, 40, 52, 56, 57, 58, 59, 60, 61, 64, 65, 66, 246
Mona Lisa (La Gioconda) 126, 130, 131, 132, 133, 137, 139, 160
Flemish copy 126, 128, 129, 130
Monnaie de l'absolu, La 95, 99
Montaigne, Michel Eyquem de 29, 34, 65, 210
Morot-sir, Edouard 85
Musée imaginaire, Le 72, 94, 95, 96, 99, 105, 114
Napoleon I 23, 24, 56, 59, 62
Nietzsche, Friedrich Wilhelm 20, 23, 68, 69, 72, 145, 146, 163
Noyers de l'Altenburg, Les (The Walnut Trees of Altenburg) 16, 17, 18, 20, 23, 40, 41, 45, 46, 50, 52, 57, 61, 65, 91, 92, 93, 144, 145, 157, 160, 245

Pascal, Blaise 15, 16, 20, 27, 29, 67, 93, 146, 213
Peyre, Henri 27
Picasso, Pablo 4, 13, 23, 59, 61, 68, 150, 163, 164
Picasso's Mask: see *Tête d'obsidienne, La*
Plottel, Jeanine Parisier 82, 229
Poetic dimension of Malraux's work 5, 7, 8, 11, 12, 13
"Poetics and Passion" 143
"Professions délirantes" from André Malraux's *L'Homme précaire et la littérature* 229
Proust, Marcel 33, 34, 39, 56, 57, 64, 196, 210
Psychologie de l'art, La 3, 155, 213, 245
Racine, Jean 32, 33, 231
Rembrandt van Rijn 13, 34, 68, 126, 136, 144, 146, 147, 158
Riffaterre, Michael 59, 60
Romanesque architecture 5
Romanesque sculpture 8, 28
Rousseau, Jean Jacques 27, 29, 34, 39, 57
Royal Way, The: see *Voie royale, La*
Sartre, Jean-Paul 30, 109, 112, 113, 117, 118, 120, 160, 199, 209, 229
Shakespeare, William 5, 34, 70, 232, 239
Spanish civil war 31, 46, 70, 76, 168, 170, 171, 172, 173, 175, 176, 178, 180, 184, 185, 190, 212, 216, 217, 218, 220, 221, 222, 223
Spengler, Oswald 28, 73, 91, 107
Stevens, Wallace 145
Storm in Shanghai 209
Surnaturel, Le 3, 9, 247
Temps du mépris, Le (Days of Wrath) 22, 23, 31, 57, 62, 92, 163
Temptation of the West, The: see *Tentation de l'occident, La*
Tentation de l'Occident, La 22, 23, 24, 25, 28, 88, 89
Tête d'obsidienne, La (Picasso's Mask) 61, 72, 201
Thompson, Brian 201
Thornberry, Robert S. 215
"Timeless Geography" 67
Tison-Braun, Micheline 155
Tolstoy, Leo 31, 199, 238
Trotsky, Leon 210, 212, 213, 216, 217, 218, 221, 222
Valéry, Paul 28, 30, 31, 39, 42, 73, 164, 229, 230, 239
Van Gogh, Vincent 10, 151, 158, 185
Vermeer, Jan 34, 135, 156
"Visual Imagination in *L'Espoir*" 201
"Voices of the Poet, The" 3
Voices of Silence, The: see *Voix du Silence, Les*
Voie royale, La 23, 60, 62, 68, 88, 90
Voix du silence, Les 3, 4, 10, 11, 12, 25, 29, 31, 47, 55, 65, 94, 95, 99, 143, 146, 147, 148, 149, 150, 246
Walnut Trees of Altenburg, The: see *Noyers de l'Altenburg, Les*
Wicker-Screen Madonna 135, 136, 137

NEW YORK LITERARY FORUM

"Fills a serious need by making each issue a symposium at a high level on a topic of central interest"
—**Harry Levin,** Professor of Comparative Literature, Harvard University
"Promises to be the most impressive literary journal in English"
—**Henri Peyre,** Professor Emeritus, Yale University, and Distinguished Professor, C.U.N.Y.

THE OCCULT IN LANGUAGE AND LITERATURE (Winter 1979)
From Apuleius to Orton. Exciting new studies on occult drama, poetry of the invisible, magic word play, numerology, ascent, death, dreams, and mysticism. The first English translation of *Visitors,* an occult Polish play by Stanislaw Przybyszewski will be featured.
LC 77-18630   ISSN 0149-1040   ISBN 0-931196-03-5   288 pages

INTERTEXTUALITY
The new, New Criticism suggesting that all writing is graft. A text bears projections from the past but also traces of future reading and writing. Twenty-one authors brilliantly present ideas with radical implications to influence our interpretation of literature and the arts.
LC 77-18628   ISSN 0149-1040   ISBN 0-931196-01-9   328 pages

COMEDY—NEW PERSPECTIVES
A thorough examination of theory together with practice, the one illustrating the other. How comedy overcomes anxiety, atrocity, and humiliation is illustrated by works ranging from Shakespeare and Jacobean comedy through silent movies and radio shows of the 1930s, modern Polish theater, Shaw, Frisch, *Candy,* Stoppard, and others.
LC 77-18626   ISSN 0149-1040   ISBN 0-931196-00-0   336 pages

ANDRÉ MALRAUX
Twenty experts, including close friends, provide new light on one of the twentieth century's most controversial authors. New text and photographs of the author, together with traditional scholarship, help resolve the current critical debate about textual truth and historical fallacy.
LC 77-18629   ISSN 0149-1040   ISBN 0-931196-02-7   336 pages

NEW YORK LITERARY FORUM emphasizes innovative and controversial studies with modern interdisciplinary concepts.

NYLF combines the definitive character of a book with the immediacy of a journal.

NYLF is published twice a year, Spring and Winter. Each volume is organized and written by a team of eminent authors and contains analytical works as well as creative writing of unusal merit.

NYLF is a lasting and valuable reference: each volume deals with just one topic, is comprehensively indexed, includes extensive notes and a bibliography, and is illustrated.

SEND CHECK WITH ORDER TO PUBLISHER NOW!
LIBRARIES AND INSTITUTIONS: $10.50, single volume; subscription and standing orders at single volume price.
INDIVIDUALS: $8.50, single volume; $15.00, 2 volumes.
Outside the U.S., please add $3.00 per volume. U.S. funds only. Prices subject to change.

Published and distributed by:
NEW YORK LITERARY FORUM
21 EAST 79th STREET, NEW YORK, NY 10021

Use this coupon. Send today for copies of this important new series.

Please send check with order to: *(only libraries and institutions may be invoiced)*
NEW YORK LITERARY FORUM, Dept. AM, P.O. Box 262, Lenox Hill Station, N.Y., N.Y. 10021

Libraries and institutions: $10.50, single volume; subscription and standing orders at single volume price.
Individuals: $8.50, single volume; $15.00, two volumes.
Outside the United States, please add $3.00 per volume. U.S. funds only. Prices subject to change.

Please send me the following copies of *New York Literary Forum:*

☐ **COMEDY: New Perspectives,** Maurice Charney, Editor

☐ **INTERTEXTUALITY: New Perspectives in Criticism,** Hanna Charney and Jeanine P. Plottel, Editors

☐ **ANDRÉ MALRAUX: Metamorphosis and Imagination,** Françoise Dorenlot and Micheline Tison-Braun, Editors

☐ **THE OCCULT IN LANGUAGE AND LITERATURE,** Hermine Riffaterre, Editor

Amount enclosed $ _____

Name _____
Affiliation _____
Address _____
City _____ State _____ Zip _____

☐ Libraries and institutions: please check here if you wish to place a standing order